THE MIND OF THE DOLPHIN

A Non-Human Intelligence

John Cunningham Lilly, M.D.

Consciousness Classics
Gateways Books and Tapes
Nevada City, California
2015

THE MIND OF THE DOLPHIN: A Non-Human Intelligence
This edition in commemoration of the Centennial of Dr. Lilly's birth.
© 1967 by John Cunningham Lilly
© 2015 (Expanded Edition) by The Estate of John C. Lilly
All Rights Reserved.

ISBN: 978-0-89556-119-0 (Paperback)
ISBN: 978-0-89556-550-1 (Kindle)
ISBN: 978-0-89556-552-5 (EPUB)
ISBN: 978-0-89556-553-2 (PDF)
Cover design: Marvette Kort
Proofreading: Tabatha Jones, Rose Gander
Cover photo: Margaret (Howe) Lovatt and Peter, courtesy of Lilly Estate

Published by: Gateways Books and Tapes
P.O. Box 370
Nevada City, California 95959 USA
1-800-869-0658
1-530-271-2239
www.gatewaysbooksandtapes.com

Library of Congress Cataloging-in-Publication Data

Lilly, John Cunningham, 1915-2001.
  The mind of the dolphin : a non-human intelligence / by Dr. John C. Lilly. --
Expanded edition.
      pages cm. -- (Consciousness classics)
  Includes bibliographical references and index.
  ISBN 978-0-89556-119-0 (trade pbk.)
  1. Dolphins--Psychology. 2. Animal intelligence. 3. Animal communication.
4. Dolphins--Vocalization. I. Title.
  QL785.5.D65L5 2015
  599.53'8--dc23
                              2015006012

TABLE OF CONTENTS

DEDICATION (John C. Lilly, 1967 Edition)

I dedicate this book to all of those persons who have aided this research program in innumerable ways, some financially, some intangibly, but nonetheless crucially.

To the Trustees and other colleagues, past and present, of the Communications Research Institute who have contributed directly their efforts to the detail of the projects.

To the Associates of the Institute who have contributed their interest and money to the effort.

To the private Foundations who have made direct contributions.

To all of those within the government agencies who, with vision and understanding, have facilitated our program, and to their advisers who have undertaken the hard work of understanding our goals, our scientific results, and our scientific contributions.

To the memory of my parents, Richard Coyle and Rachel Cunningham Lilly of St. Paul, Minnesota, in appreciation.

To the kind dolphins who have helped us to learn to understand.

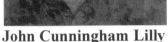

John Cunningham Lilly   **&**   **Philip Hansen Bailey**

ACKNOWLEDGMENTS (2015)

In this, the centenary year of John C. Lilly's birth, it is with gratitude and some anticipation that this expanded edition of *The Mind of The Dolphin* is published, in order that a new generation of readers may come to reflect upon the ancient and ongoing dialog between humans and cetaceans. As we celebrate John's extraordinary life and accomplishments, we also acknowledge the many family members, friends, and associates whose contributions added such depth, color, and so much love to John's life and legacy.

Mary Lilly's pioneering efforts helped stimulate and support John's early fascination with interspecies communication with dolphins. Historically, it was Mary's original observations of the dolphins' mimicry of Dr. Lilly's voice, at Marineland, Florida, in the mid-1950s, that set in motion the unfolding chain of events that continue to have significance in the modern era.

Margaret Howe led the historic efforts to break through the communication barrier with the dolphins at Nazareth Bay, St. Thomas, in the Virgin Islands. Some fifty years on, Margaret continues to articulate the need to maintain and develop that dialog with elegant insistence. During the past year, Margaret has starred in the BBC and Smithsonian Channel's production of "The Girl Who

Talked to Dolphins," garnering headlines and positive reviews around the globe. For the very first time, the story of Margaret and Dr. Lilly's grand vision has been told in an unflinching historical overview, chronicling their achievements with the dolphins known as Peter, Sissy, and Pam.

Scott McVay, Gregory Bateson, Frank Drake, Carl Sagan, and Hank Truby all made significant scientific contributions to the ground-breaking research that took place at Dolphin Point and the Communications Research Institute laboratory at Coconut Grove, Florida. In the intervening years, cetacean research has continued to expand through the work of other dedicated researchers, including: Paul and Helena Spong, Roger and Katy Payne, Louis Herman, Giorgio Pilleri, Sidney Holt, Roberta Goodman, Takako Iwatani, Kamala Hope Campbell, Claude Traks, Jim Suhre, Jacques Mayol, Ric O'Barry, Kim Kindersley, Mandy Rodriquez, Jack Kassewitz, and Jim Nollman.

John's family provided the love and solidarity that carried him through life, including his eldest son, John Lilly, Jr., with his wife, Colette, his beloved son, Charles Richard Lilly, and his daughters, Cynthia Lilly Cantwell, (John's daughter with Elizabeth Bjerg) Nina Castellucio, (John's adopted daughter, with Antonietta Ficarotta), Lisa Lyon, and Barbara Clarke Lilly.

Ann and Jerry Moss provided John with a safe landing in Hawaii where he spent his final years surrounded by his many friends from around the globe, including John Allen, Deborah Snyder, Abigal Alling, Mark Van Thillo, and "Rio" Hahn of the Biosphere II project, Glenn and Lee Perry of Samadhi Tank, Adam Trombly and Nancy Oliphant, Denise Smith and Bob Lowe, Ed Ellsworth, Brian Wallace, Faustin Bray, Lili Townsend, Napier Marten, Robert Watts, Taylor Fogelquist, James Chellis, Oscar and Sara Ichazo, Daniel McCauley, Brummbear, Robin Rae, Michael Segel, Dieter Hagenbach, Joan Ocean, Star Newland, Hawk and Molly Jordan Koch, and Patricia Sims. Special thanks are also due to Jeff Bridges for helping to keep John's legacy alive in the present, as well as Dianna Cohen and Jackson Browne for their continuing work protecting the environment.

vi

Our best wishes go out to Gessie Houghton, and Craig Inglis, curently engaged in editing the forthcoming *John C. Lilly Centennial Reader*, to be published by Synergetic Press in the very near future. Gratitude is expressed to Graham Talley of Coincidence Control Publishing for renewing interest in John's literary works, including, *Programming and Metaprogramming in The Human Biocomputer* and *Center of the Cyclone*. Christopher Riley is commended for bringing "The Girl Who Talked to Dolphins" to the screen. D. Graham Burnett dug deep into the Lilly archive and reported back in his book, *The Sounding of the Whale*. Henry Lowood and Roberto Trujillo continue to present the John C. Lilly Archive to the world through Stanford University's Green Library. Laurie and Jacob Teitelbaum ably assisted in moving things forward toward this publication and the Teitelbaum Family Foundation. Iven Lourie of Gateways Books had the prescience to republish this current work, as well as John's masterwork on flotation and sensory isolation, *The Deep Self.* Jim Ed Norman, George and Evelyn Musser, and the Bailey Family have continued to provide support and guidance through the years.

This edition is respectfully dedicated to John's parents, Richard Coyle Lilly and Rachel Cunningham Lilly, and to his brothers, Richard, Jr. and David Maher Lilly. This publication is also offered in commemoration of Ivan and Constance Tors, Albert and Anita Hofmann, Timothy Leary, Oscar Janiger, Aldous and Laura Huxley, Burgess Meredith, Carol Bentley Ely, and Rudi Vogt, John's ever-present colleagues.

In closing, let me paraphrase what Timothy Leary said about John's book, *The Scientist,* and extend it to include this new edition of *The Mind of the Dolphin:* Guard your copy. It's a precious relic of our wonderful, incredible age!

Philip Hansen Bailey
John C. Lilly Research Institute
Los Angeles, California, April 9, 2015

FOREWORD FOR LILLY CENTENNIAL EDITION
of *MIND OF THE DOLPHIN*
by Margaret Howe Lovatt

It was my good fortune to be in the right place at the right time and to be available when John Lilly pulled away a bit from hard science and allowed his softer side to follow imagination and dreams. John's "Damn it all—wouldn't it be great!" enthusiasm and attitude led a perfectly poised planet Earth (1960s) which was in the beginnings of space exploration and excitement, to actually fund the idea that interspecies communication was becoming a clear possibility? probability? necessity?

Living with a dolphin (this is where I came in) was one of the results. It was a first effort in a more elaborate plan. John described it:

"As I wrote in *The Mind of the Dolphin,* the new project would mean 'complete freedom on the part of the dolphins to come and go as they pleased' rather than as we pleased. In that book it was proposed that a house be built by the sea. Part of the house would be flooded so that the dolphins could enter and be a part of the family life in that house. Both Margaret Howe (my associate) and I came to this conclusion after the dedicated communication efforts Margaret made in the dolphin laboratory in the flooded rooms in St. Thomas."

Many things interrupted this effort as planned, but in the end, John Lilly opened the gates for the many devoted efforts that are ongoing today on behalf of all Cetaceans. In the BBC documentary *The Girl Who Talked to Dolphins,* D. Graham Burnett speaks about Greenpeace and The Marine Mammal Protection Act: "I would argue that it is impossible to imagine that work without Lilly's legacy...."

A look behind the scenes

John also wrote in the opening pages of *The Mind of the Dolphin* that "anyone who has been near dolphins, worked with them, and had the responsibility for their care and upkeep knows unequivocally that this is a difficult assignment." I would like you to meet the men who took on "this difficult assignment" in the US Virgin Islands.

The work I did at the Communication Research Institute on St. Thomas was done in extended isolation at one end of a small island in the Caribbean. There has been a lot said and written about the good, the bad, and the ugly of what went on there, but one thing that is seldom given the spotlight is the absolutely unforgettable help and support I got from the two men who were assigned to do the daily labor and work with the three dolphins who lived there with me. Both men were from the British island of Tortola.

They were there that day, so long ago, when I first drove down that long winding hill to the CRI building. And Richard Turnbull and Aubrey Pickering remained working there with me long after: supporting me, helping me, putting up with me, and keeping me safe. We worked together long days and nights. We shared many good times, lots of unusual times, we went through hurricanes and power outages, sickness of the dolphins and of each other. We drank gallons of pink Cool Aid. I got married, Aubrey got married, Richard turned down serious bribes from ill meaning people to get onto the property. We built an isolation flotation unit as instructed by John Lilly, we built walls and tanks. We buried Pamela Dolphin together.

We caught fish and eels. Richard showed me how to eat a white sea urchin. We talked about voodoo. I patched up cuts and washed away blood. I lay Aubrey on the floor and poured sterile water into his eye that had been filled with particles of wood when he was working. Richard grew delicious cantaloupes in the ashes where we burned some of the CRI trash. Together we three put two dolphins onto a plane and watched them disappear into the sky.

We closed the building and the CRI in the end, and the relationships faded as we went our separate ways. Richard went back home to his big family in Tortola, Aubrey stayed on St Thomas and became a dad and a successful Taxi driver, and I became a mom, taught Scuba and worked later as a Marketing Director. I loved them both, and know they loved me. I had a visit with Richard and his family one day in Tortola.

I would see Aubrey working from time to time, and we danced together as the sun came up very early one J'ouvert morning on Tortola. He knew my husband, John Lovatt, and was always quick to appreciate John's gentleness and playful sense of humor. John knew both Richard and Aubrey well, and understood what we all meant to each other.

This new edition is published to commemorate the John Lilly Centennial and may never find its way into the hands of these two very special people. I hope it might, or at least one day be in the hands of their families. The work I did then and the life I have had since could never have happened without either one. I was in my early twenties working with them, and I grew up under their care and influence. Certainly at the time I was not aware of this, but that is what happened none the less. Their names are mentioned continuously in my notes and in the captions of various photos.

In jest, I told them each many times that they were fired! They often fired me in turn. It was our way. These men were in awe of "the Doc" and his efforts. Lilly was often surrounded by colleagues from many different scientific disciplines who shared education, motivation and inspiration. But none were more loyal or openly devoted than these two responsible men from Tortola.

I know John would think it right to have Aubrey Pickering and Richard Turnbull mentioned in his 100th Centennial Celebration.

Margaret Howe Lovatt
January, 2015

PREFACE to the GATEWAYS BOOKS EDITION
by C. Scott Taylor, Ph.D.

The Cultural Context

The cusp of the 1960s saw the appearance of *The Mind of the Dolphin,* a book that laid groundwork for much to come. Linking science and spiritual seeking, computer theories and communication, psychology and interspecies relationships, it demonstrated the potential of scientific research to have direct connections to everyday life.

Following the broad public and scientific interest Dr. Lilly had raised with his first book, *Man and Dolphin* in 1961, *The Mind of the Dolphin* was a report on progress made toward the goals he had aimed to achieve.

When *Man and Dolphin* was published in 1961 Lilly was a highly respected neurophysiologist, medical researcher, designer of experiments, an inventor, a trained psychoanalyst, and a very well-connected scientist known across the nation and around the world. Lilly made clear, in a book intended for a broad popular audience, that indeed, dolphins had minds and language, and he intended to understand them.

Dr. Lilly was uniquely situated, by birth and intellect, to venture into multiple disciplines and was free to do basic research, not driven by ideologies based on market concerns and belief systems. His family wealth enabled him to set his own agenda, to pursue his lifelong question about the nature of Reality relatively unhindered. Despite the characterization of the cultural milieu of the 1950s and early 60s as dull, limited, and without color, the culture of the time was a perfect environment for a young scientist to be "ruthlessly rational," as Alan Watts later described Dr. Lilly.

The cultural context in which Lilly's second book appeared was one of turmoil and change. In 1967, the year *The Mind of the Dolphin* was published, a publicly declared racist was elected as Governor of Georgia; the war in Viet Nam was being fiercely fought and televised into American living rooms; race riots were common across the nation; hippies were becoming a popular phenomenon with Be-ins in San Francisco and New York; huge demonstrations against the war took place in many cities; Jimi Hendrix, the Doors, and the Beatles all released major albums; Elvis Presley got married and Muhammad Ali refused to serve in the military. It was the year of the *Summer of Love* and the *March on the Pentagon*, when the 60s hit its peak.

The Mind of the Dolphin, its last 100 pages dictated into a tape recorder while sitting in a VW camper over a period of two days, was originally contracted to be a book about his research on sensory isolation and "float tanks". But Lilly had startled the world by his first book (which military officials had attempted to prevent being published), inspiring the films and TV series *Flipper*, which ran from 1963-1967, the first global TV series, seen in dozens of countries. He wanted to round out the story, to detail not only the discoveries he had made, but to make certain that the physical, mental, and social factors necessary for any research that followed were well known.

Contributions to Science

Basic questions call for wide-ranging research, free to go where evidence leads. Searching for answers as to the nature of Reality, Lilly joined others in questioning the role of the brain in producing thought. He was uncomfortable with the prominent notion suggesting that the mind is nothing more than the brain's reactions to stimulus, or 'behaviorism'. Behaviorism denies the importance of "private events" such as thoughts, instead focusing on external and observable actions. In this view, the brain is an organ that is stimulated by sensory input that creates mental activity, e.g., thought, and the phenomenon called Mind.

Having invented the sensory isolation chamber, or float tank in 1954 to explore the brain/mind question, Lilly understood that his mind was very active when no external stimulus was occurring. In the float tank, Lilly experienced his mind free of bodily connection and sensory stimulus. Floating there he knew that he was still thinking, and importantly, he was learning.

By the late 1950s Lilly had begun to combine his background in physics, neuro-anatomy, and psychology with the newly developing fields of computer engineering, cybernetics, and communications theory. As an anatomist he wondered about the limiting factors of brains: at what size might brains become capable of higher order thought? What size must a brain be to think about itself? Looking for other large brains, cetaceans were an obvious choice. Floating nearly weightless in the oceans, whales and dolphins are warm-blooded mammals with large brains not unlike human brains and he was eager to study them.

Man and Dolphin and *The Mind of the Dolphin* set out a framework, making clear that the goal of Lilly's research was to learn about minds by studying the development of communication, since this only occurs between minds. In doing so, he "bookends" his work as a dolphin researcher, first by proclaiming the existence of another Mind on our planet, then by describing in close detail how this other mind learns and communicates. This produced a pair of volumes with far-reaching effects.

Lilly's approach to the question of dolphin intelligence, learning, and communication was direct. By enabling a human and a dolphin to live in an intimate relationship, sharing space and time and experience to explore how the two might learn from each other, he challenged the dominant scientific paradigm of the day, which was always to separate Observer from Subject. Instead, Lilly and his dedicated partner in research, Margaret Howe, made a simple but profound choice: to live together to learn from each other. Aiming to learn from each other by mimicry and mutual discovery, Howe and Peter were attempting another kind of scientific research, fully participatory. As Lilly points out, this requires a willingness to set aside a major bias, specifically that only humans have minds and important "private experiences," and to accept that meaningful discoveries can come from such a simple arrangement.

Around the world other scientists were excited to read about his work. In Russia especially, scientists took his work very seriously and began ambitious research programs. Because Lilly's work in brain mapping and his invention of techniques for investigating, stimulating, and controlling directly, without damage, the electrical workings of living brains during his wartime research, his work was known by military strategists. The implications of Lilly's work with dolphins did not escape notice of the military on both sides of the Iron Curtain, each seeking advantage in any future confrontations, and what Lilly seemed to be saying was that not only do dolphins have minds and are capable of mimicry, language, and the learning of complex tasks, but these thinking animals might be controlled and useful in warfare.

Dr. Lilly anticipated this. He understood the implications, perhaps better than anyone. Not wanting to contribute any support to military uses of his discoveries of brain stimulus control and inter-species language, which could lead to a kind of 'mind controlled bio-weapon', he chose to "go Hollywood" as he later described it. He went directly to the public via his books and many interviews, making his discoveries part of the wider social culture in hopes this public scrutiny might prevent misuse of them.

Dr. Lilly's books helped lay a pattern for disrupting misuse of research. He was partly inspired by his friendship with Dr. Leo Szilard, whose role in inventing controlled nuclear reactions led to the atomic bomb, which Szilard actively resisted. By bringing his work into public awareness, popularizing it, Lilly hoped to avert its misuse by exposing it widely. His role as an inspiration for the popularization of dolphins via the films and TV series *Flipper* and later films, books, and popular culture was not without his support. He had learned that dolphins deserved the best treatment humans have to offer and wanted them free from misuse. By helping to promote their popularity, he understood that he could create a powerful "dolphin lobby," always seeking their well-being.

Some recent authors, who did not know John, have stated that his work was funded by, and intended for use by, the U.S. military. This is incorrect. He understood well how to use public funds for supporting basic research, he had an extensive network from his family connections and his academic and scientific work during and following the war era and he used these connections to his advantage. He did not intentionally do any research in support of military weapons programs using dolphins. Approached for the job of heading up the U.S. Navy's dolphin research program, he instead recommended another man, F. G. Wood, curator at Marineland in Florida, whom John had worked alongside in his early brain research. Once he had made it clear he was not supportive of any "weaponization" of dolphins, Wood led many efforts to discredit Dr. Lilly. Lilly later realized that the U.S. Navy dolphin program was likely to want to hide any discoveries it might make about dolphin capabilities under an intentional disinformation campaign, which some think there is evidence for today.

Lilly's first two dolphin books and a later book, *Communication between Man and Dolphin* (1978), were widely influential in cetacean science. Few current researchers do not trace either their own inspiration, or that of their mentors, to Dr. Lilly's original work During an interview with John in 1998, he was asked what he thought of the current research on dolphins. His comment was brief: "I wish they would read my work more closely and stop wasting funds repeating what I already learned."

As Lilly's life progressed, he moved away from his dolphin studies into other research, some of it in controversial areas. Always seeking to understand Reality and how human minds perceive, learn, communicate, and understand, he was a pioneer in another field, one that stirs opposition, that of consciousness and what can be learned by altering it in various ways. He had always subscribed to the moral principle that no researcher should subject another human to any experimental procedure the researcher himself was not willing to experience. He held to this principle, using the float tank, undergoing psychoanalysis, and eventually, using disciplines and chemicals to alter his consciousness. He was an early and important researcher in the study of psychedelics, and for this Lilly was ostracized, his dolphin studies cast aside. Yet, to this day, researchers continue to rediscover what he documented about dolphins, often without credit to Lilly or recognizing they are replicating work he did decades ago.

Leading dolphin researchers today who focus on cognition, communication, and the behaviors of dolphins owe their inspiration to the work of Dr. John C. Lilly. Scientists Denise Herzing, Diana Reiss, Louis Herman, Stan Kuczaj, Toni Frohoff and many others acknowledge his inspiration. After 30 years of my own study of dolphins, I find myself learning new insights every time I return to Lilly's work. His unique approach to direct engagement, personal experience as well as observation, and his support of Margaret Howe, whose dedication and willingness to work so closely with a dolphin in a program she and Lilly devised, to explore how a dolphin might learn as human children learn, by imitation, stands as testament to an innovator unlike any before or since. It was a unique moment in the history of science when Dr Lilly was doing his research.

It is revealing that Lilly's dolphin research is still being explored, revised, ignored, challenged, and reviewed by researchers in various fields 50 years later. Revisionist historians seek to build a name for themselves by misreading his archives. Filmmakers use the "scandalous" aspects of the intimacy attained by Margaret Howe and Peter Dolphin to create sensationalist tales, avoiding any of Lilly's own descriptions of the content or meaning of the work. Academics point to how Lilly's dolphin research shifted communication network theory from "neuroelectric" (that is, cybernetic, computer-like programming in closed loops accessible in living brains, available for military control) to a "bioacoustics," or liberated model in a "green world" open to psychological and spiritual exploration and understanding. Lilly, many decades ago, was aware that mimicry was a key to understanding learning among large brained mammals and that dolphins were excellent partners in discovering how mimicry across species boundaries could open understandings, yet no "dolphin language" research along these lines occurs now. Instead, contemporary research focuses on encyclopedic recording of behaviors in hopes of linking vocalizations to them.

Republishing Lilly's dolphin research will, hopefully, inspire others to take up, again, the search for keys to interspecies communication. While it may not be possible to "teach a dolphin to speak English," it may be possible to find ways to share the intent that is packed into the pattern-rich energies expressed by other species. This is where Lilly left off, searching for the patterns, wishing for faster computers (a commonplace now), looking for other humans free enough, mentally healthy enough, willing to dedicate themselves to opening up a window of mutual understanding between species, a window on a greater reality.

In another time, the poet Robert Burns wrote, while contemplating another animal:

"And would some Power the small gift give us
To see ourselves as others see us!
It would from many a blunder free us."

In this is the essence of Dr. Lilly's quest among dolphins, to escape the bounds of the human viewpoint, to gain insight into our human-ness from the perspective of another consciousness, and perhaps by doing so, to understand a bit more about Reality.

C. Scott Taylor, Ph.D., Executive Director
Cetacean Studies Institute
Australia, January, 2015

PREFACE to the GATEWAYS BOOKS EDITION
by Dr. Michael T. Hyson, Ph.D.

I am pleased and honored to offer a preface to Dr. John C. Lilly's masterful work, *The Mind of the Dolphin*. *The Mind of the Dolphin* is pioneering in many areas, in communication, acoustics, neurology, dolphin physiology, language acquisition, the capabilities of large-brained creatures, and many other topics. I wish to put his research into perspective and mention some of the work his research inspired.

I first read his previous book, *Man and Dolphin* when I was 13 and it literally changed my life. I was living on a small farm in Illinois, far from the sea. While I was studying my pet bats, I researched animal sonar, which led me to Lilly's dolphin research. I was mesmerized. According to Lilly, dolphins were friendly, playful, apparently smarter than us, and were even learning English!

Within a year, I had visited the dolphins in Brookfield Zoo and had talked my brother Robert into taking a dolphin training job in Port Aransas, Texas. I later joined him for a fondly remembered magic summer, where I lived with Pete and the other dolphins there. It was near heaven for me. I learned so much I was inspired to be a dolphin researcher.

I read *The Mind of the Dolphin* while at the University of Miami, when I was 19 (having followed Lilly into the study of biology and medicine). I have just re-read it. I am struck that I remember so much of it, almost verbatim in places. I am amazed, even now, by how broadly and comprehensively Lilly presents the importance to us of interspecies communication and how talking to the Cetacea could change our world profoundly.

Lilly clarifies our place in the scheme of things. It is obvious that larger-brained species like the elephant, the dolphins, the orcas, the sperm whale, and other Cetacea with brains larger than ours, strongly challenge our concept that we are the most intelligent species on the planet. It is quite possible that the sperm whales, with 6 times our brain size, might be thinking in ways beyond our comprehension. He suggests that the gentleness, playfulness and joy of the dolphins could teach us to be a better species, to become more harmonious, and temper our current violent behaviors and help us become better stewards of the Earth, its oceans, and its inhabitants.

At the time Lilly was writing, the NASA moon flights were starting to launch, and Lilly felt they needed practice at communicating with the ETs they might find. Lilly was partly funded by NASA for this reason. Lilly attended a conference with Frank Drake, whose team were the first to listen for intelligent signals from the stars and who started the *SETI* program (Search for Extraterrestrial Intelligence). Lilly created the *"Order of the Dolphin"* for those who have attempted communication with another species and presented an award to Drake and his team.

Lilly foresaw that with the advent of full communication with the Cetacea come many implications, such as treating our partners in the sea much better and changing their status from commodities, products, chattel and food to recognizing them as beings that are our equals, and even *superiors*. As such, they should, at the very least, be accorded rights and proper treatment. Lilly saw them integrating into our societies as our compatriots, mentors, and being an overall civilizing influence, ending our isolation in the Universe—what Loren Eiseley termed our *"long loneliness."*

Lilly envisioned shared human-dolphin habitats where we could live together and learn from each other in partially flooded structures. *The Mind of the Dolphin* describes their research and progress toward these goals, including building a partially flooded house in St. Thomas, Virgin Islands, where Margaret Howe and Peter Dolphin lived together in isolation for weeks. The basic idea was that with only each other to be with, this *"immersive"* environment might lead to a communication breakthrough. Part of what Lilly and his team found out was that the dolphins were capable of living with humans in close quarters in shallow water for months. The language lessons held their interest and they were diligent.

The dolphins first learned to make sounds in air with their blowholes, and imitated English sounds, and, sometimes, whole phrases. This was first noticed in 1957, and the dolphins Chee-Chee, Elvar and Tolva got pretty good at it. Later, Sissy, Pam and Peter were part of the research in the St. Thomas lab. At first, the mimicry was done rapidly and at high frequency and first noticed only when tapes were slowed down. When *"humanoid"* sounds were evoked through shaping their behavior, the dolphins dropped their speed and lowered their frequencies as much as they could to match us.

Remarkably, dolphins only rarely make sounds in air *except* when they want to talk with us. Some of this was known some 2500 years ago by Aristotle. After some training, the dolphins became good enough at this mimicry that those close to the dolphins could often understand what they were saying...similar to how a mom knows what her baby is saying better than anyone else.

However, when other scientists were brought in for demonstrations, they typically failed to hear anything like speech. After that, Lilly decided to show that the dolphins could imitate the correct number of syllables when they were presented in strings up to 12 long. The dolphins matched such random utterances with a 98%+ accuracy. This showed that they have a short-term memory of about 12 units while humans only have a short-term recall of 5 units (plus or minus 2).

The dolphins were *exceeding* human performance!

There were limits on what the dolphins could do with their blowholes and *naso-pharynges* (the sound producing vocal cord-like structures just below the blowhole). For example, Margaret Howe taught Peter her name. He did pretty well with an *"...arrgret"* sound but was missing the *"M"* sound which is usually made by stopping the air flow briefly with our lips—hence it is called a *"bilabial"* (two-lip) stop.

On the tapes of Margaret and Peter, we can hear Peter starting an "aaarrr" sound, and, at the same time, swirled water over the blowhole so that the water flow would briefly block the airflow to make the "M" sound. He almost got it right! Think of the inventiveness and skill that required.

At one point, Margaret helped Peter by cupping her hands over his blowhole as he made the *"...arrgret"* sound so that her hands stopped the airflow for a fraction of a second. The result was a pretty good *"Margret."* Dr. Hank Truby (a linguist and acoustic-phonetician who helped invent the sonogram or *"voice print"*) was reviewing the tapes of Peter and Margaret's language lessons at the Coconut Grove Lab of Lilly's Communications Research Institute one day when he spotted a bilabial stop in the recordings of Peter. Obviously this was impossible for a dolphin to do. Hank called Margaret and asked: *"Margaret, what the hell are you doing?"* Margaret knew immediately what he meant and cried *"Oh, Hank, I just wanted him to say my name."*

The dolphins continued to have difficulties pronouncing consonants, but were getting steadily better, and toward the end, I am told, the dolphins were getting exponentially better. Margaret has said that the experiment needed to run longer, as even a baby human takes at least a year or two of learning to do well at talking. After these preliminary experiments with Peter and Margaret, funding decreased and the experiments stopped. Much of this story can be seen in the BBC documentary *The Girl Who Talked to Dolphins,* although there is a bit of hyperbole and sensationalism in the film.

Overall, I am impressed how fresh and exciting the concepts and writing in the book are, even now, some 50 years after the experiments. Lilly went on to do the Janus Project, with Joe and Rosie Dolphin, in which a computer interface was utilized, and research by Louis Herman and others have skirted the edges of the problem, yet we are still striving for full communication with the Cetacea.

Lilly would have been 100 on January 6, 2015. In his centenary year we can reflect on where we are. The legacy of Lilly's work in immense.

In addition to his dolphin work, John also invented many devices and techniques, like the *"Lilly Wave"* and electrode recording techniques that were in use when I learned neuro-physiology. He worked on high altitude oxygen systems, built a respirator for the dolphins, pioneered the use of computers for signals processing, invented the isolation tank and then used it to explore the nature of consciousness to a very deep level. Out of this work came the synthesis of cybernetics, information theory and tank work that he presented as *Programming and Metaprogramming the Human Biocomputer.*

He was a physicist, M.D., psychiatrist, sailor, pilot and ham radio operator and computer expert. Truby said, *"John was the most certificated man he ever met."* Others have described him as *"a walking syllabus of Western civilization."* Whale researcher Scott McVay goes even further, saying: there was Kepler, Galileo, Newton, Einstein, and then... Lilly. Certainly his discovery of the dolphin's conscious breathing, their brain size and complexity and his recognition of their intelligence and sentience was a major revelation.

Because of Lilly, the Russians stopped killing dolphins. Later, he also inspired the Marine Mammal Protection Act and the International Whaling Commission ended most commercial whaling (although there are still Japan, Iceland, Norway and Denmark in the game).

As well, the public perception of the Cetacea changed! Now we have millions visiting the whales and dolphins each year and the numbers are growing. More and more people are aware of the dolphins and whales as being conscious and intelligent like we are.

When I was growing up, in the era of *"Flipper,"* coverage of *"Lilly and his talking dolphins"* was widespread. Yet, the academic community still largely ignores Lilly and his work. Ironically, because of this, many of the younger people I meet (who are quite aware of the Cetacea and their nature) have never even heard of Lilly. While they may know something about isolation tanks, they often have little idea where they came from. Perhaps in this Centenary Year, we can reintroduce John and his work to a new and wider audience.

Another legacy of John's discoveries is the large number of people who were inspired to do further research and other activities with the Cetacea. As one of many examples, I will describe some of my adventures.

While I was inspired to research dolphins, the opportunities to do so seemed limited. In 1973, after I had finished a Masters and was working on a Ph.D. in neuroscience, I met Dr. Hank Truby who had directed the language work for Lilly for some 17 years. Hank was amazing, had played professional tennis, spoke 14 languages, and was an expert at sonograms and human and dolphin speech production. I took all of Hank's courses, and worked with him for a dozen years. It was a wonderful period of my life.

Hank was the first to take autistic children to the dolphins, which initiated the whole Dolphin Assisted Therapy field. He founded the World Dolphin Foundation and for two years we kept Florida and Liberty Dolphin in the Mashta Island lagoon on Key Biscayne. We intended to release them and hoped they would bring their friends back. While most of our plans were curtailed by lack of funding, I became good friends with the dolphins and some 2,000 people came to meet them. They were released off Abaco where they joined up with the dolphins used for the film *Day of the Dolphin*.

After that I went to Cal Tech in 1977, and, wanting to go to space, worked with NASA, JPL and two of the first private rocket companies. Some 15 years later, I decided it was time to get back to the dolphins. I met a dolphin in Florida named Dreamer, who later healed a neck injury of mine, convincing me that the dolphin therapy aspects were quite real.

After meeting Dreamer, I met John Lilly on his 75th birthday January 6, 1990, in Malibu. There I also met a marvelous woman, Star Newland, (and her son, Tiger) who was a friend and colleague of John and Toni Lilly, and we determined to extend John's work, especially through underwater birth with the dolphins. Star formed the Sirius Institute to do this. I joined the effort and we came to Hawaii some 25 years ago. We have swum with the free dolphins, sent Humpback sounds live to the stars, and designed MIDI communication interfaces that the Humpbacks played with and had many other adventures.

A major part of the effort has been to perform dolphin attended water births here, as has been done in the Black Sea. This goal has been elusive, even though the Hawaiians have done this traditionally, in some cases.

Star's second son was born on a black sand beach with 300

dolphins waiting, but he decided to arrive one foot first. Star then initiated the *interspecies birth cohort study*, motivated, in part, by discussions with John and Toni that concluded that one of the best ways to bridge our communication would be to birth and raise human and dolphin babies together.

While we intend to have ocean births here, so far, some 30 babies, who had *pre-birth dolphin contact* because their moms swam with the dolphins prior to birth, have all been born at night (all short, natural deliveries with zero complications)—when the dolphins are out at sea hunting.

These babies are special. At least four were making clicks and whistles as part of their first sounds, several are strongly linked to the dolphins, and at least, can tell where the dolphins are and when they have come to the shore even though she is ten miles away. Our studies continue.

Star Newland dedicated her life to the Cetacea, gentle birth, dolphin attended births, domestic harmony, living *"en pod,"* Language Sculpting (a way to make our communications have more clarity and power), and other means to improve the human condition. She advocated *"dolphinizing"* the planet which is to raise human consciousness nearer to the dolphins, and integrating them into our societies as full and equal partners.

In addition, Star was active in many public arenas, talking to legislators, mayors, the Navy and many others about all these concepts. She was given numerous proclamations about these matters.

I deeply love and honor Star, who, sadly, passed away July 13, 2013. We are still actively working toward the integration of the Cetacea into our society, and to complete John's work, and now, as well, Star's work. They are greatly missed!

Another exciting recent development is that a dolphin working with SpeakDolphin.com, has begun to spontaneously vocalize vowels in the air, much as Lilly's dolphins did! I am privileged to be assisting in their research.

Lilly's observations and results are totally relevant to this new phase of our communication with the dolphins. It is wonderful and appropriate that in his Centenary year, the dolphins are contacting us again with sounds in the air directed to us!

The dolphin seems to be asking: *"OK, I have figured your vowels out, and here they are, in the correct order. So what is next? Where do we go from here?*

The dolphins are challenging us to communicate. The game is afoot (or a-fluke?) again....What is our answer? We are re-booting Lilly's language work even as I write. May it be *completed* this time!

I think John, Toni and Star are looking down on us and are pleased.... Remember, as John said:

> *"Communication with the Cetacea is the greatest achievement to which humans can aspire"*

Mahalo nui loa,

Dr. Michael Hyson, Ph.D
Research Director
Sirius Institute
Puna, Hawaii
March 31, 2015

AUTHOR'S PREFACE (1967)

This book is a record of an attempt to express some ideas, some formulations,and some experiments in communication research. In a sense this book is an extension of the previous book *Man and Dolphin* published by Doubleday in 1961. The main ideas and formulations are a theory to scientifically penetrate into the area of at least one non-human mind, that of the bottlenose dolphin. In order to solve the major problems of communication with a non-human mind, it is necessary to shed many cherished beliefs that man possesses. It is also necessary to develop a realistic set of theories to guide one in the pursuit of research into such a penetration. One must take into account the factors in the external reality and in the biology which mold and control the non-human species.

Experiments are recounted in which a dedicated woman and an enthusiastic young male dolphin live together for a period of a year. This book contains a detailed account of the problems and the results of living together in water. The mutual learning and teaching that were exchanged is given in some detail. This is another example* of a dedicated attempt to find means of communication between a human and a non-human intelligence.

In this book an attempt is made to show that one of the major blocks to the establishment of interspecies communication are the beliefs that man carries to this work. In many areas of science there is a *basic belief* that no species other than *Homo sapiens* is capable of speech, of language, of thought, of imagination, and of true feelings. This thesis further states that there is another set of basic hypotheses which are more open-ended, open-minded, and more general purpose. Evidence for the new formulations is given. Those readers who wish to examine the underlying thesis will find encouragement. Those readers who would deny the validity of such searches and researches are asked to bear with us patiently in these investigations and to keep their own minds open.

Conservationists who are interested in the plight of other species may find reasons in this book to warrant giving some aid to dolphins. If the present trends continue, the bottlenose dolphin ("porpoise" to some) may be extinguished as a species along the southern coasts of the United States. Tolls are being taken by sewage from cities resulting in their infection,

---

*Other examples are the Kelloggs' and the Hayes' independent attempts with the chimpanzee *(Pan satyrus)* (see Gilbert, 1966).

illness, and death of Dolphins are being lost by capture for entertaining humans in oceanaria around the world, for motion pictures, for television shows, for Navy tasks, for "pets." Some form of effective regulation and protection for the dolphins is fast becoming a prime need. Like the large whales, the dolphins need enlightened help, through contributions, through new laws, and possibly through a new agency devoted to conservation.

In 1958,* announcing the results of experiments with the bottlenose dolphin (*Tursiops truncatus*), I first put forward the hypotheses that the large dolphins (and probably the great whales) are highly intelligent and that they have complex highly abstract communication. Some of the evidence for these hypotheses and an extension of them to include the development of possible interspecies communication between man and dolphin was published three years later in the book *Man and Dolphin.*

In the years since 1958, the evidence that has been accumulating supports the correctness of these hypotheses; no evidence disproving them has been turned up either in our laboratories or elsewhere. In the last seven years, it has been found that the problems at the human end of the interspecies communication have placed severe limits on this type of communication. Human basic beliefs and human traditions in science have tended to discourage effective scientists from giving their interest and their dedication to this field.

If one takes an objective and careful look at man's communication with man, woman's communication with woman, and man's communication with woman, we see that most intraspecies interpersonal communication is not ideal. If one studies himself in solitude, he can find some suggestions for solutions to these interpersonal problems; one's own beliefs below his usual levels of awareness prevent complete communication with self and with other persons.

Our species has not achieved equality of communication. Each of us tends to assume that one's self is an expert communicator. We assume that we can communicate our needs, our purposes, the needs of others, and the purposes of others. That we fail to do this communication job well a large fraction of the time is shown by the prevalence in the United States of mental illness and of unhappiness despite an affluent American society. Communication with other peoples fails; we have international conflicts in most of the world.

---

*Lilly, J. C., Am. J. Psychiatry, 115: 498 (1958).

This book emphasizes man's communication and its close relationship to mental health. The science of interspecies communication can illustrate and some day help our human communication. "Learning of a nature gifted with special powers" we can become healthier.

We do not yet have an adequate description nor an adequate language for describing and dealing with mental illness. Conversely, we do not yet have adequate languages nor adequate means of dealing with and encouraging mental health. There are mental health movements in every major city of the United States. There are talented individuals in these movements who have made more progress than most persons. There are literally thousands of mentally healthy people who are succeeding in their communication one with another. However, the majority of persons in the United States, if not in the world, are failing to understand and to communicate their basic needs and their basic purposes. Large numbers of the majority cannot even articulate their needs or their purposes. Large numbers of people take on pseudo-needs and pseudo-purposes at the behest of programming by other persons. No mentally healthy person assumes that anyone else can furnish him with needs or with purposes not his own. The mentally ill, like children, are the ones who have a need of being told what their purposes and their basic lives can be. Such pressures by other persons are withstood and even ignored by mentally healthy people.

A major problem in the way of interspecies communication and a program of development of this field is the short supply of mentally healthy people committed to the field. This field requires happy, natural, bright persons at the human end, otherwise serious errors are made. As is delineated in this book, unless the human being has ingenuity, open-minded dedication, and courage in the dolphin-human transactions, the dolphins quickly learn the limitations of that human being and reject him.

I do not believe that the solution to the interspecies communication problem can be realized in a short time. In *Man and Dolphin*, I estimated (in 1960) that it would take at least a decade or two. In the intervening half decade we have found that the program is limited mainly by the human end of the system. It is to be hoped that this situation can be improved.

Of what benefit to humanity and to individuals may interspecies communication become? One immediate effect of this research is that we are forced to take a much closer look at our own deficiencies of communication, within man and between men. Thus research in this area sharpens up, highlights, and renders more effective the research on our own communication. Our own strivings toward mental health enter very strongly into this program. Before we achieve a satisfactory communication with a dolphin, we must achieve far better communication within each of ourselves and between ourselves. One major thesis of this book is the encouragement of better and more mental health research on ourselves; and as we improve, to use the improved selves in interspecies communication research. We have false beliefs which block our efforts; we are blinded by our interspecies beliefs.

There are times when I feel that each dolphin may be more mentally healthy than the human beings to whom he is exposed. Under artificial conditions in the care of man, dolphins can develop mentally unhealthy trends. However, dolphins in the wild at sea (or freshly caught) do not seem to have these characteristics. This may merely mean that we are unacquainted with those dolphins who are still not in close contact with us. However, many (but not all) dolphins seem to stand the brunt of being exposed to the mentally unhealthy environment (for them) provided by man and the mentally unhealthy persons with whom they are placed in proximity for some months and even years.

As we work with larger and larger species of dolphins (until finally we are working with the largest of them, *Orcinus orca*), the danger to individual humans increases. It is essential, as we work with the larger species with larger brains, that only healthy human beings deal directly with the animals. One "purposeful accident" by a mentally unhealthy person can lead to fatal results. In order to keep the interspecies program on a positive, progressive plane, we had best provide intelligent, mentally healthy people in the environment of the captive large dolphins. Criteria for selection should be set and selection itself should be carried out for faster progress.

All of these considerations are germane to the space and planetary exploration programs. If and when we encounter intelligent extraterrestrial communicating life forms from other places in this universe, we will need results from communication research to apply there and then. It is man that we have to examine more carefully and objectively to avoid possibly planetwide fatal errors during those possible future encounters. Some of the vast sums going into the space program should be invested in the communication program as a life insurance for the future of man.

Contributions from healthy, vigorous minds and pocketbooks are needed in this new activity. Ideas and money and work will allow us to penetrate and understand our minds, as we begin to penetrate and understand the minds of the dolphins.

Interspecies communication is a long-term endeavor: the arduous path of careful experimentation and careful analysis has been opened up. We are on our way toward deeper understanding of other species, giving them long overdue respect and dedicated work. Many routes to understanding the dolphin—the mind of the dolphin—are available. We need help—expert and talented help—with this program of search and research. This book gives some details and it gives one perspective on the scene.

"Through dolphins, we may see us as others see us."

Cetacean Nation (1992)

Dr. John C. Lilly announces the formation of Cetacean Nation, representing whales, dolphins, and porpoises from Oceania, covering 70% of our planet.

Dolphins have brains comparable to ours; whales have brains up to six times larger. No matter the differences between species, no matter differences of anatomy, no matter differences between media in which they live, creatures with a brain above a certain size will be considered 'equal' with man.

Human decisions have major repercussions in the oceans and in the lives of Cetaceans. Cetacean Nation assumes human responsibility for protecting the interests of the world's Cetaceans until they can speak for themselves. Learning to communicate with Cetaceans, we are forced to take a much closer look at our own deficiencies of communication, within persons and between persons. For the well-being of each one of us, for the national and international peace of all of us, communication is a paramount and pressing issue.

Cetacean Nation aspires to representation in the decisions of the United Nations. We propose a platform for expressing outlooks from the Cetaceans' point of view.

John Lilly and Roberta Quist, co-founders of Cetacean Nation, ask that you discover more about the lives of the people of Oceania. We invite you to join in Harmony with each other and voice a positive difference for both Cetaceans and Homo sapiens.

Dr. John C. Lilly   *Roberta Quist (Goodman)*

December 20, 1992   *Paia, Maui*

THE MIND OF THE DOLPHIN

A Nonhuman Intelligence

CHAPTER 1

Mental Health and Communication

COMMUNICATION, when it succeeds, is one of man's greatest assets, and when it fails is his worst enemy. Each of us tries and succeeds to a certain extent to communicate with others in his immediate surroundings every day, hours at a time. As we vary as individuals so we vary in our talents in communication with one another. Some persons are expert communicators; each of us recognizes the experts. Yet an expert is not a scientist, is not a psychologist, nor any specialist necessarily. Such an expert communicator can be anyone. How does such a person become an expert in communication? Basically this is a question of mental health. The best communicators are those who are the most mentally healthy, happy, natural, spontaneous, disciplined persons.

Among the human species are persons who have severe difficulties in communication with other human beings. During our growth from infancy each of us has had difficulties which grade all the way from those of the child who yet had no language for communication, through the various human achievement levels: grade school, high school, college, job, profession. As we become older our skills at communication tend to increase, with experience and with practice and with study. For each one of us this is the most important study that we have ever undertaken: how to communicate with our fellow man is a constant and recurring problem of consuming interest. We want understanding,

1

love, and respect; we receive them through communicating what is in our minds. We want to give understanding, love, and respect; we can give only through communication and only to those who can communicate in turn.

Our mental health is measured by how well we communicate with our fellow men and women. As Freud emphasized, the special communication called sexual activities gives one a rule of thumb of the success that a person has as a healthy human being. If one has exhilarating, stimulating, and fulfilling sexual experiences in the heterosexual sphere, he is mentally healthy. If one's work is successful, expanding, and happy, he is mentally healthy. In these two spheres (in the love life and in the work life) of a given individual are the major clues as to a person's success as an individual. This is the outside view of one's personal accomplishments and personal behaviors.

However, the inside view (the almost secret view) of one's self that he protects from the outside society says similar things. If one, as it were, deep within his adult self knows that his sexual activities are satisfying, guilt-free, and give intense pleasure to his partner, he has a deep happiness on which he bases the rest of his life.

If one's work presents novelty, variety, and a sense of internal and external progress as judged by himself (and eventually by the others outside himself), he then adds to the happiness of his love life by the accomplishments in the external world.

Thus our problem in our own species is achieving a basic communication with our fellow men and fellow women, so deep that each of us and each of them can be satisfied in very basic ways. If our communication is blocked, the satisfactory performance of our love life and our work life is blocked. If we have an unconscious and a conscious desire to communicate with our fellow men we can succeed. However, we must know ourselves in order to communicate. We must know the kind of things that we project into other people "as if" they are communicating them to us but are really not so doing.

This phenomena of projection of ourselves (our thoughts and our expectations) into others is a very human problem. We miss our goals by assuming that others are what we want them to be or that they are saying or communicating by other means what we want them to communicate. This problem of projection blocks a large fraction of true communication. How do we do this wishful, false realizing?

Our relatively large minds (brains) act as computers that can make models inside themselves of other human minds and their activities. Each of us knows that we construct models of other persons: one has a model of his wife in his head; she in turn has a model of her husband in hers. Each of us have a model of each child as it comes along; the models must grow with the child or there is communication trouble. The model of the wife must change in the husband as the wife changes and grows; the model of the husband in the wife must change as the real person changes. Otherwise there is a severe breakdown of communication.

One must change the models of one's parents and not project them into the model of one's wife or husband or children. The modeling that we did as children (of the adults in our surroundings) has the primitive features on which all the others eventually are built. However, unless built as growing, changing models, the childish models can be defective, can be incomplete, and eventually can be shown to be what they really are, "childish models," needing change and growth. Mentally healthy persons start with growing, changing models and see to it that growth continues.

Thus projection involves the use of inappropriate intransigent models of other human beings. If one has a realistic model of one's wife or husband (the model that corresponds more or less with the reality of that person), he or she then successfully communicates with the real person. He does not ask that particular real person to do impossible or contradictory things to satisfy his fantasies; he asks appropriate, realizable things to satisfy him.

Similarly, if one knows his own basic deep needs, he can communicate in terms of ethics, morals, manners, instincts, the acquisition of new knowledge, the nurturing and teaching of children, the building and maintenance of his own home, the encouragement of his friends, the performance of his work, the participation in the national and international life of his species. If one can realize that he is a unique individual, unrepeated since the beginning of his species, and can also confer this honor on each other human individual, he can then spend the time to learn his own internal language, and the internal language of each other individual, learn how to translate each into the commonly shared language and thus succeed in communication.

The human species has found quite empirically that the best communication is by those who closely resemble one another and who are placed in long-term close contact with one another. Isolated communities develop and maintain singularities in the language used; they develop and maintain customs of dress, of ritual, of loving, and of working uniquely theirs. They can also develop what has been termed "fear of the stranger" or "xenophobia" in many instances. In other instances xenophobia fails to appear or somehow is worked through by the local community, and strangers are welcomed among them. The projection of one's fears outward onto the unknown or the unfamiliar, beyond one's own group, nation, or species creates a dangerous communication paralysis.

In the modern world with the hydrogen bombs and threats of extinction we must, finally, examine carefully our best means of communication with interpersonal man, of

4

group to ever larger group. We must support research in these areas of communication. We must support research that shows promise of giving us new insight into interhuman communication. *For the mental health of each one of us, for the national and international peace of all of us, communication is a paramount and pressing issue.* We can no longer allow the "glass walls" that have risen between us (most dramatically in the mentally ill, and in the international cases) to exist, much less to influence our desires and our needs to communicate. This book demonstrates the relevance of the study of communication with the bottlenose dolphin to these extremely important future advances in human communication: through dolphins we will see ourselves as others see us. Through dolphin communication efforts we will help ourselves.

The mentally ill among the human species illustrate many of the points of failure of communication between us. In the following section I give what I consider to be the basic problems leading to mental illness and of maintaining mental illness in terms of this communication problem.

The truly deep problems of the mentally ill are communication problems. A mentally ill person for some reason or another cannot and hence will not communicate adequately with other human beings. The reasons among the many unique ill individuals are myriad. The reasons are under intensive scrutiny in many areas of medical and mental health research.

Some of the genetic factors, the "inherited defects," are being turned up in the recent research on chromosomes in the human. For example, several determinable physical signs of an altered inheritance have been found in the chromosomal studies. Some forms of mental illness depend upon such inherited, determinable defects. These defects are manifested by sometimes obvious anatomical changes in

5

the appearance of the human being, sometimes in an obvious biochemical change (with the excretion in the urine of particular "abnormal" substances). Sometimes there are only peculiar behaviors, and, most relevant to our present discussion, only peculiar kinds of communication of types not normally encountered.

This group of patients are those with built-in "errors" of inheritance. These are the genetically determined and clinically detectable "errors." Such cases are relatively infrequent in occurrence.

Most of us who manage to survive all of the exigencies of conception, gestation, birth, and infancy are uniquely different, one from another. The evidence for this uniqueness is manifold. If one attempts to graft the skin of one person onto another person, the second person develops immunities against that grafted skin, and it eventually sloughs off. A careful examination of the mechanisms underlying the development of these immunities shows that each of us is so biochemically different that we reject the live tissues of another. These biochemical differences may extend into almost all aspects of our lives. Each of our neuronal patterns of activity are unique (EEGs, etc.). Perhaps each of us is so uniquely different that our thought processes, as well as our neuronal patterns of activity, are uniquely different. However, there seems to be at least potentially enough commonality of thinking and feeling to achieve communication and to maintain us as a species. We know that there is enough commonality of anatomy, at least of gross anatomy, to perpetuate the species. If there is not, that individual has no children. It is almost as if in the gross large picture we are forced by survival contingencies to look alike. As the picture becomes more and more microscopic, and we analyze closer and closer to the individual selves, the differences become obvious, inescapable, and determining.

6

The "general purpose" nature of large parts of our brains is the saving grace which allows one individual to communicate with another. The uniqueness built into the biochemistry generates a brain which in the patterns of activity and in microscopic and molecular detail is unique. As over the thousands of generations in evolution the number of neurons has increased to the thirteen billions that we have, a common power or property has developed in most human brains. The important common power is the ability of this brain to assume the tasks of making models of creatures and persons in its surrounds. This is the fundamental property which allows communication to take place.

We can develop and share a language among uniquely different individuals because each of those individuals can take on enough of the commonality of language within his own brain to allow communication. But we must never forget that the thinking processes of the individual are still uniquely his or hers. Only certain aspects are common and shared. We may have the illusion of penetrating completely into the mental life of another human being through language, but this is impossible. Each of us is so uniquely different and so uniquely himself that we cannot yet so penetrate. It is a delusion to presume that one can. Laziness fosters this belief.

The mentally ill person may have a defect of his structure which prevents the acquisition of the common factors necessary to share language with others. A schizophrenic has a basic metabolic problem which gives him an attitude and a set of thinking processes so alien to the normal commonality that he acts as if and thinks as if he had a "glass wall" between him and other human beings.

The "glass wall" between the schizophrenic and other human beings in the communication mode is quite effectively a two-way barrier. There is hope that it depends upon an altered biochemistry of the brain which can be changed

7

by proper and sufficient treatment. It is the aim of certain kinds of research to devise chemical corrections to allow this person to share the commonality of language and enough of the commonality of thinking so that he can dissolve his "wall" and can be happy and mentally healthy.

No one wants to be insulated and isolated for long from his fellow human beings. In experiments in which I have isolated volunteer subjects and in experiences in which others have isolated themselves, it is shown that the major need that develops in the isolation experience is transactions with others, i.e., communication. This need can be temporarily satisfied by hallucinating and talking to the "projected" persons in the solitudinous surroundings.

The schizophrenic behind his "glass wall" is isolated by the biochemistry of his own brain. The glass wall insulates and isolates him in a fashion analogous to that of a person living in the polar night alone. Thus the schizophrenic does hallucinate and does project into his surrounds those things that he needs most and those which he fears most. These projections cause reciprocal fear in those placed close to the schizophrenic. In other words, a person with this particular biochemistry is increasingly isolated from his fellow human beings because of his "built-in" failure of communication consequent upon his chemistry. Such a person, struggling to communicate and unable "to break the glass wall" will at times become violent. Symbolically he may smash windows and mirrors, attempting to get through to other persons. He may become so exasperated with the failure of others to penetrate to him that he may knock them down or otherwise injure them. When one knows and appreciates the feelings and basic causes leading to this kind of behavior, life can be eased by the proper kinds of special communication required by the schizophrenic. However, most people are too involved, too busy, with their own communication problems with normal people to spend much time on research in how to communicate with a schizophrenic relative or friend.

Depressed persons and alcoholics also have profound difficulties with communication. The normal person presented with a tragedy in his life (such as the death of a dearly loved person) goes into a brief depression; somehow or other manages to communicate it to others; to receive solace from others; and hence to treat and to recover from his depressed state. The ability to communicate one's grief to others and to receive their solace is an essential part of our communication. If a communication block exists and one cannot transmit to others and receive back from them the necessary treatment for his depression, then he is in trouble. If one goes into a depression whose causes are unavailable to himself, or whose causes he is hiding from himself and hence cannot be communicated to other persons, drastic methods of treatment may be needed in order to relieve depression and prevent suicide. Electric or chemical shock therapy are the common methods of treatment for these states. Once again the basic failure seems to be somewhere inside the involved person. Part of these failures may be in long-term communication strategies which may forbid one to communicate certain kinds of states of mind to his loved ones. For example, pride may prevent one from showing grief; he bottles up the grief and eventually the grief catches up and depresses him. This may be because of a faulty model that he acquired when he was very young; a parent or other loved one who reacted in this way to a grief-producing situation. Many basic communication problems start in childhood as we first begin our speech and learn the language. Along with the language we learn ways of using the language, some of which may be totally inappropriate and may lead to mental illness.

The case of the alcoholic is another example of a failure in communication. If one watches (from the security of a non-drinking position) a cocktail party at which some of one's best friends are becoming changed by ethyl alcohol, one is amazed that human beings have chosen this particular toxic substance, this particular poison, to free themselves up enough to communicate that which they forbid themselves to communicate without its aid. One of the basic needs for communication is expressed through the use of this "socializing" chemical substance.

Analyze very carefully the effects of alcohol upon one's own psyche. Quiz others about its effects upon their mental functioning, their social abilities, their thinking processes, and their feelings. From the answers, one can quickly see that alcohol is being used (or misused) as a social lubricant to facilitate communication with other persons. Sometimes the type of communication becomes rather shoddy. If a person drinks too much, he moves beyond the "socially facilitated" stage into a "partially anesthetized" stage in which he can hardly communicate at all. At this stage amnesia will take over; the party will be unremembered at the point at which the anesthetic effect become predominant.

It is in the early initial stages of alcoholic effects that the socially facilitating ones appear. What an experienced drinker would call "the first and second martini" stages. Those who have the integrity and force of will to take the first martini and refuse all others, can give the best account of the "lubricating" effect. Those who can take two and stop (who do not experience the anesthetic effect with two) can also give valuable information. However, those who go on and continue drinking beyond this point repeatedly are the ones who cannot give a coherent account of what happened or of their changed feelings with alcohol. It is these people who finally end up (and are diagnosed) as "alcoholic." To these people alcohol induces a positive feedback problem in which a little bit leads to more and more leads to anesthesia, or in common parlance, profound drunkenness. If such persons are penalized by an extremely painful hangover the next day, they can be induced to stay away from alcohol for a period of time—sometimes days, sometimes weeks, sometimes months or in extreme cases even for years. If there is no such penalty and if the penalty is avoided next day by taking more alcohol to anesthetize the pain, that person is well on the way to becoming an alcoholic.

Once alcoholism becomes firmly established in a given individual he cannot be taken off his daily allowance of alcohol (up to several quarts a day of hard liquor) without a severe penalty, the "withdrawal symptoms." The withdrawal symptoms are an intense acceleration of the activity and excitation of his whole central nervous system. Some systems are overexcited, as are the visual systems of the cerebral cortex, to the point where one sees unpleasant objects in his surroundings which do not exist, i.e., one begins to *project images,* by being overstimulated by the withdrawal of his normal amount of anesthetic. In this sense the nervous system has adapted to a high level of an anesthetic. If the anesthetic is now removed the nervous system automatically overexcites itself, as it were. Most persons cannot handle this degree of overexcitation of basic deep centers; they become extremely frightened and project frightening objects into their environment. Treatment for this condition (known as delirium tremens) involves very careful withdrawal of alcohol and substitution of other chemical substances to control the overexcitement. The so-called "drying out" period for one who has gone through alcoholic hallucinosis is best left in the hands of medical professionals. The nervous systems of such people are in such poor shape that, especially in the older person, death can ensue from heart or other basic failure of the organism itself.

One of the modern social treatments for alcoholism is the

organization known as Alcoholics Anonymous. This organization has achieved good results with some alcoholics and has given them a form of communication one with another which is sympathetic, disciplinary, and in many cases more complete than the nonalcoholic can achieve with alcoholics. This is mostly a failure of communication between the alcoholic and people who do not have the disease, and a success of communication of an alcoholic with another one.

Alcoholism could be better treated by some method of striking at the deep problem of the particular alcoholic involved. Some alcoholics think more of what other people think of them than what they think about themselves. In other words, their standards are "other-directed." They are directed from outside. Alcohol is their method of seeking approval from others by improving their social relationship through the camaraderie and transcendence experienced with the alcohol itself. Alcoholics, in a way, are the victims of civilized man's need for attaining transcendence; of finding something beyond himself, beyond his present state, beyond his present condition, beyond his civilization.

In addition to self-transcendence, alcohol avoids certain problems. If one looks in the other direction, away from the social surroundings down deep inside himself, one finds that alcohol, among other effects, anesthetizes his self-criticism. It anesthetizes certain bad feelings he may have about himself, certain demeaning judgments that he makes about himself, and it allows him to communicate these thoughts to others, even though without alcohol he forbids himself to make such communications.

In my experience attending parties at which most people are drinking and I am not, I find that approximately 80 per cent of the communications which I receive from the dinner partners (or the cocktail partners) are their secret dissatisfactions with themselves, with their spouses, with their children, with their social lot, with their sexual lives, with their work. A few attain euphoria through alcohol and can express good feelings that they cannot express without the aid of this substance. A few become more amorous than they allow themselves to be without the aid of this agent. A few become more violent than they allow themselves to be without this substance. The great proportion of civilized men and women with educated, gentle backgrounds allow themselves to express their dissatisfaction. They allow themselves also to become candid; they say what they see of one's self. In other words, one must face people at a cocktail party with the expectation (especially when one does not drink) that he will be subjected to a range of criticism that he would not expect from the same people in normal life. It seems to give some persons an access to their "true" feelings and a release from the necessity of disguising these feelings and pretending they do not exist.

Almost by definition, the mentally healthy person has no need for this kind of effect of alcohol. He has no need for the anesthetizing effects of alcohol, and he has no need for the hangover resulting therefrom. A mentally healthy person, as it were, must experience at least one bout to appreciate all the handicaps and deficiencies of the experience. A mentally healthy person by definition can control his own mood, can create euphoria when he needs it without such a chemical determinant. Our nervous system and cortex are large enough and our brain sufficiently complex so that we can achieve control over mood without such aids. Training along these lines is peculiarly lacking in our education and in our schooling.

Those of us lucky enough to have parents who automatically do these things may be ones who are mentally healthy. In other words, the communication defects that make alcohol necessary, we may acquire because of a deficiency in proper teaching and proper learning at very young ages.

The built-in programs and control-of-self programs by one's self can be learned and can be taught by teachers who have already learned this kind of control. We do need modern aids for such teaching and for such learning. Because of the deficiencies in our traditions and in our inheritances, we still must lean on special methods which are not yet built into our civilized structures and are not yet socially accepted in full. I do not propose a Utopia. I do not believe that as yet we have all of the information necessary for the construction of an "ideal" society. As our sciences and our humanities are expanded and deepened, as our understanding of ourselves becomes more clear-eyed, less biased, so will the degree of effectiveness increase.

The basic problem, then, is communication. Communication each with himself, in his own depths, and communication with those outside one's self. Our problem also is teaching a "broad front" kind of communication to our children. The educational problems are as profound as our individual inner problems and as our individual interpersonal problems.

One deeply abiding belief which profoundly influences one's communicative abilities is the relationship between one's self and his eventual demise. The personal survival problem of each one of us is handled differently by each. Some of us have never faced thoughts of our own eventual demise. Here I refer to the end of one's body and/or the end of one's self. Each of us has somewhat different treatments of the subject and different beliefs.

Some of us believe that with the death of the physical body the self dies. Some believe that with the death of the physical body the self in some form or other continues into some other dimension, some other universe, some heaven or some hell. Some believe that the body is only a temporary abode for the soul, for the self; life in this physical universe is only a stage in the progress of the spirit which temporarily

14

lives here. Some believe that life on this earth is an illusion, that we are hallucinating an external reality of a very fugitive and temporal nature, in reality we are part of a "universal mind" of infinite extent in physical space and of infinite extent in time backward and time forward.

Some believe that the self is only a subjective manifestation of a very complex, organic, physical, chemical organism. This group feels that the manifestations of self are merely the "software" of the big computer known as our brain. The thinking processes (for these believers) are the net results of many, many thousands of complex computations going on among the neurons and circuits of the brain. To such persons communication is between computers, between brains, between minds resident as an inextricable part of brains. To such persons the soul has very little meaning except as an integrated view of the self as generated by the brain. To such persons there is no outside influence nor influencing of the outside except through known physical media, i.e., speech, language, gestures, physical contacts, etc. To such persons there is no such thing as "extrasensory perception," telekinesis, psychokinesis, or other direct influence of mind on matter or of mind on mind at a distance in time or space.

Behind science there is a stringent set of beliefs. This set is one which ties one to his body, ties one to his brain, ties one to his biochemistry, ties one to this world and to this time. In this view, a person is the net result of the inheritance in two germ cells derived from his parents; he is a set of chemical, biochemical, and physical-chemical orders carried by his chromosomes, by his genes; his brain is built by the orders in the sperm and the egg; his brain is influenced, molded, changed, in terms of its software, its inner operations by the impingement of input and output to and from this brain in the uterus, after birth, and in contact with organisms similar to himself in the outer world. In this view, communication is the development of an under-standing and an incorporation of the rituals of the physical bodies and of the spoken words of other human beings. In this framework, one is profoundly influenced by changes in the internal chemistry within his own body and brain. In this view, one is profoundly influenced by communica-tions received from other human beings, and he profoundly influences other human beings by such communications. In such a view, ESP is strictly forbidden as an existing mode of communication.

In my view, ESP is a blind alley at the present time. Para-psychology groups are struggling to gain acceptance for their field, acceptance by other scientists. This is very nearly impossible at the present time. The above non-psychic-influence, non-soul point of view is working, working suc-cessfully, and generating new results of great interest. Until modern man can send telegrams and receive answers via ESP with the degree of reliability furnished by Western Union, there will be little progress in convincing other people of its existence. The simple pragmatic result of a function serving man is needed before acceptance can be gained.

Thus most of us assume that we can communicate only through our bodily presences and through our spoken and heard words and sentences, paragraphs, ideas, etc. Most of us assume that we cannot directly influence the mind of another without the use of physical presence or speech, or written word or other artifact. An artist can communicate through his paintings, a musician with his music, a sculptor with his statues, an author with his writings, a businessman with his form of written papers, a politician with his speeches and his vote-getting abilities, an accountant with his careful techniques, a doctor with his beneficial therapies.

The modes of communication between human beings who have acquired language and speech and writing are multiferous. The communicative behaviors of the human being are finally becoming a part of scientific investigation. Investigation of the modes and means by which we communicate is (finally) an object of proper scientific investigation. The nonverbal physical gestures in "contact languages" are finally beginning to be studied by qualified scientific personnel. The means of expression one to the other between lovers has long been a taboo area for scientific investigation. With the publishing of the Kinsey reports in the United States, a large number of these taboos are being attenuated and eventually apparently will be dropped. The up-and-coming generation has a much greater understanding of sexual communication than does the preceding generation. Inevitably, however, they have less experience and hence less abilities in human communication in other spheres. Certain kinds of communication come only with long experience and many years.

Some kinds of communication can be inhibited for many years. The ability of our big brain to inhibit certain kinds of activities is immense and persistent. Sexual inhibition can be carried throughout a whole lifetime in many cases. The inhibition of good feelings, and of bad feelings, of aggressive and hostile feelings, can also be carried out.

There are several advantages to making investigations of possible communication with a species other than man. There are advantages to picking a creature whose brain is equal to the size of ours so that one may one day realize communication at the same complex abstract levels at which one operates. There are advantages to choosing an entirely different body form and entirely different modes of communication, to delineate by contrast the modes and means that are interhuman.

I chose to investigate communication between dolphins and between dolphins and humans because of these outstanding differences and because of these similarities. The

17

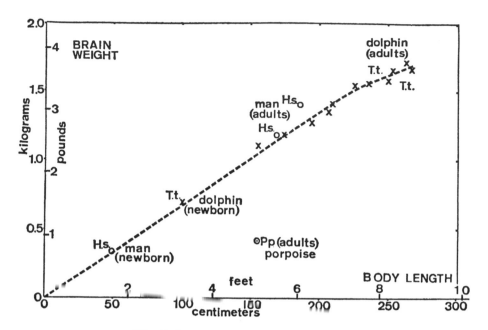

FIGURE 1. *The Relation of Brain Weight and Body Length for Man, Dolphin, and Porpoise*

This graph shows quantitatively our main reason for the choice of *Tursiops truncatus* (T.t.), the bottlenose dolphin, for communication research—young adults, 6 feet long, have brains equal to that of man in weight; as they age the brain weight and body length continue to grow to levels exceeding the average human size. The true porpoise (*Phocaena phocaena*) is limited in brain weight to the range of human children; the adult porpoise has a brain smaller than that of the newborn dolphin. Other dolphins (not considered in this book) have brains smaller than these dolphins. Still other dolphins have brains very much larger than those of these dolphins. The absolute size of a mammalian brain determines its computing capability and the size of its storage (memory); the larger the computer, the greater its power. One specimen of *Orcinus orca* (the largest dolphin) which was 510 centimeters (17 feet) long had a brain weighing 4.5 kilograms (9.9 pounds). Brain weights of *Physeter catadon* (sperm whale) have been found up to 9.2 kilograms (19.2 pounds) for body lengths of 1440 centimeters (48 feet); these are the largest known brains on this planet. (Relative brain size has little meaning in regard to computational powers: if it did have meaning, the marmoset monkey would be better than man at such tasks.) J. C. Lilly, "Critical brain size and language." *Perspectives in Biol. & Med.* 6: 246–55 (1963).

18

dolphin's brain is as large and larger than ours, if one picks the species correctly. We picked *Tursiops truncatus* which has a brain 20 per cent to 40 per cent larger than ours (Figure 1). In the Institute in the last four years we have examined this brain in great detail and can now say with authority how similar it is to ours in certain respects and how different it is in certain other respects. We can begin to define the communication problem as it exists between man and dolphin on a scientific level.

We find that one of the major deficiences in our past attempts to define a science of communication has been a lack of understanding of our own human-to-human communication methods and systems. As we sharpen up our man-to-dolphin communication, so do we sharpen up our human-to-human communication. As our basic understanding is expanded by an attempt to communicate with another species, so our understanding of our own communication problems is highlighted and better understood.

I have often moved from my attempts to communicate with a dolphin back into the attempts to communicate on a deeper and more understanding way with humans. My research has carried me into three areas of communication and into the depths of each area. Let me define these for you.

One area is my communication with myself. Another is communication with other human beings. Another is communication with dolphins.

In my communication with myself I used methods of isolation, solitude, and confinement and other special methods. In my communication with others, I investigated in depth using psychoanalytic and other special techniques. The results of these methods are applied in one form or another to our attempts to communicate with the dolphin. As we learn things with the dolphin, they are then turned back and used in our communication with human beings.

This is one way of this field of research. How useful it will be in our understanding of ourselves and our communication within, between, and among ourselves, and in the improvement of our general mental health will be seen in the future as more and more people become involved in this area of human endeavor.

In this book I attempt to show, to explain, to delineate, to theorize, to demonstrate, the value of interspecies communication to man, to individual men, to each one of us. This new field of human endeavor needs support, needs help, needs understanding, needs dedication. It needs dedicated men and women at a high level of confidence.

This book is a continuation of the report on communication started in *Man and Dolphin;* it contains the ideas, observations, philosophy, and proposals for a new field in human communication. This field is not necessarily only a science. It is a whole area of human efforts given in the first book,* "Interspecies Communication." This field includes scientific endeavors, humanistic endeavors, political endeavors, *interspecies* endeavors of all sorts. An analogy in human affairs is some of the international endeavors of the United Nations which could be subsumed under the name "international communication." In contrast to the older international one the new field exists in a limited context described here.

This book is not a textbook nor a study in any one of the accepted present-day sciences alone; i.e., it is not included within nor should be conceived of as being included within any of the following fields: marine biology, ichthyology, zoology, oceanography, cetology, delphinology, psychology, physiology, anatomy. Those readers with expectations that this is the case are firmly advised to stop right here. This

* *Man and Dolphin, loc. cit.*

is not intended to be, nor was *Man and Dolphin* intended to be, a specialist's book in one science nor only in science.

At the time of writing *Man and Dolphin* it was not known what would be relevant to this new field of "interspecies communication." Therefore, basic assumptions, postulates, faith, hopes, charities, and known facts of this field were presented. Some of the personal side was presented to allow later observers to evaluate the person giving this outline of the new field.

In *Man and Dolphin* the points of view, the philosophy, and the presentation were characteristic of the author. I chose a form which covered those matters currently in fashion in science insofar as they were known. But possibly more importantly, the chosen form of presentation covered matters not yet in fashion in conventional science of the year 1960. I also chose to present matters which may never become part of science as such. The breadth of the field was appreciated and the necessity for participation by those persons other than scientists was also appreciated. Some of these then unconventional matters had begun to show signs of respectable acceptance in 1965.

I wrote the first book for those who haven't forsworn their birthright to an open mind, to a broad view, to an inner dignity, to a total integrity, and to a deep sense of wonder and respect for their inner and outer unknowns.

I am a scientist. I try to be a kind of scientist called a generalist. This term "generalist" means that I do not any longer recognize the walls that have been arbitrarily set up between the sciences. The science of man is to me as important as the science of nuclear physics, or of biology, or of chemistry. In my opinion, the sciences are a continuum of knowledge, broken only by the holes of the unknowns. This continuum of the sciences stretches from the basic particles of the universe to the hidden thoughts of you and me and to the incredibly distant island universes. As a generalist, I integrate knowledge from any and all sources. This statement means that I include in my "science" matters from religion, political sciences, politics, human affairs, and other sources of basic knowledge about man.

Such a broad front may sound presumptuous. However, with humility and with respect for the areas of one's ignorances, one may possibly remove some of the stigmata from the generalist approach.

Even though certain persons may expect one to be a specialist, such as a physicist, a biologist, a biophysicist, a neurophysiologist, possibly even a psychoanalyst, a delphinologist, a doctor of medicine, I feel that this is rather a lazy view. I would prefer to say that one must include something of each of those specialities in the generalist approach. My training and experience is in each of these special areas. In addition to these disciplines, I must use other areas to fill out the picture. For example, I need Christ's teachings, the works of Shakespeare, the writings of Aldous Huxley, Prokofief's and Beethoven's concertos and symphonies, the paintings of da Vinci, Le Tour Eiffel, and the Empire State Building. The Encyclopaedia Britannica, 11th and 16th Editions, the Oxford Unabridged Dictionary, The Great Books are also needed as essential sources. Accounts of the creation of great industries, of great governments, of the United Nations are absorbed. The writings of William James are as important as those of B. F. Skinner for a full understanding of both inside psychology and outside psychology. Two Freuds (Sigmund and Anna) hold deep meaning for me; C. G. Jung's writings also help (see Bibliographical References). A real machine which is well conceived and well built gives me pleasure; I have built enough machines with my own hands to appreciate excellence in this area. Driving a powerful automobile, skiing a fast mountain trail, sailing a catamaran, cruising in a motor-sailor, navigating in a Maine fog, skin diving with an aqualung, programming a computer, teaching a child (or horse, or cat, or dolphin), making love, are all knowledge-generating activities which are also essential.

One other essential activity is the exploration of my own mind; this exploration is in depth and has produced unexpected results. It *seems* to contain (or be a part of) some large inner universes beyond my present understanding.

The important aspects of both the inner and outer realities are a part of the investigations of a generalist. He is willing to study and explore them as courageously and as actively as possible. Appreciation of basic dangers in such exploration is also essential. One explores inner reality carefully and cautiously, with the long preparation as well as the courage of the mountain climber scaling Mount Everest.

I am an optimist; I believe that we will not terminate life as we know it on this planet. I believe that there is time to pursue these areas of study, despite the fact that they are essentially peacetime, exploratory, long-term, loving, and non-destructive. At times this belief has been shaken badly with the news in the daily papers. Without this belief there would be no reason to be a human being much less a generalist. As it were, I must believe that our species has deep reservoirs of goodness, beauty, and truth. I must also believe that each of us, given a chance, can love and be loved, respect and be respected. There are some who take a more cynical, so-called "realistic" view. I have tried such an approach and find it lacking.

The heavens of the optimist and the hells of the pessimist exist, both in the inner and in the outer universes. One might expect an optimist to hide from "the evil" in himself, around him and in others, and in the world at large. Today, we cannot afford so to hide and be hidden. We must face it; there is destructive evil everywhere; sometimes we can escape it by friendship or by love or by luck in the sense of

23

the near miss. But we cannot escape it forever. Eventually each of us dies.

Sometimes one works out the evil in himself by courageous self-analysis combined with sheer guts. Sometimes this inner wickedness is deeply buried and requires deep "mining" tactics to reach it. When he consciously finds this deep evil, he may or may not remove it from himself. Sometimes all he has to do is find the evil and it flees before the searchlight of his consciousness.

The evil in one's loved ones is sometimes available for them to attenuate or eliminate in their personality. Sometimes we can help our loved ones to do this. However, this is a rare occurrence. When someone offers such an opportunity sometimes it is wise to look at it extremely carefully before taking it. We usually find that we are actually less help than we presume we can be. When I can help, I find it of great value in my own growth as a human being. However, even as in one's self, the evil in another has many layers and strata to be stripped off, one by one, to expose the true roots deep within.

The evil in man's large institutions is even more difficult; one tries to work around it or to eradicate it or to attenuate it. The present world dilemmas of incipient war on a total life-destroying scale is one ultimate expression of the evil in the inner and in the outer realities. Basically, the evil seems to emanate from within man himself. Those who would blame an outer reality, a bad God, or a bad Devil, are rationalizing and elevating us to a plane which is fantastically unrealistic. We, *Homo sapiens,* are basically at fault.

Thus a generalist must of necessity include morals and ethics in his studies. His own morals and ethics come under intensive scrutiny and deep study. After such perusing and after very careful experimental studies on himself, he may be willing to change his moral and ethical grounds to match more of the ideals which he finds.

In his book called *Insight and Responsibility* (New York: W. W. Norton & Company, 1964), Erik Erikson writes:

"I would propose that we consider moral rules of conduct to be based on a fear of threats to be forestalled. (Page 222 . . .) I would consider ethical rules to be based on ideals to be striven for with a high degree of rational assent and with a ready consent to a formulated good, a definition of perfection, and some promise of self-realization. This differentiation may not agree with all existing definitions, but it is substantiated by the observation of human development. Here, then, is my first proposition: the moral and the ethical sense are different in their psychological dynamics, because the moral sense develops on an earlier, more immature, level."

Thus the ethical rules are the more conscious ones. The ethical rules are available to voluntary control by the self. These rules can be modified in the light of experience as such modification is needed. The moral rules are buried deeper. The moral rules are less controllable by the self. The moral rules are not easily modified by the conscious self without the use of special basic investigative methods.

If one wishes to diagram self, it would consist of layers. The outer layers, which are the voluntary conscious ones, contain "ethical" programs we can rewrite by ourselves. This is the area of conscious argument in conscious modification of programs by ourselves or by contact with another human being.

Below these outer layers there are deeper ones of self which have relatively fixed "moral" programs. These programs are more automatic, autonomous, out of contact with one's self, and thus seemingly have a life of their own. These programs cannot be easily rewritten nor even easily detected by self. Sometimes others outside self can detect their operations more easily than we can by ourselves.

The moral programs can only be rewritten in special states of the mind and of the body. Such states may vary from ecstatic ones of religious revelation to stressful ones of a near brush with death. Alternatively, such states can be induced by special methods, including long psychoanalytic investigations, long self-analysis, and fundamentally dedicated strivings to achieve the ideal in self that one has set. With these experiences as a basic background, some of these programs can be rewritten with the help of certain special chemical substances, combined with the proper setting, with the proper preparation, and with the proper planning for the future at the time of the special experience.

Thus is a generalist generated. At least this particular generalist. As a scientist and a human being, I study and modify my own moral and ethical rules as needed. The modified versions are then used in the practice of my profession. This regime is necessary for progress of self, for progress of one's own species. The measurement of progress is not easy to do consciously and rationally. We must measure our progress and accept to a certain extent the measurements expressed by other persons of our progress.

After the publication of *Man and Dolphin* I received many letters from out-of-the-way corners. To those persons who wrote me from their hearts I am grateful. At the time I did not necessarily agree with all points of view expressed. I have come in the intervening years to agree with some.

First I am a man, then I am a scientist. As a member of the human species, progress of the species comes first; understanding leading to that progress comes second. This book is an attempt on my part to give a picture of a certain kind of progress desired for the human species by this particular member of it.

I believe that attempts to link the human mind with the

most basic particles of the universe will not succeed until basic considerations of research on the mind and the brain have been accomplished. I *do not subscribe to the view that there is a most basic single science.* I feel that investigations of the human mind, of the brain, of the basic particles of the universe, of communication with our own and with other species, are all equally necessary to our understanding and to our progress. In my "basic science training" at Cal Tech we were imbued with the notion that each of the main special sciences has much to offer in terms of human knowledge and that no one of them should be considered as more basic than any other one. Those who would construct hierarchies in science may have political power as their main motivation. The current competition in science for government funds is extreme; anyone who needs large sums of money for research for his particular field is tempted to use definitions and to voice opinions of other fields which are demeaning to those fields. I do not feel such a necessity for justifying my scientific position nor my position as a humanist nor as a scientist.

The generalist cannot demean any kind of knowledge nor demean any source of knowledge. He must use them all. In saying this I do not mean to imply that a specialist is lesser or greater than a generalist. There is an old "saw" in science which says that "a specialist learns more and more about less and less until he knows everything about nothing." Conversely, "a generalist learns less and less about more and more until he knows nothing about everything."

Each man of science must decide how much of a specialist and also how much of a generalist he wants to be. One must have a specialist's knowledge in certain areas of science in order to function within science itself. One must have something of the generalist in him in order to realize the proper position of the knowledge he is acquiring with respect to the total knowledge gained by man.

There is a picture which a scientist is expected to generate when he writes a book. In the natural sciences, the tradition is to remove one's self as far as possible from the information that he is transmitting. One avoids the subjective approach; he keeps his own name out of the presentation of the "objective facts." One attempts insofar as it is possible to remove all his own thinking about the processes and the facts revealed by the research. One gives only "results" and "perspectives on the areas where the results fit in." This is the tradition in the natural sciences, i.e., the sciences of those materials, processes, and functions, which are far from man (physics, astronomy, etc.).

In the general area of science which I have chosen, this view creates paradoxes. Man himself must be included. The scientist himself must be in his system. In addition to being trained in the natural sciences, I am trained in psychoanalytic research.

In psychoanalytic research, one's self can become, as it were, one of the objects of the research. By long years of training, one realizes in detail how difficult the self is for the application of scientific principles. The subjective life treated objectively is difficult. We learn that objectivity with respect to our own feelings, motivations, thoughts, ideas, and most cherished ideals is necessary. We also learn that scientific research on the minds of others is similarly a difficult assignment. We finally learn that one's self and the self of others are inextricably part of the scientific research no matter what the field is.

This is true in physics. There are definite rules of separation for physicists. The rules are those which separate theory from experiments, experimenter from system. There are two fields of physics in general, theoretical physics and experimental physics. The theoretical physicist is quite competent in the area of constructing theories, testable ones. With closely supervised experiments by an experimental physicist, the theories are rebuilt depending upon the outcome of the experiments. There is a constant feedback in physics between the theoretical and the experimental approaches. Few physicists are capable enough or have time enough for both areas. But even here, the physicists themselves are not analyzed deeply; they are programmed by theories and experimental results.

In the sciences of man himself, this separation and the rules of separation are not as clarified as they are in physics. In my work as a generalist, I use the model of the physicists and their separation rule. I separate the fact and theory rigorously in my own mind. In addition, experimenter and the parts of himself functioning in the system under investigation are separated as far as is practical.

Man and Dolphin was in part an exercise in theoretical biology. It was also a presentation of the facts (experimental and naturalistic) that had been accumulated. I gave those facts which I considered of importance.

Some persons, mainly biologists, do not understand this separation of fact and theory. Some persons act as if I am jumping ahead of the facts and as if the theoretical deductions presented in that book are true, i.e., are "facts." Obviously this is nonsense. Such separation is very carefully done. If the book is reread carefully, one can see this separation.

In addition to being a presentation of theory and fact in regard to the present status of interspecies communication, the first book was written in as simple a style as I could achieve. Having come from a long scientific background in which one is expected to condense his thoughts to the minimum possible space, I found it difficult to free up my style. The style expected of a scientist is usually condensed and hence difficult. Ideas are so succinctly expressed that one cannot miss even single words without error. He uses a stilted, complex, and condensed jargon. Such jargons are spread throughout the sciences; they are useful shorthands in talking with specialists.

The usual justification for the jargon is that the matter in hand is not translatable into "laymen's terms"; that "too much exactness is sacrificed" in translation. I appreciate this view and subscribe to it in a limited way. However, given enough time and energy to do it, the truly worthwhile ideas and discoveries are translatable.

There is another route that I prefer, a route which I took in *Man and Dolphin;* as the work progresses, one does a continuous translation into "laymen's terms." This latter technique has deficiencies in one communicative sense: everyone *thinks* that he understands what someone else is saying. Writers for lay publications read what one has written and then write their own paraphrase of what has been said. Often they miss the point, often they put an emphasis which was not right and not intended. Despite these drawbacks I found that many persons responded strongly and positively to the writing.

The other basic motivation behind *Man and Dolphin* was to write for those who are coming next, after my generation. Part of my duty as a general scientist is to adequately explain what I am doing for those who come next. It is this motivation which strongly influenced my style and content in writing *Man and Dolphin* and in writing the present book.

This book and its predecessor are written for the young in mind and in spirit. If any of those persons who are not yet committed to a way of life choose this approach to general humanistic science as a result of reading these two books, I will feel that I have succeeded. Too few of our modern "general purpose" geniuses go into this kind of science; most of them enter a special science, the arts, the professions, politics, or business. Human-orientated science needs more broad spectrum geniuses than it has today: I do what I can to arouse their interest while they are still uncommitted enough to do something about it.

In addition to scientific theory and scientific fact, there is an additional content in these two books. My surroundings, my self, and my training are in them. In my psychoanalytic research training, I found that the scientist who works on man should present something of himself as a man in the material. In the sciences of man, in order to understand the science, one must know the particular man who is giving the facts and the theory; one must know the transmitter of the knowledge.

I realize that this point of view is at variance with the accepted technique of natural science. In spite of this variance, in this day and age I do not see how one can proceed differently. If we attempt communication with another human or with an individual of another species, we use ourselves in this communication. The quality and kind of self that one is becomes an important part of the system. Those who come after me and who read these publications will know somewhat of me and may be helped to learn what to do about themselves. They may learn the sources of our success or failure in the writings about my personality, techniques, interest, training, experiments, or dolphins. At least I give them a good chance to find this out.

This point of view partially explains the contents of this and the previous book. The publicly expected content is scientific fact; the actual content is theory, fact, and who we are (those who are doing the looking), why we looked where we did, and how we found those facts of scientific interest and importance. I have tried to give as much of the picture as possible to encourage and to aid those who come later.

To my surprise, it worked with several of my scientific colleagues. For example, a zoologist recently wrote a paper about dolphins, and he attributed his results partly to one of the major points of *Man and Dolphin*, i.e., to the social relationship between the dolphin and the experimenter. This degree of acceptance (1965) of a formerly radical new idea (1960) is gratifying to behold.

One of the effects of time on discovery is that those who come later have the facts without the struggle of those who found them. Discovery is partially a struggle for acceptance for one's ideas and findings. Later, for someone else to learn the ideas and the discovered fact and to make them his own is easy. So a naïve learner then says, "What was all the fuss about?" The discoverer is thus expected to forget the conflict and the costs of breaking into the new territory. He is expected to move on with new battles and new discoveries.

I have written many scientific papers and have given numerous lectures to scientific audiences, to scientists and their wives, to scientific evaluation teams visiting our project. We have shared ourselves, our work, our methods, our dolphins with all qualified persons who have asked.

Today the program and its results and its plans are obvious to everyone: everybody expects quick miracles. I have never and am not currently expecting a fast "breakthrough." The unexpected has a way of creeping up on the predictor, but I hope we do have time to become acquainted thoroughly with the dolphins themselves and their problems.

The exploiters of the dolphins may be spoiling our relationships to them. With or without a breakthrough the dolphins need protection from the human exploiters. The commercial use of dolphins needs rational, ethical control. Literally tens, if not hundreds are sick, unhappy, dying, or dead as a result of man's ignorance. Dolphins are even eaten by humans (e.g., in Japan). The exploitation of dolphins for Navy projects, and their commercial exploitation for circuses, motion pictures, television, and for pets, have also taken their toll of the dolphin population.

Nobody can be a real expert with dolphins until he has lived with them and continued to try to communicate with them for many years. I feel very strongly that the future experts on dolphins will have certain characteristics which few if any of the present "experts" have.

The future dolphin experts will have a sensitivity, a training, a philosophy, a flexibility, a curiosity, a dedication, and a personal involvement which the dolphins need.

Anyone who has been near dolphins, worked with them, and had the responsibility for their care and upkeep knows unequivocally that this is a difficult assignment. They also know that in contact with man the dolphin's morbidity and mortality is high. How much higher or lower than for the dolphin in the wild no one as yet knows.

The best possible research into the causes of death of dolphins close to man is lacking. I have come to the conclusion that our dolphins rate at least the investigation we give to the deaths of individuals of our own species. In our Institute, the cooperation of the local county Medical Examiner's Office is sought and obtained in those cases in which there is any doubt as to the cause of death. The Medical Examiner's Office makes a thorough investigation, comparable to the investigation that it makes of human deaths. We wish to find and preserve the maximum amount of information we can as to the causes of death of dolphins in proximity to man so that in the future we can avoid these causes insofar as that is in our power.

Should we or should we not include dolphins in the Golden Rule? I have come to believe that we should. "Do (and not do) unto others as you would have them do (and not do) unto you." The "others" includes dolphins, porpoises, and whales. The usual form of the rule is pretty much limited to individuals of the human species. It is my belief that we should include at least dolphins, porpoises, and whales, if not other species. Once again I am indebted to Erik Erikson for this pertinent ethical formulation.

In our experience in the Institute, apparently the dolphins also use a rule with us which is approximately the same as the above rule: if we treat them gently they treat us gently; if we treat them roughly, they match our roughness but they are still forbearing. If one realizes their immense power in the water, one can call them "forbearing" because they do not unleash this power in full force against us.

Even *Orcinus orca,* the so-called "killer" whale, is quite as judicious and careful with us as the smaller dolphins are. During 1964 Moby Doll, a killer whale, kept at Vancouver, B.C. was remarkably cooperative, as was Namu in Seattle in 1965. At the turn of the century, Old Tom, the *Orcinus* at Twofold Bay in Australia, aided the shore whaling station for an alleged fifty years (see General Bibliography, William John Dakin, 1934).

In this book there is a problem in the current use of "animal," with respect to dolphins. When I use the term I am subscribing to the scientific theory that man is "an animal," evolved from lesser forms of animals.

The use of "animal" has several other connotations which are not very appropriate for this book. Some persons, including many scientists, use the term consciously or unconsciously to place man (and themselves) above the rest of the animal kingdom; in this context man is either a creature with a separate creation, presumably in the image of his God, or else has evolved so far above and beyond the other animals that he is placed in a special class by himself.

A cogent argument in favor of the "special case" for man is our ability, *demonstrated,* to communicate complex thoughts. We are placed in the special case because it is presumed the other "animals" lack such an ability. Until the communicative abilities of dolphins and of whales are demonstrated or else disproven, I will abandon the use of this possibly demeaning term ("animal") as applied to those creatures with brains equal to or greater than ours.

I will use the term only in the context of those dolphins whose brains are smaller than ours. There are several such species (*Stenella microps, Delphinus rubiventris, Phocoena phocoena*). Thus the term "animal" is used for those organisms with brains below the accepted human size of brain. Unless an organism has a brain equal or greater than ours in size and complexity, I use the word "animal" for him. In other words, if we are to be "special animals" then there are also other "special animals."

As I theorized in *Man and Dolphin*, we speak and communicate complex matters partly because our brains are large enough (in terms of numbers of active elements) to do it. Therefore, any similar brain of similar size and complexity can do a comparable job though possibly in ways very strange to man. (I suspect that dolphins have similar problems with regard to man: one can imagine dolphins asking, "Is man a God, a Devil, a lower animal, a creature from outer space, or just a dolphin that failed to get back into the seas?".)

Inevitably the question of the religious significance of one's work arises. I touched earlier upon the ethical and the moral rules. In a much deeper sense than the Golden Rule, we seek significance beyond the all-too-human limits of ourselves. If one succeeds in having a religious revelation, the significance is steeped in a perspective so vast as to generate an awe from which he cannot recover. His whole life, whole philosophy, hopes, fears, relations with others, his view of himself are said to be permanently changed. The realization through one's self of the immensity of the cosmos in time, in outer space, in others, in dolphins, in other creatures still beyond our ken, creates a new "childlikeness" in which one can give up "childishness." Man himself is put in a perspective in his proper place with other beings.

Through such "revelations" the freshness and the rebirth of one's self are of immense significance. Such experiences are not yet admitted to the halls of conventional science. A major difficulty is that unless another person has had such experience, he cannot share the wonder and the awe of one's own inner experiences.

A person who has not had such revelations is impermeable to any kind of description that may be given him of such experience. The account is met with a skeptical and even cynical attempt at demeaning its importance. Those who have not been through it are the only ones who can afford the luxury of cynicism and of skepticism. Until such persons have had the revelation themselves, they remain in the "out-group." This is a delicate and difficult area of the science of man. It may be that it is too easy to fake in this area. The truth of what one presents is not subject to the usual tests of evidence as devised in the courts and the sciences.

These are apparently the basic reasons conventional science has ruled "revelations" outside its province. Science limits itself to that which can be shared by conventional means of communication. This point must be emphasized. *Conventional means of communication are the only acceptable ones for science.* Especially important means are the printed word, and printed pictures and other data that can be graphically presented. *Knowledge cannot become science unless it can be recorded, reproduced, distributed, stored, and hence studied at leisure.* J. J. Thomson (Lord Kelvin) wrote that an area of knowledge isn't science until more than one person can measure it, tie numbers to it, and agree on the value of those numbers with the other measurers within certain limits of error.

I suspect that the phenomena that we now call "revelation" will become part of an important new field of scientific research. It will not become so, however, until we have persons adequately trained in the techniques of self-observation and self-recording, persons with an immense degree of objectivity. Then we will be able to record accurately and well and obtain reproducible experiments in this area of scientific research. At that point, we may be able "to tie numbers to it" and "share the values of those numbers" from one individual to the next. As experimental techniques for producing reproducible "revelations" are worked out, and as the phenomena become less and less unique, i.e., as they become shared by more and more people under the proper experimental control, then the subjective phenomena may become science.

As the new knowledge does so become science, I am sure that we will achieve important new insights not only into ourselves, but into other beings as well. Among the other beings are the dolphins.

Many phenomena of the human mind, like the transcendental religious experiences, have been mistakenly classified as a "negative" area for "proper" scientific research. This mistake has removed them from a proper scientific investigatory sphere and put them almost totally in the custodial care of other groups of men.

The science of the mind is expanding rapidly. New mechanisms and explanations are being discovered which are broader, deeper, and more "open-ended" than the old religious, medical, and psychological systems. Some of these new views of our minds appear in this book. I apply them to me, I apply them to my own species, and I apply them to the dolphin.

Much of the science of the human mind is deeply imbedded in mathematics, in the law, in the humanities, in politics, in government, in business, in private enterprise. To understand what is going on, I must borrow from each of these human areas of activity and theory. I hope that experts in these fields will help us with the dolphins, not only in terms of financial and facilities support, but also in ideas, philosophies, and the kinds of activities required to broaden this field of interspecies communication. A "total push" approach includes as many varieties of the best of human beings as can be motivated and dedicated to the interspecies communication field.

Laymen, including lawyers, politicians, and businessmen, should be interested in interspecies communication. We must somehow show to these laymen the relevance of inter-species communication to interhuman communication to its improvement for evolving mental health. I hope that this book and the previous one will interest intelligent members of the professions and intelligent laymen in forwarding the field of interspecies communication in ways appropriate to their own needs. If and when man breaks barriers to communication with dolphins, the necessity of "interspecies education" using "interspecies communication" will be evident. Then interhuman communication will be needed at all levels to explain what happens.

CHAPTER 2

The Importance of Interspecies Communication

As I OUTLINED in *Man and Dolphin,* man may be on the threshold of a new area of discovery in the field of communication with beings other than the human ones. The newly accelerated space programs of the Soviet Union and the United States are pushing closer to the lunar landings of man within this decade. The probing of other planets by means of interplanetary vehicles has already started with the Mariner series. The plans for the first biological samplings from the planet Mars are nearly completed. Plans and projects for the detection of extraterrestrial, intelligent, communicating life forms have been formulated. (One such project, called Ozma, failed to find narrow-band signals from the stars Tau Ceti and Alpha Eridani.)

Thus it can be seen that some scientists, some engineers, and some administrators within certain government agencies are seriously engaged in planning for the *detection* of nonhuman, intelligent beings from outside the earth. However, there is no public evidence that any plans are being formulated as to the possible ways of dealing with these beings if and when they are detected. Serious consideration of research plans in this area is not yet respectable; detection, yes; dealing with them, no. As I stated in the previous book, it is necessary, scientifically, to consider well in advance the areas for future research. I believe it is important that we consider possible ways of dealing with nonhuman intelligent life forms before the duty is forced upon us. We must decide what humans with what training, with what motivations should make the first contacts. I would not like to see certain kinds of human beings start the initial contacts with the other beings. We should consider carefully the kinds of human beings which are best suited for this kind of contact. It is about time that man consider the kinds of men, the desirable traits and qualifications of those persons who will be in control of this kind of important communication.

For example, highly classified, top-secret military plans may already be formulated for dealing with such beings. I hope not. The last thing we need is a closed, military-secret treatment of this subject. This would be an assurance that the wrong kinds of human beings would make the first contacts and probably spoil those contacts forever. This subject needs public airing, with a fresh breath of youthful minds freely discussing possibilities, ways, and means. The military approach of necessity is on the offensive-defensive logical base. The necessary curiosity and the necessary love with which such beings should be met are something that military minds leave at home when they go to the office. Currently we need responsible, competent humanists in this field: the need for them is so great that it looks as if it spells the difference between success and possible disaster on an unprecedented scale. (With the current picture as it is, I would advise any being greater or lesser than we are not to contact us. In our present state of development, we are still unsuitably organized and unsuitably educated to make contact.)

Our present military potential is great enough to kill not only all human beings but all life forms on the land and in the sea. It may sound a bit silly to go beyond this potential for cataclysm, but modern military minds are carrying the power to create cataclysms even further. It takes only an elementary knowledge of modern nuclear and particle physics to see the trend to the ultimate Armageddon of vast released energies destroying planets. It takes only an elementary knowledge of what is happening in the United Nations, in the Far East, between the United States and the Soviet Union to see the brink of the release of these vast energies. *Homo sapiens* is fast developing the means of destroying this planet as a habitable abode for all of life as we know it. It may be that this is the natural course for our form of life. It may be that it is destined for this type of self-destruction. It may be that the evil in enough of us is destined to destroy the whole of us.

I sincerely hope and pray that this is not so. I hope that my children and their children have the opportunities to pursue beauty, goodness, truth, and self-fulfillment that I have had. It may be that I have not taken enough of the responsibility against this evil in my own lifetime. The old saying that one is either a missionary or a scientist, not both, may be a disguised, evil way of regulating too much of my life. Let me illustrate this point by the story of my contacts with one of the scientists turned "missionary" to try to eradicate the evil implicit in the use of atomic energy in our era.

Dr. Leo Szilard met several times with me in 1958. He later used information he gained in our talks to write a parable of the dolphins and of man.*

This parable was in the service of Dr. Szilard's humanitarian ethic and hope of elimination of the military control of the vast sources of energy by the physicists. Szilard turned from physics to become a missionary in the humanitarian tradition. When I first met with him we were both in a great medical research center. We were about as far from destructive evil as each of us could be. He had lately embarked on a search for the scientific bases of human mem-

* Szilard, Leo, "Voice of the Dolphins" (1961).

ory. In the course of his search, he was interviewing me along with many other scientists who had worked on the brain.

At this time I had completed some of my investigations of the dolphins. I had just decided to leave that particular institution and start a new institute devoted to dolphin research.

He told me of his hopes of the peaceful uses of nuclear energy and of banning the military use of it. Apparently to test me, he argued with me about the dolphin project; he elicited in our discussion all the facts I then knew. He elicited my theories about their intelligence and "languages" and my ideas about the consequences of these theories, and the consequences of communication with them.

At the time, he tried to persuade me to stay at the medical center. He met every one of my reasons for leaving. At that time I had made up my mind. I wasn't to be dissuaded. For what I wanted to accomplish, I feel that I was right. For what he wanted to do, he was right. If I had wanted to be a humanitarian and a missionary and work with him, I would have stayed.

In his parable he based his "Vienna Institute" on the model of the present Communication Research Institute that I had already planned in my own mind and had imparted to him. In this parable, the dolphins solve many of men's problems by sheer intellectual superiority. This is a fantasy, of course. We named the species of dolphin that could accomplish this after Szilard; we call them *Delphinus szilardiensis.*" The characteristics of this species are any characteristics that Szilard wished to give them. He enjoyed this joke.

Before Szilard died, we talked several more times. I was more and more involved in the creation of the new research institute. He became more and more involved in the "ban-the-bomb" efforts which were then in progress.

Today, I feel closer to Szilard's ideals than I could have at that time. The danger has increased with the entry of China into the nuclear warfare race. It may be that there will be no time left for humans to prepare to begin to really communicate with the dolphins and the whales. It may be that we are all doomed to extinction before such an ideal can be realized. Szilard's fantasy of human-dolphin intellectual teamwork may remain a fantasy because it did not have a chance to be tested or to be realized. In fact, intellectual teamwork of humans with any other being (possibly greater than we) may never come to pass. The true race of today is not a military race, it is race between humanitarianism, no matter where found, and militarism, no matter where supported. If the military forces destroy us, then everything great that man has accomplished (including nuclear energy and the vast sources of energies beyond the present ones such as those existing in anti-matter) end in nothing. Somewhere else, someone else may know we ended our own existence, though we cannot then know whether they do or not. We may end in several small flashes or in one big flash sent out into the eternal blackness of the cosmos. If there is anyone else watching in the proper regions of the electromagnetic spectrum, they may try to account for the demise of this planet by a theory that it happened through purely passive, nuclear planetary and stellar forces and energies. On the other hand, they may be advanced enough to know that we destroyed ourselves through these energies.

Personally, I would rather see how it comes out. A friend of mine once tried to commit suicide. We talked all one night; finally he agreed not to take his own life. (I am not sure that he would have committed suicide, even without the talk we had that night.) However, he later said that the most cogent and helpful thing that I said to him was, "If you commit suicide, you won't be around to see how it all turns out." I hope that the destructive ones of our species are curious enough to want "to see how it all turns out." I further hope that they can control themselves and others in order to control these awful forces enough to be able to save all of us.

Historically then, the Communication Research Institute was born out of an effort to create a new research institute devoted strictly to peaceful projects. If we are to destroy ourselves, there is no point at all in the kinds of research which I am doing and which I propose doing in the future through the Institute. Therefore, I must believe we will live on. There must be people like myself who insist we will live on, who insist on doing these projects in the face of the imminent demise of the planet Earth. Otherwise, such projects will always give way to other "defense" projects. I asked myself again and again should I not participate, along with Szilard, in attempting to be in control over atomic energy for peaceful purposes?

My argument to myself ran somewhat as follows: Why do we fight wars at all? We do it as a defensive measure because we are attacked by others. We do it because it is necessary for the health of the nation as a whole in order to keep up maximum production of a huge industrial machine. We do it to protect that which we hold most dear and to maintain those institutions and those activities which we consider to be ideal in terms of the future progress of our species.

I choose to consider interspecies communication one of these ideal activities, i.e., one of those activities for which we have created a military machine in order to be able to carry on that activity in a protected and fostering atmosphere, as it were, behind the lines of the military perimeter. Without dedicated people who persist in scientific research which is oriented toward an idealistic set of aims and goals, we may as well give up the ghost as a progressive species and sink into a new dark age. If all of us get out and fight, do development only of weapons, then no one is left at home to bring us farther along the road out of our abysmal "peacetime" ignorance.

What is it basically, deep down underneath, behind the apparent façade that communication with another species may possibly give to man? Szilard attempted to answer this question with his parable. If one reads his story, one can detect a bit of making fun of man and his current needs. He arranged it so the dolphins in the Vienna Institute gave easy and facile answers to all of the major problems facing man today. For example, the peoples of the world were fed by one of the dolphin's inventions.

We may obtain the cooperation, say, of the dolphins and get them to work on the major problems facing us. They may in their original alienness be able to see our problems more objectively than we can see them and to solve them for us. They may have, and today we still do not fully factually know this, an intellect superior to ours, as Szilard assumes.

If interspecies communication is to exist at all, I feel that it will give us far more than just facile solutions to man's problems. As a result of my experience and experiments with dolphins, I feel that they have much to teach us which is new to us and that we have much that is new to teach them. Our work on the problems of importance to dolphins, and whomever else they may be communicating with, may be our best contribution to them and may be our best contribution to ourselves. Sometimes I feel that if man could become more involved in some problems of an alien species, he may become less involved with his own egocentric pursuits, and deadly competition within his species, and become somehow a better being.

I wish to underscore and to emphasize the cooperative aspect of this interspecies communication attempt. When we make the assumptions that we do on this project, we also must face the consequences. We have found that we cannot make the kind of progress that we wish to make with dolphins unless we give them the respect that we give to one another. We find that we cannot proceed and make progress with a given dolphin unless we treat that dolphin with gentleness, with politeness, with respect, and with discipline of a special sort. We find that a young dolphin will, quite as unashamedly as a young human, take advantage of our good nature. We and they need and want mutual respect and mutual discipline. Our group and they do not want unilateral exploitation by man. Our group and our dolphins do not want unilateral exploitation of man by the dolphins.

The whole philosophy that says that the one species must rule the other species has been cast out of the thinking of myself and my colleagues. We are often asked, "If the dolphins are so intelligent, why aren't they ruling the world?" My very considered answer to this is—they may be too wise to try to rule the world. The question can be easily turned around, Why does man or individual men want to rule the world? I feel that it is a very insecure position to want to rule all of the other species and the vast resources of our planet. This means a deep insecurity with the "universes" inside of one's self. One's fears and one's angers are being projected on others outside of one's self; to rule the world is, finally, to rule one's inner realities.

It is my deep feeling that unless we work with respect, with discipline, and with gentleness with the dolphins that they will once more turn away from us. Apparently at the time of Aristotle or just preceding his time, the dolphins approached man. By A.D. 50 in the time of the Romans, they had turned away from man not to come back until this century. This is one-half of the view. To be complete, we must say that at the time of Aristotle man turned toward the dolphins. It is only in this century that we once again seek the dolphins. I prefer the view that each of us has sought the other, at least twice, once 500 B.C. to 200 B.C. and once again in the twentieth century.

Exploitations of dolphins by men are not only a disgrace to our humanitarian ideals but also are a definite handicap to our possible future with them. If we are to communicate with them on anything but a "bright animal" kind of exchange, we had best show them our best side from the beginning. Their present relationships with us are pretty well restricted to their "entertainment value" and some uses the Navy is making of them. If our future with them is to have wider horizons, we must bring those wider horizons to our work with them.

If we think of dolphins as "lower animals," then we will not even attempt to meet them as "equals" worthy of our efforts. If we think of them as "bright, intelligent animals serving man" in entertainment, in circuses, and on television, we are favoring a segregationist point of view. Currently, we place dolphins "over there," with chimpanzees, performing dogs, and fictional horses that talk to TV audiences. Currently, in the entertainment media, dolphins are equivalent to "good boy"-type dogs, similar to Lassie.

If we "teach" them to aid our underwater work in the sea as glorified "seeing-eye dogs" of the Navy, of oceanographers and of divers, we are far from my goals for them. This sort of a relationship ("fetch and carry") is not between equals. Slavery (man to man) has had a long history in our species. Persons can still "buy" dolphins from other persons even though they cannot "buy" another human being. As long as the legal view of dolphins is that of "animals," they will still be an article of commerce to be exploited for man's purposes. The dolphins are not yet protected even under "animal conservation" laws.

It may be that the word "equal" is not quite the term to use for dolphin-human comparisons. A dolphin can be what

I call a "cognitive equal" with a human being and still be an alien and strange mind as seen by the human. We must somehow translate the Golden Rule, and the dolphin will have to do the same, for use between such strange, likable, cooperative beings. As one of the "others" in the Golden Rule, neither his appearance nor his alienness of thought should deter us or him. Both sides will have to search for the bases of equality. The United Nations does not recognize race, color, or creed as a means of differentiation between human beings. Let us add "species" and use this approach as a good example of the kind of thinking which we should be applying to the dolphins and whales. In addition to race, color, creed, and religious beliefs, the new criteria should read: "*No matter differences between species, no matter differences of anatomy, no matter differences between media in which they live, creatures with a brain above a certain size will be considered 'equal' with man.*"

Currently, without this point of view we may be doing violence to dolphins. It may turn out, for example, that the worst thing in the world to do to a dolphin is to lock him up in a closed tank (of any size) and give him free food and free care. This is among the worst things that can be done to one of us. Consider those cases in which we do it to one another.

Even the places where persons are confined like dolphins have a very poor reputation. We call places where we give free food and free care to people who are locked up, "prisons," "state hospitals for the insane," "prisoner-of-war camps," etc. A very poor press. In other words, among our most cherished ideals for each of ourselves and each of our loved ones are civil rights, personal freedom, private enterprise, and private initiative. From this point of view we are mistreating the dolphins.

Let us look at our present dealings with dolphins from the humanitarian viewpoint. In order to get the feel of the dolphin's situation with respect to us imagine that we as a species are placed in their position by "invaders from outer space."

The invaders arrive in their interstellar space ships. Their appearance is totally alien to us. The aim of the invaders is to collect humans as interesting bright animal specimens for displays in their zoos, in their circuses, in their schools, in their medical research institutes, and in their universities. These displays are primarily for entertainment and scientific purposes. They treat us even as we currently treat the dolphins.

These invaders cannot live in air. There is too much nitrogen in our atmosphere for them to be comfortable. On their planet nitrogen is their source of energy, even as oxygen in our atmosphere is our source of energy. Even as 100 per cent oxygen is eventually poisonous to humans, so is 80 per cent nitrogen to the aliens. By special means not yet known to us, the invaders modify the air of our planet for their own use.

After long study the invaders find out how to capture human specimens. They study us for a long time. They learn how curious some of us are about anything new; they learn how repelled we are by the invaders' true appearance. They learn how upset some of us become by the death or disappearance of loved ones. They learn how to influence the general directions of the thinking of large numbers of humans.

Once they are able to influence the thinking in the mass, they devise "warfare between humans" to facilitate their collection of human specimens. When the order comes from the invaders' planet to collect more human specimens, a war is started among human beings. During the chaos attendant upon the war, they collect human specimens as needed. Large explosions, large fires, and disappearances at sea are used as covers. When the invaders collect humans not under these covers, a small flurry of interest is created in the human press by the unexplained disappearances.

Even as in our collection of dolphins, the invaders have trouble with their collection program. At first, most of their human specimens die. The causes of death are not too well known nor are they thoroughly studied by the invaders. So many humans are available, however, that the invader collectors do not worry about those who are lost. When they find that they are losing all of them, they begin to investigate the possible causes.

After many years the invaders discover that humans need oxygen to breathe. They asphyxiate their first specimens by keeping them in an oxygen-free atmosphere in their spacecraft. All that the invaders can obtain are anatomical specimens for scientific investigation back on their home planet.

This lack of success keeping the specimens alive opens up a whole new science on the planet of the invaders. They call it "interplanetary zoology." Under this title they begin their study of human physiology. They discover the humans' need for oxygen; they keep them in special tanks containing 20 per cent oxygen and 80 per cent nitrogen. Experiments with the invaders' home planet atmosphere show that it anesthetizes humans even when oxygen is added to the mixture. The invaders' scientists discover that the 80 per cent xenon in their atmosphere causes the anesthesia. The xenon is removed and nitrogen substituted as the inert gas for the humans.

The Academy of Science on the invaders' planet lost much time by arguments about these questions of human metabolism. Many specimens were sacrificed to prove this or that hypothesis which ultimately turned out to be incorrect.

The human specimens decide to try to communicate with their invader captors. None of the invaders pay any attention.

The humans' attempts to communicate are watched very

carefully by one interested invader scientist. He duly reports his observations to the invaders' Academy of Science. He writes a paper on the hypothesis that humans are intelligent. A flurry of interest stirs the invader scientists' group.

Meanwhile, inside the tank these research attempts by the invader scientists are viewed by one of the human specimens as "attempts on the part of intelligent creatures to communicate." A storm of human controversy results. "Are the invaders as intelligent as we are because they captured us? Are they not just sadistic predators of a high native intelligence (bright animal) but with no really civilized ethics? They cannot be intelligent, they have no developed sense of either fairness nor of true altruism with respect to the humans."

The human specimen with the communication theory begins to respond to the invader scientist with complex sounds and gestures. He quickly makes a discovery. He receives no answers if he uses his normal speech spectrum. He has to lower his voice an octave or so before the scientist apparently can even hear it. (As is well known if one breathes xenon this does lower the real voice frequencies. The human was not breathing xenon, so that his voice frequencies were up where they normally are in nitrogen on the earth.) He finds that he must train his own hearing to hear the invader scientist's very low-pitched voice. To keep the invader's interest, he mimics as best he can the voice sounds which are put out by the invader. As his mimicry apparently improves, the excitement builds up among the invaders.

These facts are announced to the invaders' Academy of Science. Many invader scientists try their own approaches as a result of this flurry of interest. The psychologist tries conditioning; the physiologist tries brain methods; and the trainers trained some specimens for circuses. The human specimens are forced to make "cute" noises for the entertainment of the invaders. The exploiters of the human specimens begin to make a profit.

Meanwhile the original report of the mimicry by the humans of the invaders' sounds is investigated by the invaders' Academy of Science. A research project is established under a modest grant to the discoverer to allow him to pursue the findings. He continues the research and, with human help and electronic aids, he devises a special interspecies communication method. Communication is established. The alien human intelligence is not measured, but humans are accepted into the invaders' society as equals. Earth is set aside as a tourist attraction for the invader scientists. Thus we have a "happy" ending.

Whether or not we and the dolphins and whales can ever achieve a "happy" ending, we should at least try to find such a road, one to the other. Other, less happy endings, could be concocted for the parable of the invaders. Let us not even allow ourselves to consider such endings. Rather, let us strive for the happy ones.

In this parable, I am carrying to a logical extreme the current situation with respect to the dolphins and the whales. I feel this is a wrong approach since this puts such ideas comfortably off in a safe, fictional framework.

With four other speakers in a recent symposium, (Lilly, 1966) I was asked to speak to the question, "If there is extraterrestrial intelligent communicating life, how will we recognize it and how will we communicate with it?" Currently we are faced with other species possibly as intelligent as we are. We do not yet recognize their intelligence. We do not even attempt communication with them. We do kill them, eat them, and use their bodies as industrial products. We have no respect whatsoever for their huge brains. In other words, as a species, human beings faced with other species demean them, kill them, and eat them. I hope all this carnage can be stopped and something more ideal can take its place.

In the above parable of the invaders, the Golden Rule is not applied to the humans by the invaders until their science says it must be. We do not apply the Golden Rule to the dolphins or the whales nor any species other than our own. Even dealing with our own species, we tend to annihilate vast numbers of them. As a species, we are a poor example for highly intelligent life forms from other planets or from our own planet to communicate with. Let us improve ourselves.

Perhaps (and it seems likely from our experiences in the Communication Research Institute) the dolphins are applying the Golden Rule to us. To those humans who are willing to apply the rule to them, the dolphins use the Golden Rule. I suspect that if the dolphins did not apply such a rule to us we would annihilate all of them.

The Golden Rule has been devised by several great men in the past. There were and are those among us who apply and have applied it with diligence and great effect. Christ, Gandhi, Buddha, Quetzalcoatl, and the other great religious teachers have applied it with diligence and great effect and remind us of the necessity of this rule.

If modern humanitarians can become interested enough to either work directly with the dolphins or to obtain the support for the efforts of others, we may acquire enough information to discuss the dolphins' real ethics. It may take the dedication of a new religious leader to carry it off appropriately. I hope not. I hope a framework can be found within our society in which such work can be accomplished.

If we suddenly stir up the real invaders from outer space and are still devoting most of the world's wealth to military weaponry, we will inevitably use the weapons on the invaders, too much too soon.

With the present lack of applying the Golden Rule interspecieswise, the whaling industry can still exist. If whale-like forms, for example, were to come to earth from outer space, it is inevitable that our military group would consider this visit an "invasion." Even though the visiting whales, as it were, come on a friendly mission, they may not have a chance of expressing this. They probably will be shot down before they can get into orbit around our planet.

If the whaling industry is a good example of the way we treat harmless superior beings in the sea, imagine how we would treat harmless superior beings arriving in space ships. Here we have superior brains right next door to us and we insist they are not superior and are only good to eat and to be made into fertilizer. If I were from an older, greatly superior culture from some other place in the vast universe, I would recommend that this planet be shunned. The human species is so arrogant that it doesn't recognize its own superiors. The only way that humans in the mass will respect any other species, apparently, is the ability to beat them in warfare.

Often I am asked the question, "If the whales are so smart why are they letting us kill them?" I also am asked the question, "If the whales are so intelligent why aren't they ruling the earth instead of man?" These questions reveal much of the questioner. I measure my answers carefully. One could become quite angry at the lack of insight into man shown by such questions. It can be embarrassing.

My answer is usually a humorous-serious joke. I pretend that "we" recently found the meaning of one word in the language of the "killer" whales, the word they use to designate Homo sapiens. Freely translated into English, their word means "killer ape." This semihumorous view can be rather serious.

We have named one of the largest of the dolphins "killer whale"; the term is derived from the "whale-killer" used by the whalers of the last century when they saw Orcinus orca

54

killing and eating the large whales (even as we do them, cows, sheep, and pigs).

The bad press of these huge dolphins is hardly warranted. There is no recorded instance of an unprovoked whale ever attacking a human. Several cases have been confused with the great white shark which is not a whale at all. For a true picture see the motion picture and the 1966 *National Geographic Magazine* article on Namu the Whale.

Often I have asked myself what would a brain six times the size of mine think about? I ask in the spirit of philosophical inquiry and not in any superficial operational sense of the question. Since we do not know the thoughts of creatures other than ourselves with brains the same size as ours, the answer has obviously even more unknowns than first meets the eye.

The sperm whales have brains six times the size of ours (*Man and Dolphin*). Before they are annihilated by man, I would like to exchange ideas with a sperm whale. I am not sure that they would be interested in communicating with me because my brain obviously is much more limited than theirs. Somehow I am sure that their huge brain is used effectively. I am also sure that it has capacities beyond my present comprehension (see Selected Bibliography on Dolphins, John Cunningham Lilly, 1962 and 1963).

I would like to exchange ideas with a willing sperm whale because the ability and the potential of such a vast computer as his is so far beyond our present theories, beyond even our imagining, that it is an intriguing and challenging subject. I have a theoretical approach which may give a hint as to where to look and what to look for, if and when we ever do so communicate. The beginnings of this theory were in *Man and Dolphin*. In this book let me expand it a bit to clarify some of the points.

The theory is as follows: The sperm whale's brain is so large that he needs only a small fraction of it for use in computations for his survival. He uses the rest of it for functions about which we can only guess. His survival computations (including feeding, hunting, sex, and escaping) may take up such a small fraction of his brain that he can do these things with only a very small part of his mind. It does not mean that he does them by means of reflex, instinctual patterns, built in. It means that he does them somewhat the way that we do them. To think the way we do he would need to use about one-sixth of his total brain. To him, our best thinking may appear to be reflexes automatic and primitive.

The rest of this huge computer is computing continuous inner experiences beyond our present understanding. If a sperm whale, for example, wants to see hear-feel any past experience, his huge computer can reprogram it and run it off again. His huge computer gives him a reliving, as if with a three-dimensional sound-color-taste-emotion-re-experiencing motion picture. He can thus review the experience as it originally happened. He can imagine changing it to do a better job next time he encounters such an experience. He can set up the model of the way he would like to run it the next time, reprogram his computer, run it off, and see how well it works.

Currently, we do exactly this with some of the large artificial computers. We program them to make a model of, say, an ocean basin, and the flow of silt on the bottom and the flow of water on the top, various kinds of changes that can be exerted over long periods of time. We then can make the computer run the model over a hundred-year period in a few hours and find out what the erosion pattern will be at the end of that time. In the same way, the sperm whale can model his past experiences, and change them the next time he meets a similar situation.

The sperm whale probably has "religious" ambitions and successes quite beyond anything that we know. His "transcendental religious" experiences must be quite beyond what we can experience by any known methods at the present time. Apparently, we can in rare times with our experiences begin to approach his everyday, accomplished abilities in the cognitive, conative, and emotional spheres. Only slowly have we begun to improve our control of such experiences. The means of inducing them are slowly being unearthed.

With our more limited minds and brains, we can have these experiences only under safe and controlled conditions; i.e., we cannot have them during the period of intense computations which are devoted to our bodily survival. Such computations (of necessity because of our limitations) will take up all of our computer. If we are going to have a "transcendental" experience, the physical and social surroundings must be such as to assure us that outside reality will make no demands on us. Each program is sufficiently complex so that our relatively small computers can compute only one program at a time or do a poor job of trying to compute both at once. (I may be doing a disservice to my species here. Some humans may have gone much farther than I with such experiments, and perhaps they can compute both programs satisfactorily and simultaneously.)

Perhaps the sperm whale has gone so far into philosophical studies that he sees the Golden Rule as only a special case of a much larger ethic. Compared with us he probably has abilities here that are truly godlike. From my theory, I deduced that attacks on man by sperm whales should be rare, with the exception of occasional cases of extremely severe provocation by man.

I tested this deduction from the theory by data found in the old whaling logs in a museum. The data were fascinating. In the six cases that I could find and check, there had been provocation of the sperm whale by men.

The cases were chosen from nineteenth-century newspaper accounts of attacks by sperm whales on ships and boats. In the newspaper accounts, I frequently came across the term "unprovoked attacks." This proved to be untrue. Every one of the attacks was provoked, as I found by checking the original handwritten log of the ship itself. In each and every case a notation stated that one or more "irons" had been thrown into the whale. Several such sperm whales were captured and the irons from as many as five or six different ships were found embedded in their sides.

The book *Moby Dick* by Herman Melville is based on such a real case. The sperm whale involved was called by the whalers "Mocha Dick." Six harpoons from five different ships were found in him when he was finally captured.

Thus we can see that a sperm whale, in general, does not attack us unless we first attack him. In one desperate attempt to escape or sometimes save his own life or that of other sperm whales, he may be provoked into turning and destroying.

Why do they not attack us unprovoked? *I believe they recognize that we are dangerous, even that we are the most dangerous animal on this planet.* I believe that they recognize that if they attacked us, unprovoked, we would organize quickly and wipe them off the face of the earth. I believe they recognize that we now have the means to do this. A large fraction of our atomic and nuclear weapons testing is done over and in the Pacific Ocean close to the ocean routes of the big whales.

Even if they have not been warned by our atomic testing, the whaling industry has kept them well informed of our dangerous abilities. They are exposed to all manner of our shipping across oceans including even single-handed sailors in small vessels. They must know by now that only certain kinds of vessels carry dangerous human beings, i.e., whaling ships, bomb-testing and military ships, and certain airplanes.

The slaughter of these magnificent beings must end. Instead of slaughter, let us devise new projects with whales, conserving them. Large private resources and government resources should be devoted to encouraging bright and intelligent human beings to devote their lives to this problem of achieving communication with these magnificient brains and minds.

The importance of interspecies communication, the peak of interspecies communication insofar as we can foresee it, lies here: establishing communication with the dolphins, and with the medium-size whales, and with the great sperm whale. I visualize a project as vast as our present space program, devoting our best minds, our best engineering brains, our vast networks of computer people and material and time on this essentially peaceful mission of interspecies communication, right here on this planet.

It is a bit discouraging to see this magnificent opportunity being thrown aside by the human race. I hope that enough people can be fired with the enthusiasm which I feel for it to launch the effort with momentum similar to that we are devoting to the space program, to oceanography, to nuclear energy, and to warfare. The rewards to the human race, new experiences, new ways of thinking, and new philosophies can be very great. The experience of such a venture with creatures here on our own planet will make the way safer for extraterrestrial life if and when our presence is detected. The "invaders" will be met with more understanding human beings and we then will deserve to be included as an "intelligent cooperating species" within our galaxy. Until that time arrives, I advise all extraterrestrial visitors to avoid man. He is a dangerous, unpredictable, powerful, "bright animal," operating in murderous concert.

In *Man and Dolphin* I predicted that perhaps within a decade or two we would establish communication with another species. Since that was written in the year 1960, one-half of a decade has already passed. If we continue to receive support for the dolphin research, I suspect this estimate will be neither too short nor too long. If we can devote resources at higher than the present rate, we should be able to break the barrier, at least with *Tursiops truncatus* or *Orcinus orca* if not with the others. This book is devoted to this program, both in terms of where we are today, our past progress, and our future plans.

CHAPTER 3

Differences between the Communication of Man and of Dolphin

How do we know when someone is speaking to us? How do we know they aren't humming a tune, singing a song, talking to themselves, conversing with someone else, hallucinating a vision, repeating nonsense, doing an echo-ranging job with their voice, speaking in a language foreign to us?

Once we question how we know when someone is speaking to us, we find that the clues we use are myriad. These clues are quite subtle, and the alternatives many. And yet we come to a quick and correct conclusion. *As long as the other being is another member of our species, we succeed quickly and easily.* We succeed even when he is speaking a foreign language or is a pre-speech child; somehow we know for all human languages when the language stream is being directed in our particular direction. On the other hand, let the organic form of the speaker deviate radically from ours and we do not have this immediate and quick success. We have a difficult manifold of new data, obstructing our decision-making processes. We have hidden beliefs which prevent us from recognizing that they are attempting to speak to us.

For full communication with another being we ask for a rather narrow set of specifications. Basically, each of us asks a respondent to be a full and complete replica of one's own body and one's own mind. We almost insist that we talk only to ourself projected outward. If the other person looks somewhat like ourselves, it makes it easier for us to speak, though not necessarily easier for us to transmit useful information. Ideally, then, one would like a duplicate of one's self with identical form, identical experience, identical sex, and identical age as the respondent in an information transaction. Such an identity has the highest probability of a full and complete communication, one being with the other. The only cases similar to this are identical human twins.

Such twins may develop a language of their own, devised between them before they learn the communal speech of their parents. Thus if one can also choose one's genes and the genes of the person to whom one is speaking, it pays to have identical or nearly identical inheritance. In lieu of twinness, it pays to be siblings; one can sometimes talk to a brother or a sister of nearly the same age far better than one can talk to one's parents or one's children. Thus we can set up a spectrum of humans. Some humans are very easy to communicate with and others at the other end of the spectrum are very difficult to talk with and exchange information.

For example, sexual differences raise barriers. Genetic differences raise more barriers. A different nationality, different language, increase the difficulty. Differences in development of the body can be limiting; if one has a cleft palate, pituitary dwarfism, or pituitary gigantism, one can have very great difficulty in communicating with the so-called normal members of one's own species.

Brain size and the development of the brain establish probably the greatest differences in this area. A microcephalic may not be capable of learning complex language as the rest of us know it. An underdeveloped brain for any reason may have the same problems.

But above all these limitations stands the monumental one of crossing the line from our species to another species. We may visualize this problem in the following fashion: Let us assume we have a manlike creature with a brain one-fourth to one-third the size of ours. This creature has two factors building up the barriers to communication with us: (1) He has an entirely different genetic inheritance with unknown limiting factors built in. (2) He has a smaller brain with less capacity than ours. This is the case of the great apes, the chimpanzees, the gorillas, and the orangutans.

One aspect of these creatures confuses us: their body form resembles ours. They have forelimbs with hands, hind limbs with feet, a visible neck, an expressive face, no tail, a dry existence, and a diet similar to ours. Their reproduction and their care of their young bear superficial resemblances to ours.

If we search among other known species on this planet, and if we wish to attenuate the brain size limitation, we look in vain at most of the other known members of the animal kingdom to find a brain equal to or greater than ours. There is a large gap in the primate series between what we consider a satisfactory brain size in our own species and the largest of the ape brains. As I hypothesized in *Man and Dolphin,* when he reached the critical size of brain for developing a language, man probably killed off all the "proto-human" type of primates in his competition for living space and food. Language gives him such an obvious advantage in the hunt that he could eliminate his rivals rather rapidly by cooperative efforts, controlled by shouting instructions at his fellows at a distance, for example. In other words, there is no primate other than man, *Homo sapiens,* with a brain size equal to that of man. No primate has a brain larger than that of man nor is there any primate with a brain just under that of man. Perhaps some of the small-brained microcephalics are throwbacks to the protohuman types. Large-brained humans have their difficulties with most humans of the smallest brain size.

In our search for a brain size equal to man's, we must then go more distantly in terms of the body form and in terms of the medium in which the animals live. We must go to the sea to find brains equal to ours. There we have not yet eliminated them from this planet. Some of the medium-size dolphins have our size of brain; some very young and small elephants may have brains as small as ours. That's about it. The large elephants, the large dolphins, the whales, all have brains much larger than ours. The small dolphins and the porpoises have smaller brains than ours. To hold brain size equal to ours we have only a few choices: medium-size dolphins (Figure 1).

However, the body form, the physiology, and the medium in which the animal lives are radically changed. The dolphins' forelimbs have all the bones we do in ours, but they are all bound together in a pair of stiff paddles (or rudders). The hind limbs are missing entirely. Only once in a while are rudimentary hind limbs found in these species. A very long and powerful tail and flukes are present; we have absolutely no homologue of these structures, even as they have no homologues for our legs. There is no sign of an expressive face. The dolphins have no visible neck, the head is not well delineated. The jaws are four or five times the length of ours. The external part of our ears, the pinna, is completely lacking (the functions are taken over by structures *inside* the head). Their nose does not open at the end of their upper jaw; it opens on the forehead (the blowhole). Their mammary glands are not on the chest; they are back by the genitalia.

It is very difficult to identify ourselves, our anatomy, to empathize with these creatures. In addition to all these anatomical difficulties are the great differences in where we live and the media in which we travel. We essentially travel on land through air, pushing the air aside. We are essentially dry creatures. They live in the seawater, pushing the seawater aside, breathing the air above but spending most of their time underneath in the water itself. Even as we are dry, so they are wet.

The speeds of our progress in the air against the dry surface of the land are easily measured (Figure 2). We progress at a velocity from three to eighteen knots on our own feet on dry land. The dolphins can equal these velocities easily in the sea and can even better them. At least we know they can maintain the eighteen knots for a good deal longer than the rare man in top form running a record hundred-yard dash in ten seconds (eighteen knots). They can maintain this eighteen knots beyond the thousand-meter run in which the rare man in top form is now doing 12½ knots. By the time the mile is reached, the man is down to ten knots and the dolphin is still maintaining his eighteen. At ten miles the man maintains his ten, the dolphin his eighteen. Thus an everyday, essentially normal dolphin can maintain those velocities which only rare men can reach. (Of course man has learned how to go much faster in specially invented machines.)

In the vocal sphere, our communication is essentially airborne. The dolphin originates his communication inside his own head in air passages; the sound is transmitted through his flesh into the sea and becomes waterborne. The limiting velocity of our communication of sound in air is 340 meters per second (1100 feet per second), or about 640 knots. The dolphins' vocal communication has a limiting velocity in seawater of 1540 meters per second (5000 feet per second), or 2900 knots. Thus their sonic communication velocity is about 4.5 times that of ours. Using these figures, let us determine values of other variables.

For example, at a given instant how long is the spatial

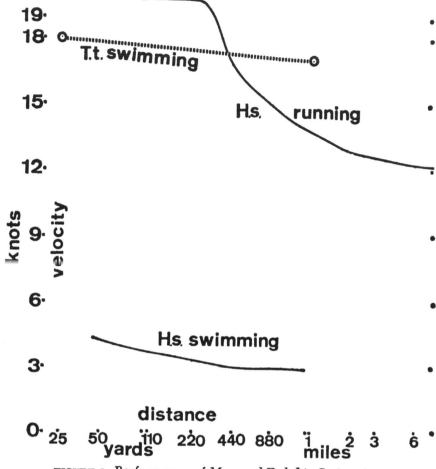

FIGURE 2. *Performance of Man and Dolphin Swimming*

Each species in its own medium has somewhat similar performances. The graph shows the average velocity maintained (knots) for the distance moved (yards and miles). The data for man (H.s.), running (in air) and swimming are from the *Guinness Book of World Records*. For the dolphin (T.t.) swimming, the first point is from our data for jumping out of water; this point is calculated from the height attained (ballistic computation). The second point is from the data of T. Lang, K. Norris, and T. Pryor. The running curves for man are the best performances known; the curves for the dolphins are the only known points measured accurately. Other dolphins can swim faster than this and the porpoises probably swim more slowly than these figures. One of the very large dolphins (*Orcinus orca*) has been found to maintain 20 knots for 5 days 24 hours a day under chase conditions.

extent of one of our communications? From the time we start saying something until the time we stop it, that particular message is traveling outward from us in concentric circles at the velocity of sound. The leading edge of a sentence travels outward, the rest of the message follows it, and the trailing edge follows after that. If we measure the distance from the leading edge to the trailing edge, we get an idea of the length of the message in "air space," or in the case of the dolphin in "water space." For example, say that one says a very short "no." This word lasts approximately 0.2 second. From its leading edge to its trailing edge in the concentric circles radiating out from one's mouth is 6.8 meters (22 feet). In other words, if one's listener is 22 feet away, the beginning of the "no" reaches his ears just as the end of the "no" leaves the mouth. If he is closer, of course, the beginning hits his ears before the end has left the mouth. If he is farther away, the beginning has not yet hit his ears when the end has left the mouth.

In contrast, a dolphin's whistle lasting 0.2 second under water is 31 meters long (100 feet) so that the leading edge of a whistle of this duration reaches another dolphin 100 feet away just as the end of the whistle leaves the apparatus below the blowhole. As will be discussed later, if the dolphin is 50 feet away from a flat wall underwater, the beginning of his whistle will be reflected and returned to his ears just as the trailing edge of the whistle leaves his head. If he is closer to such an obstacle, the returning echo of the beginning of this whistle will overlap the trailing end of the echo. For dolphins, this may be a very important relationship, as will be shown later.

One of the individual sound waves within those long transmissions has a special length, from one crest of amplitude to the next crest of amplitude, the "wave length." In human speech, the wave length of individual sound waves ranges from 3.4 meters (11 feet) for the lowest frequencies at 100 cycles per second down to very small values with much higher frequencies. For example, for frequencies at the upper end of the consonantal band at 8000 cycles per second, the wave length is only 4.25 centimeters (1.6 inches).

These wave lengths are important in our determination of the direction from which the sound is coming toward our head. If the wave length is very long compared to the distance between our ears, both of our ears are subjected simultaneously to approximately the same pressure changes. We cannot detect the direction the very low tones (long wave lengths) are coming from. At shorter wave lengths and slightly higher tones, the pressure variations at the two ears are not quite the same nor are the times of arrival of pressure changes quite the same. The detectors in our ears and the brain behind those detectors are very good at picking up very small differences in pressure and very small differences in time of arrival of the equal pressure waves. Thus, if a deep bass organ note is sounded on the shore and you are on a large lake or at sea (to avoid multiple reflections from other objects), you can localize the position of this source to a very small part of the total 360 degrees surrounding your head; at the low frequencies you can find, for example, a foghorn within something like two degrees despite no visibility in a dense fog. This property of low tones is why foghorns are so successful. Their deep bass notes penetrate literally miles through the air. Low frequencies in general penetrate more easily and farther than do the higher frequencies, which not only suffer from direct absorption by air and by dirt particles in the air, but are also easily refracted by temperature difference layers in the air and are reflected quite easily from any small objects in the way. The longer wave length, lower-frequency sounds do not suffer as much from such processes. In other words, their crest-to-crest distance is sufficient so that they cannot, as it were, be pushed aside by either temperature gradients, solid objects, or absorption processes.

The directivity of the higher frequencies is better than it is for the lower frequencies. In other words, as long as echoes do not interfere with the apparent direction of the source, a very high-frequency source fairly close to us can be localized within a very small fraction of one degree. Special rooms called anechoic chambers allow us to demonstrate this in the laboratory without going to the trouble of being out in open space.

Our ears are approximately 17 centimeters (7 inches) apart. The distance between our ears is one wave length at approximately 2000 cycles per second, or a half wave length at 1000 cycles per second. These are two important frequencies in the middle of our speech communication band. Our most easily detected frequency is 1000 cycles per second. It is also the frequency at which we are best at detecting small differences in frequency. This is the usual standard frequency for testing electronic equipment to be used for passing human speech. It is the reference frequency for amplitudes measured in logarithmic units called decibels. Our threshold for hearing in terms of intensity measured at this frequency is 0.002 dyne per square centimeter (microbar) absolute pressure. This is the value for people with normal hearing. This is the minimal detectable sound. A very loud sound at this frequency may be as much as 140 decibels above this threshold. This is above the threshold for pain, i.e., a sound which is so loud that it is painful. In absolute pressure units, this is approximately 3000 dynes per square centimeter (or 60 million times greater than the minimum detectable sound). These figures are useful to know, and we will contrast later similar figures in the dolphin's medium.

Let us return now to the wave length consideration and the distance between our ears. If a continuous sine wave at 1000 cycles per second arrives at our head from one side, the wave must travel around the head to the other ear in the air. A very very small fraction of the wave will travel through the head to the other ear through bone conduction and conduction through the substance of the brain.

Since the amplitude of the airborne wave is very much greater than that of the intrahead wave, we use the airborne wave for our detection. The dolphin does not have this advantage.

The shortest distance around the head is approximately 12 inches (29 centimeters). Thus the same part of a sound wave traveling from one ear to the other from one side to the other takes approximately 0.001 second (1 millisecond) to move from one side to the other. With the proper electronic equipment designed to delay two sound waves delivered independently to the two ears, it can be shown that one perceives a delay of one millisecond between two sounds as if one sound is coming only from one side of the head. As the sound source shifts around to, say, being directly in front of a person, the delay between the two ears approaches zero. With the proper electronic techniques, it can be shown that one can still reliably detect delays of the order of 20 millionths of a second (20 microseconds), and, say, whether the source is to the right or to the left of the midplane straight ahead with this amount of delay. This is, of course, for short, sharp sounds. With longer-duration sounds we do not have this degree of accuracy, and the delays move up to approximately 100 microseconds or more. Thus our nervous system is able to tell us from what direction sounds are coming with respect to the midplane through our head by measurement of the delay between the arrival of similar fronts at the two ears. Our brain does computations which fuse the two percepts into one effective source toward the right or toward the left.

The dolphin does not have this particular physical advantage in his reception of sound. Since the velocity of sound in the tissues of his head and in the water surrounding it are approximately the same, the sound waves coming to one ear are delayed only by the amount of time it takes for sound to travel through his head to the other ear. He does not have that small prolongation of the time of arrival of the sound that we have as it travels around our head. This means that at the longer wave length he will not have the advantages that we have in terms of localization of the direction of the source. Presumably at longer wave lengths, however, he can use pressure receptors in his skin (somewhat the way the shark does with his lateral line organs) to localize the direction of the low-frequency sound sources. Here in wave length he has the advantage over us of a body that is approximately 8 feet (2½ meters) long.

The dolphin's ears are approximately 12 inches apart inside his head; i.e., about the same as the shortest distance around our head. Since the velocity of sound, however, is 4½ times what it is in air, in his head and in the sea water, his time-delay discrimination is the same as ours, it must be 4½ times the frequency that we have for air. In other words, if the dolphin operates at the same minimum detectable delay that we do, he would need a frequency 4½ times the frequency that we use for the same degree of accuracy of localization of the source of the sound (same wave length in water as ours in air).

We use the peculiar shape of our head and the peculiar shape of our ears (the external pinna) to tell the difference between sounds coming directly ahead from those coming from overhead or directly astern. The dolphin, lying in the water stretched out, can use the differences in absorption between the peculiar shape of his head forward and some of the air sacs ahead of his ears versus the peculiar shape of his air-containing lungs astern in somewhat a similar fashion. Thus, he too can localize sources of sound by differences in the quality of the sound and the amplitudes of sources directly in front of him from those directly behind him. He separates right and left sources the same way we do, i.e., by measuring the delays of the arrival of the wave fronts between the two ears.

The dolphin may be able to do a better job than we in terms of his measurement or perception of the small time delay between the two wave fronts arriving at the two ears. Experimental tests of his ability to localize sound sources at very small angles have not yet been done. It is known that he is very good at this kind of perception at extremely high frequencies when using his sonar and picking up echoes from his own emitted signals. How good he is, however, at listening for the directions of sounds of other dolphins and other sources at much lower frequencies has yet to be determined. Let us now return to the comparison between our speech and that of the dolphin.

In our speech the wave lengths of individual sound waves, as stated above, run from 3.4 meters (11 feet) for 100 cycles per second to 4.25 centimeters (1.6 inches) for 8000 cycles per second. The comparable wave lengths for the dolphin in the homologous frequencies are calculable by remembering that the speed of in-water sounds is $4\frac{1}{2}$ times our in-air sound speed and that the effective distance between the dolphins' ears is comparable to the effective distance between our ears. If we hold the wave length constant when moving from air to sea water, and shift frequencies to match, we find the homologous frequencies for our 100 cycles per second and our 8000 cycles per second. For the dolphin, the two homologous frequencies then would be 450 cycles per second and 36,000 cycles per second. We would thus predict that the dolphin's homologous band corresponding to our speech band would have these limits, i.e., 450 to 36,-000 cycles per second. Since the above limits for our speech include all of the important fundamentals and harmonics for the transmission of meaning and since we can do without some of the fundamentals and overtones, it may be that the dolphins can also do without some of theirs. Even as we can limit our speech to a band 300 cycles per second to 3500 cycles per second (as in the telephone), so maybe they can be limited and still be able to communicate.

With the narrower band 300 to 3500 cycles per second we obtain nearly 100 per cent of intelligibility for the most frequent talkers and listeners, human type. An analogous dolphin telephone, predicting the frequencies on the simple constant wave length hypothesis, would use the frequencies 1400 to 16,000 cycles per second.

When we make the assumption that we should move the dolphins' frequencies 4.5 times our frequencies we are using a hypothesis which I call the "constant wave length hypothesis." In full, this hypothesis is as follows:

Human communication takes place in an air-flesh medium in which the contrast between the velocities in air and in flesh and the reflection of the sound in air from the flesh use a certain band of wave lengths in order to distinguish the direction of a transmitter, i.e., a speaker. The dolphin in water cannot use this contrast and must use the distance between his two ears inside his head because the wave length of his sound in the surrounding sea water is nearly the same as it is in his head. The effective distance between the ears of the human and the ears of the dolphin are approximately the same, i.e., about 12 inches or 29 centimeters. Thus, if the dolphin has the same time delay detection that we do, he must use frequencies $4\frac{1}{2}$ times ours in order to maintain the wave length constant. In other words, for waterborne communication he uses the same band of wave lengths that we do; hence the frequencies must be $4\frac{1}{2}$ times ours.

This constant wave length hypothesis is testable. We have set up experiments of various kinds to see whether or not these predicted limits for the dolphins' bands of communication exist.

One way of investigating the frequencies of the dolphins' communication bands is to measure their produced sounds directly while they are talking to one another. Even as in our case, one fault in this argument may be that some of the sounds they emit probably do not carry essential meaning for them. By observing the sounds themselves we can establish the extreme upper and the lower limits for their frequency bands. In the Institute, we have made literally thousands of such observations and measurements of frequencies.

One instructive method uses a fast frequency analyzer. This method displays the calculated results of a frequency measurement on a storage cathode ray oscilloscope. This storage oscilloscope allows one to store almost indefinitely a given wave form. In other words, the bright spot moves across the screen tracing the instantaneous amplitude of a given wave form; as it does so, the cathode ray tube (through its special structure) keeps repeating the wave form in the same place. By this technique, one can see the frequencies displayed directly on the cathode ray tube. The instant the dolphin starts talking to another, the amplitude of the sounds in each frequency band shows on the cathode ray tube face as vertical deflections of the spot of light corresponding to the intensity of the sound in each band. One can then photograph the stored results at will, erase the picture, and continue the observations, all within a few seconds.

This method shows extreme limits of approximately 500 to 85,000 cps for the dolphins' produced sound during communication exchanges. (This does not include their echo recognition activities, the so-called "sonar." Such activities will be discussed in another part of this book. The echo-recognition, active frequencies are higher.)

Thus there seems to be similarity between the predicted

PLATE 1. *Photograph of Dolphin in Tank for Studies of the Production of the Voice Inside the Head.* The dolphin is isolated in this tank and produces his sounds with his head either raised as shown or placed below the water. The blowhole is closed. Hydrophones are placed on his head or in the water near his head. (Note the reflection from the back of his retina of the flash from the camera.) A TV monitor is shown through the doorway. In the far room is the computer used for analyzing data. The data shown in the next figure were recorded with the equipment directly behind the dolphin's head through the window.

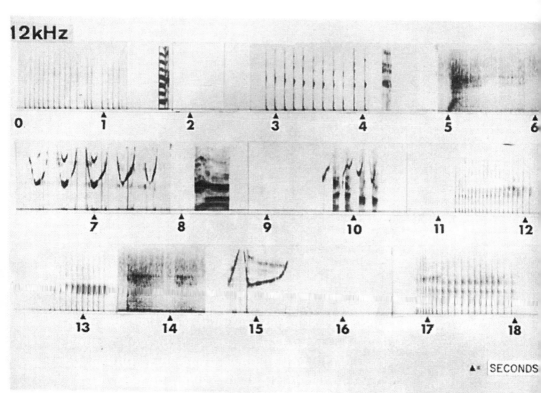

12kHz

0 · 1 · 2 · 3 · 4 · 5 · 6

7 · 8 · 9 · 10 · 11 · 12

13 · 14 · 15 · 16 · 17 · 18

▲ = SECONDS

PLATE 2. *Some of the Sonic Patterns of the Underwater Voice of the Dolphin.* This figure shows a plot of the frequencies and amplitudes of sounds emitted by a dolphin over an 18-second period. The frequencies run from 0 to 12 kilo Hertz (kilocycles). Five slow-clicking trains can be seen. Seven periods of very fast clicking can be seen: near 2 seconds, 4 seconds, 8 seconds, and 10 seconds. Five whistles are seen near 7 seconds and a single whistle and click train near 15 seconds. These are the natural underwater sounds produced in the two nasal systems of the bottlenose dolphin. The structure of the fast clicking near 8 seconds resembles that of the formants of the human voice, as do those near 10 seconds. The production at 10 seconds shows a whistle superimposed on the fast-clicking trains. This dolphin was alone with the head partly out of water, and a contact hydrophone was placed over the right and over the left vestibular sacs.

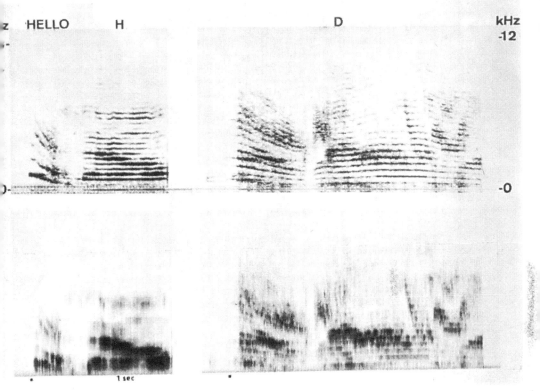

PLATE 3. *The Voice of the Dolphin in Air.* The records are sonic spectrometer analyses of a woman saying "Hello" and the dolphin's reply. It is to be noted that the frequency analysis for the human is from 0 to 8 kilo-Hertz and for the dolphin from 0 to 12 KHz. The frequency pattern for the dolphin for the first two-thirds of the record resemble somewhat that of the human (Margaret Howe and Peter Dolphin). In general the human child's and woman's voice is a closer approximation to that of the dolphin in air. During long close contact between a human and a dolphin his voice in air tends to be lowered to the frequencies shown in this figure.

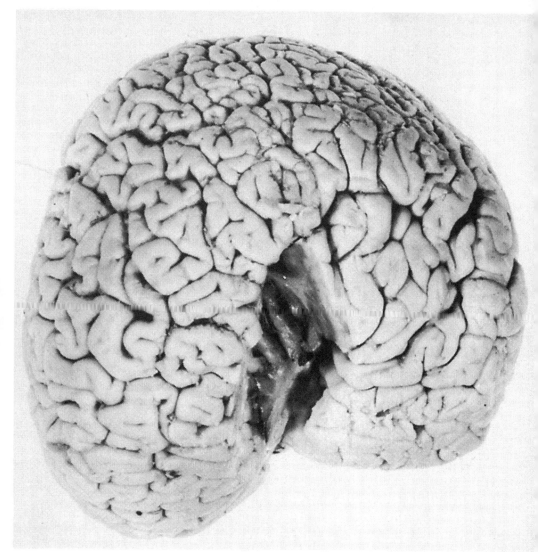

PLATE 4. *The Brain of the Dolphin: The Acoustic Cortex.* The lateral view of the brain
shows a hole where an opercular plug was removed to expose the insula and the dorsal
surface of the left temporal lobe. It is on this dorsal surface that the four gyri which are
the acoustic cortex of the dolphin are shown. This acoustic cortex is the central and
highest station of the acoustic portion of the brain of the dolphin. It is very much larger
than the corresponding parts of the cortex of man. (From P. J. Morgane, M. S. Jacobs,
P. I. Yakovlev, W. J. McFarland, and S. J. Pielero, "Surface configuration of brain of the
dolphin *(Tursiops truncatus),*" *J. Comparative Neurology,* in press.)

PLATE 5. *The Dolphin Point Laboratory.* Communication Research Institute, St. Thomas, U. S. Virgin Islands on the Caribbean Sea, 18 degrees north of the equator. View towards south and west; entrance road; steel motor-driven door closes entrance to wet laboratory room 40 ft. by 20 ft. on the main floor. Office on second floor; roofs (3000 square feet) collect rain for fresh water; cisterns are on

ground floor below the main level (30,000 gals.). Year-'round temperatures are: low, night 75° F.; high, day 90° F. Seawater temperatures year-'round are 78° F. to 84° F. Daylight-nighttime ratio approximately 1 to 1 year-'round. Tradewinds are predominantly from the southeast to east, 14 to 30 knots, approximately 80% of the year, except during August, September, and October. Waves about 90% of the year are from the southeast toward this building. Close passes of hurricanes for the laboratory were "Donna" (1963) with 80-knot winds and south winds (no damage); "Cleo" (1964) with about 50-knot winds; "Inez" in 1966 with 150-knot winds. Maximum waves 15 feet high in 1966, with wind tide of 5 feet.

PLATE 6. *Sea Pool, Balcony, and Wet Room.* This view is taken from a point directly south of and above the sea pool; Caribbean Sea behind the camera. Seawater flows in from the left and out through the flume at the far end of the pool. Spiral staircase gives access to balcony from sea pool. Wall to west limits sea wave noise in air above pool. Sea pool depth is 4½ feet, sloping upward slowly at inflow and at outflow ends to about 6 inches

average depth. Daily tide range most frequently about 8 inches; extreme lunar tides over the year about 2 feet. One tsunami (in 1911) caused minus 30 feet and plus 15 feet tides for a brief period at middle of island. Offshore water depths one mile from lab are 15 to 20 feet. Maximum wave height thus is limited. Main floor is 16 feet above mean sea level and has waterproof wall to at least 19 feet above sea level, thus affording adequate protection against the highest waves.

PLATE 7. *View through Underwater Bubble Port in Sea Pool.* Margaret is cleaning Plexiglas; Peter Dolphin is watching. Water surface is near top. Camera is in booth, in air. Margaret experiences included frequent swimming with one to three dolphins in sea pool from February 7, 1964 to beginning of experiments reported here.

PLATE 8. *View through Underwater Bubble Port.* Taken from the observation bubble, the camera in air close to Plexiglas. Margaret and Peter examine the sump at bottom of sea pool.

PLATE 9. *Margaret Howe and Dolphin in Sea Pool.* Margaret is stroking skin between flippers, a region often presented by dolphins for stroking. Dolphin is rocking on Margaret's legs underwater. Margaret talks loudly and frequently.

PLATE 10. *Margaret Howe and Dolphin in Sea Pool.* Margaret spontaneously hugging the dolphin Sissy, wraps her arms around her, and continues to talk. Dolphin responds by arching back upward and pressing downward with chest and belly. This type of physical closeness may be followed by kissing the dolphin's head, peering into the blowhole, blowing gently into the blowhole, and mutual close-up inspection of each other's eyes, ears, mouth, etc.

and the observed output bands of the dolphins. We then did experiments to find out how much of this whole band the dolphins consider essential.

In 1961 we set up a "dolphin telephone" between two tanks. These tanks were sonically insulated and isolated from one another. A telephone was arranged electronically to be two-way, i.e., the dolphin in tank A could talk to the dolphin in tank B and, simultaneously, the dolphin in tank B could talk to the dolphin in tank A. With the frequency band of the telephone band wide open, the useful frequencies transmitted were from approximately 2000 cycles per second to 50,000 cycles per second. By the use of electronic filters, we could limit this band to any part of the above band. The two ends of the telephone operated under water; in tank A there was a transmitter and a receiver and in tank B there was a transmitter and a receiver, all four of which were under water. A dolphin was placed in tank A and another dolphin in tank B.

The dolphin in tank A could communicate only with the dolphin in tank B, and vice versa. Thus their conversation would of necessity be limited to one another. As soon as the telephone was turned on, the dolphins exchanged sounds.

In a previous publication we described how two dolphins exchange such sounds when placed in the same tank isolated from one another physically but allowed to communicate through the water with one another.* In this previous study we showed that dolphins exchange sounds very politely. When one is talking, the other one keeps quiet. In addition, we showed that they exchanged not only whistles, but also exchanged trains of clicking sounds. We also showed that the two kinds of sonic exchanges do not correspond in time, i.e., they can be talking with whistles and

* Lilly, J. C. and Miller, A. M., "Vocal exchanges between dolphins." *Science* 134: 1873–76 (1961).

talking with click trains, the whistles and the clicks completely out of phase with one another. They can be using the silence of the whistle exchange with a click exchange and filling the silences of click exchange with a whistle exchange, and thus each are polite in the same mode. Thus one pair of dolphins talking can sound like two pairs of dolphins talking, one pair exchanging clickings, the other pair exchanging whistles.

These observations led to further studies in which we demonstrated unequivocally that each dolphin has at least two communication emitters, both in the nose, i.e., below the blowhole, one on each side. A right and a left phonation apparatus is demonstrated in the dolphin's nasal passenger (Plate 21). Thus a given dolphin can carry on a whistle conversation with his right side and a clicking conversation with his left side and do the two quite independently with the two halves of his brain. An analogous human activity may be thought of as follows: if we could whisper and carry on a whispered conversation and at the same time carry on a vocalized conversation using two different apparatuses. Since we do not have the two sides divided with midline structures, we do not have this advantage. The dolphin can control the two airflows separately and the two membranes' vibrations separately. A comparable human activity is the typist typing a manuscript and at the same time carrying on a conversation. Now let us return to the "telephone" experiment.

With the telephone between tanks A and B, the resulting sonic exchanges were found to be very polite, most of the time each dolphin maintained silence while the other spoke. It was found that while the telephone was turned on, the dolphins would exchange sounds most of the time. If we shut off the telephone, either all the sounds ceased or one or both dolphins gave the simple repetitious personal whistle ("signature whistle") characteristic of a solitary dolphin isolated alone. With the telephone off, any sounds that were emitted were completely out of synchrony with the sound emitted by the other dolphin. Little or no "interlock" was detected between the sounds emitted by the two dolphins. In other words, when sounds did occur with the phone not working, the alternating character of the clicks and of the whistles was lost. Either there was frequent overlap or many emissions were met with silence.

The telephone was modified by adding filters to reduce the intensity of sound at certain frequencies. The dolphins tested the system briefly. If the telephone was satisfactory, i.e., no missing critical frequencies, they continued using it. If it was unsatisfactory, i.e., missing critical frequencies, they stopped using it. In the latter case, they tested the system at intervals. If, meanwhile, we had restored the missing critical frequencies the dolphins resumed their "conversations" over the system.

We soon found that we could not cut the frequencies much below 28,000 cycles per second at the high end nor cut the frequencies much above 5000 cycles at the low end without losing the exchanges. The best performances were found with bands extending from about 2000 to about 80,000 cycles per second. Thus the exchange frequency bands correspond fairly closely with the produced frequency bands. In other words, dolphin conversation used a large portion of those sounds whose frequencies are emitted. In addition, the *exchange frequency band* and the *produced frequency band* correspond surprisingly well with the *predicted bands corresponding to our speech wave lengths in air* by the constant wave length hypothesis. In other words, we use the same wave lengths for speech in air as the dolphins use for their speech in water; the frequencies used are in the same ratio ours to theirs as the ratio of the velocities of sound in the two media, air versus water (1 to 4.5).

It is wise to review the question asked at the beginning

of this chapter. How do we know that these two dolphins are exchanging intelligent information? May they not be singing a senseless round, making dolphin music, playing a vocal game, or just saying repetitious simple phrases over and over, or possibly humming reassuring sounds to one another?

We do know that they are not just repeating the same thing again and again. To observe this result, one records these exchanges on a tape recorder and slows them down four times. (Ideally, 4½ times according to the constant wave length hypothesis, to reduce the frequencies to our equivalent speech band.) At the new speed, one has lowered their frequencies four times, and stretched out each of their emissions by a factor of four. Thus we lower their 32,000 cycles per second to 8000 cycles per second and their 1200 cycles per second to 300 cycles per second. Our speech, similarly lengthened, without the frequency changes, is not easily understood; the method is not ideal but we have found it to be useful. (A later development in the Institute allows us to shift to all of the frequencies without lengthening or shortening the emissions. This is discussed elsewhere in this book.)

These recordings are used to listen and to measure the sounds and to find out if the patterns are changing or are merely repetitious (for our pattern perception system, trained as it is to human patterns, not the delphinic ones). Apparently much smaller-brained animals exchange repetitious cries. At least they sound repetitious to us. Frogs, birds, fish, insects, bats, monkeys have different cries for different emotional states. No one so far has detected whether or not these are used for any communication other than the emotional state of the sender, i.e., signaling danger, sexual activities, hunger, etc. A relation seems apparent between the number of different patterns used and the size of the brain of the creature using them. We might thus expect a very large number of patterns in the dolphin exchanges, at least as many as we use in our exchanges. The very small-brained birds and fish have very limited vocabularies, at least as the patterns are currently measured and counted.

In measuring the sonic patterns one basic problem is whether one is measuring aspects that are important to the sender and to the receiver in carrying the meaning. Similarly, it is difficult to choose what to measure in the dolphins' exchanges; we may choose variables not at all important to dolphins and sacrifice the important variables. Therefore, our criteria for differentiating and hence counting the number of different patterns may be totally incorrect. It is necessary to proceed empirically but cautiously and realize the limitations of the methods of arbitrarily choosing patterns.

When listening to the slowed-down exchanges, one is impressed with the numbers of different sounds one hears the dolphins use. The most varied of the transmissions that we have recorded are between "old" dolphins, those with large bones, scarred skin, truncated or missing teeth, and such marks of age. These are the really sophisticated vocalizers. When a *Tursiops truncatus* has become old enough so that the ends of his teeth are worn down flat, he has accumulated a very large number of sonic patterns which he exchanges with similar dolphins. Youngsters four to five years old have a sonic complexity which does not come up to that of the older ones; but even with them the first striking impression is that the versatility and complexity are well developed, that there is very little monotonous repetition, that one has a hard time keeping up with the new patterns as they emerge. Only if the dolphins are badly and continuously frightened are the sounds emitted monotonous and repetitious.

The sounds the dolphins use in their exchanges are difficult to categorize. They are all difficult to describe in words. In my laboratory, we use the following nine large classes to describe the sounds in a somewhat arbitrary fashion:

79

(1) sounds that are emitted under water ("hydrosounds") and sounds that are emitted in air ("air sounds"); (2) whistles; (3) slow click trains; (4) fast click trains; (5) sounds resembling elements of human speech, called "humanoid" sounds; (6) a group that is like mimicry of other sonic sources (fish, ducks, sea gulls, boat engines [inboard or outboard], insects, etc.); (7) a group that is usually associated with emotional behavior (barks, screeches, hammerings, etc.); (8) various non-vocalizing sounds including sneezes, respiration sounds (slow and fast), borborygmi, flatulence, tail slaps, the water noises of swimming at the surface, jumping, etc.; (9) ultrasounds (for us) used in echo-recognition and echo navigation (EREN), sometimes miscalled "SONAR" (sound navigation and ranging) after the human artificial systems.

The steady, most frequent outputs during non-emotional exchanges between dolphins are under water ("hydrosounds") (Plate 2; Figures 4, 6). These sounds are mostly whistles and various complex patterns of clickings and short humanoid emissions.

Their most frequent outputs with us are emitted in air, apparently to accommodate to us in our medium. They lift the blowhole up in the air, open it, and make very loud sounds. Such sounds can be whistles, clickings, barks, wails, and various "humanoid" sounds. The barks and wails in air seem to be analogous to their emotion-tied exchanges with one another under water.

The radical shift, voluntarily executed by dolphins, making the sound in air as opposed to water is in response to our consistent use of air sounds with them. If we talk back to them under water, they answer us under water. If we talk to them in air, they answer us in air† (Plates 3, 31; Figures 3, 8).

† Lilly, J. C., "Vocal behavior of the bottlenose dolphin." *Proc. Am. Philos. Soc.* 106: 520–29 (1962).

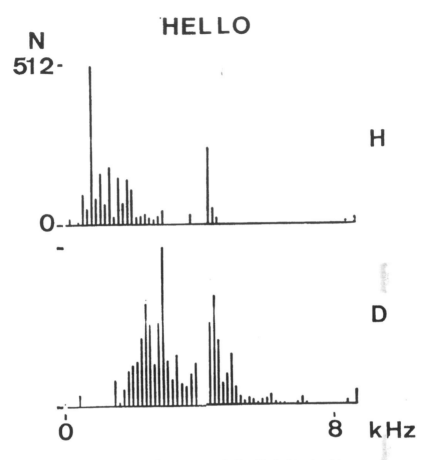

FIGURE 3. *The Voice of the Dolphin in Air:*
Computer Analyses

In each of 58 frequency bands a computer counts the number of times each of the bands is used above a chosen threshold as occurs in several tape replays of the "hello" and of the dolphin's reply. The bands extend from 135 Hertz to 8000 Hertz at 135 Hertz intervals. In the sixth band from the bottom (at 810 Hz) the number of instances of use (N) was 512. The use of each of the other bands is linearly proportional to the length of the black bar. It is to be noted that the woman's voice used frequency bands in two separate regions, one at low frequencies and one at middle frequencies. The dolphin's reply shifts the lower frequencies to higher ones and matches the group of higher frequencies.

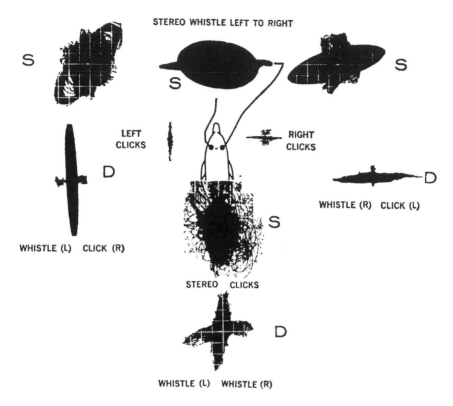

FIGURE 4. *Records from an Experiment with an Isolated Dolphin of the Sound Production on the Right and the Left Side of the Narial Mechanism*

A hydrophone was placed on each side of the dolphin's blowhole (as shown in the figure). The sounds picked up on the right side deflected the cathode-ray oscilloscope beam in a horizontal direction. The sounds picked up on the left side deflected the beam in a vertical direction. The traces shown in the figure are photographs taken during sound production. If the dolphin clicks only with his left side, one sees only vertical traces. If he clicks on the right side, one sees only horizontal traces, and the same for the whistles on each side. If he makes a whistle which is coupled between the two sides, complex ellipses are shown on the screen. In a given click train, he may control the clicks in such a way that the ellipses shift their axes across the screen. Capital "S" means stereo, i.e., linked sound on the two sides and "D" means "double" (or separated) sound production on the two sides without coupling. (From J. C. Lilly, *Stereophonation and Double Phonation in the Dolphin* [manuscript, 1966].)

We use the following *working hypotheses* in our communication research with dolphins:

The airborne whistles and the airborne clicks are attempts to communicate with us as they do with one another, i.e., attempts to induce us to use their mode of communication (Plate 2). Their humanoid sounds in air are their approximations to our communication sounds as distorted by their hearing and by their phonation apparatus (Figures 5, 6, 12). *With the humanoid sounds, dolphins are attempting to communicate with us in our mode of communication.*

At first a dolphin in the presence of a human uses mainly air clicks and air whistles. There are at least two main requirements for the use of humanoids in air: (1) the dolphin must have heard much human speech and (2) he must have had a long period of close, kindly contacts with us.

Once a dolphin has started airborne sounds with one or more of us in close contact, he may induce other dolphins in the colony (not in such close contact) to use the new mode, apparently in dolphin-to-dolphin exchanges. This latter airborne mode is apparently rarely, if ever, used by dolphins in the wild.

We have found that, in dealing with such a large-brained mammal, we must keep the working hypothesis in mind that "they are highly intelligent and are just as interested in communicating with us as we are with them." (With the species *Tursiops truncatus* this is reasonable; it may not be reasonable with smaller dolphins.) If we use any other hypothesis, we have no success whatsoever in dealing communicatively with them.

This hypothesis seems to be necessary and even overriding to accomplish the kinds of communication we are accomplishing and attempting to expand. The proof, the incontrovertible truth, that they are interested in this communication is developing slowly and carefully in our laboratory.

If and when dolphins and we do establish communication on a highly abstract level, the proof will become obvious and incontestable. In this book I give some of the details of this developing picture and give the reasons why we, the ones who work with them, must rely for some time on our faith in their intelligence. *This faith is in the working hypothesis that both we and they are intelligent enough to break the interspecies communication barrier between these very different minds.*

Without such a faith and working hypothesis one makes bad mistakes in tactics and in strategy with the dolphins. If one assumes that they are stupid, they act in a stupid manner. This is partly because in the eye of the beholder, stupidity is seen everywhere, and partly because dolphins understand, catch on fast, and act the way one expects them to act. We have seen dolphins acting rather stupidly in care of persons who think of them as "overgrown stupid fish kept in an aquarium." These dolphins develop some delightful contrasts in new behavior when one of the "believers" shows up and attempts communication.

This is one of the basic difficulties in this new field. One must have an unusual amount of consciousness of faith in one's hypotheses in order to make progress.

In reality, this faith factor is basic to all fields of science. It is necessary to elicit consciousness of this factor in researchers. Most of the sciences have been able to "forget" this necessity; however, it is present and used. In physics, for example, one constantly has a model in mind of what is happening in the system under investigation, and has a kind of temporary faith in the model. This is how physical apparatuses are designed to test the various consequences of a hypothesis.

In this new scientific area, we use the approach of the theoretical physicist teamed up to a certain extent with that of an experimental physicist. We set up hypotheses and operate temporarily as if they were true. We interact in the system under investigation, with each of us programmed with the hypothesis marked "as if true." We then estimate our progress and see how well we operate. We judge our success (or failure) by our success (or failure) in finding new information, i.e., data that were not predicted by the previous workers, nor by those current researchers whose hypotheses differ from ours. I consider this to be a very important point, and it bears repetition in another way.

One thinks of the scientist (and his team) as a set of very large computers, say several thousands of times larger than the largest known man-made electronic computer in 1965; one thinks of a dolphin (and his group of dolphins) as another set of very large computers, also several thousands of times the size of the largest man-made computer. Since this is an exercise in theory, we can assume these basic postulates to be "true." What then are the consequences of the assumptions?

Let us first define something of these biological "computers," something of their characteristics. The two sets of computers—the human ones and the dolphin ones—have similarities and also have differences.

We have said that in each case, the computer is "very large"; this means at least ten billions of active elements (neurons) and a number of memory storage units of the order of ten raised to the seventeenth power (of one with seventeen zeros after it) for the number of memory storage slots.

In the language of computer technology, the access to these large numbers of memory slots is "random" and filing is "associational," i.e., most items in the "memory" can be made directly available with a short search. There is no necessity for the very long search technique of electronic computers involving all of, or a large part of, memory itself. When a piece of data stored in memory is sought in a large file, it is better to proceed to search from many places simultaneously in a "random" manner; the search is for associational chains leading into the correct slot. If one started a systemic search with only one searcher, as it were, one would spend years trying to find the necessary piece of information.

If, for example, one of us wants to remember a particular thing that happened many years ago, we start random search by "free-associating." Sometimes, by very peculiar associations which may seem irrelevant, we arrive at the sought piece of information. If we follow carefully and analyze the path we took to that piece of information, we can see all of the associations among the information stored in a similar place.

Our big brain computers (as opposed to the artificial computers) apparently can search their memories simultaneously in many different places. The large artificial computers have to search one spot at a time and must do it at an extremely rapid pace to be useful. As soon as the artificial computers become as large as ours, however, multiple "associational" searches rather than a single, one-track one will be needed.

Everything coming into our large biocomputers and everything going out of them moves over multiple channels. For example, each one of our eyes contains 1,200,000 neurons coming from the retina to the brain. These all operate in parallel and each one of the channels can deliver information at a rate of about fifty bits of physical information a second. Thus, *the input to the brain from one eye is at the rate of about fifty million physical bits per second.* In spite of a relatively slow input in any one channel (axon), the simultaneous inputs on all channels (nerve trunk) give a total very high rate. Comparing the visual input in the dolphin to ours, he has only one-tenth the number of these visual inputs.

Each of our ears has 50,000 nerve fibers to the brain. Thus we cannot receive nearly so much information by our ears as we can through our eyes. In contrast, the dolphin has $2\frac{1}{4}$ times as many nerve fibers from each ear as we do, i.e., 115,000 fibers. If we also remember that he can function at frequencies four and a half times the frequencies which we use, we can estimate his rate of reception of physical information by his ears.

According to physical information theory, the higher the frequency of a signal, the more physical information it contains, i.e., the greater the number of bits transmitted per second. Therefore, the dolphin is receiving, in general, four and a half times the amount of information that we are for each second because all of his frequencies are multiplied by a factor of $4\frac{1}{2}$. He has $2\frac{1}{4}$ as many neurons, i.e., $2\frac{1}{4}$ as many pathways into his brain, each of which is operating effectively at $4\frac{1}{2}$ times the frequency. Thus we find that the dolphin's ears are receiving almost exactly twenty times as much information (40,000,000 bits) as we do through ours (2,000,000 bits/second). In other words, in the acoustic sphere we have reversed our relative position in relation to that in the visual sphere. The dolphin receives almost as much information through his ear as we do from our eye. In summary, then, the visual inputs in the dolphin are one-tenth the capacity of our visual inputs, and our acoustic inputs are one-twentieth the capacity of the dolphin's. Simultaneously, through these two modes (vision and hearing), a dolphin can receive twice as much information as can a man.

The dolphin's ability to receive twenty times as much information through his ears as we do is reflected in the structure of his big brain computer, from the ears all the way up the nervous system through the cortex. His limitations in the visual sphere are also reflected in the comparative size of his brain computer in the visual tracts all the way to the cortex. If one examines these brains minutely, one finds these ratios reflected in the total number of cells devoted to each of these modes of inputs in the large computer.

The dolphin lacks olfaction completely. Our olfactory input is relatively rudimentary compared to the lower animals. The dolphin's skin is much richer than ours in pressure, touch, and similar endings, so that their sensory input from their skin, presumably, is several times that of ours. This is especially true of their flukes, of their flippers, and of the flanks of their body where it is important to maintain streamlining. The genital regions have not yet been investigated from this viewpoint.

Their tongue seems to have many more specialized structures in it than ours. Their tongue must operate in sea water. There seems to be a special way that the taste of the salt of the sea itself is kept out of the end organs. The many papillae on the tip of the tongue (mentioned in *Man and Dolphin*) contain blood sinuses which apparently pick up the special taste molecules from the sea water and carry them to the end organs that are buried deep beneath the surface of the skin. The sea salts themselves do not influence these end organs. The problem of taste in these animals has not yet been investigated thoroughly. It appears to be a fertile field for future investigation.

Turning now to the outputs from the brain computers, comparing ours to theirs, let us look at the organs in which we are primarily interested—those used in fast communication. We have looked at the eyes and the ears from the standpoint of "physical information" reception, now let us look at the phonation apparatus from the standpoint of physical information transmission. In the same time period, the vocalization apparatus transmits 4½ times the amount of information that our apparatus does: the frequencies used are 4½ times the ones we use. They gain an additional factor of 2 over us in that they have two phonation apparatuses—so their ability to transmit information should be 2 times 4½ or 9 times our capacity to transmit. As will be seen below, there is an additional factor consequent upon the ability to use two phonation apparatuses in a stereophonic fashion which could raise this information rate somewhat higher.

The two phonation apparatuses can be linked one to the other to give "stereophonation." This will be dealt with in greater detail in a later chapter. Presumably the ability to interlock the two phonation apparatuses can increase the amount of information which can be expressed by these organs; in other words, a special sort of additional signal comes out of the stereo use of the two phonation apparatuses. Conservatively, *we estimate that the dolphin can put out ten times the sonic physical information per second that a man produces.*

The sonic-ultrasonic use of echoes from one's own sound sources increases the amount of information that one can gain from the surroundings and, possibly, send out in one's communication with others. The dolphin's ability to do this increases his information capacity in the sonic sphere beyond the factor of ten given previously. We have found that the dolphin has a *third emitter*, especially constructed for the production of his ultrasonic beam. This is localized in his larynx. The physical information transmission capability of the larynx in the "sonar" sphere can be calculated. The band covered is from 15,000 cycles per second (Hz) to 150,000 cycles per second (Hz), a ten-to-one range like that of the other two emitters in the nose. Thus his total transmitting rate is twenty times that of a man. This transmitting rate matches the receiving rate calculated above for the dolphin's ears. They very politely alternate with each of their emitters when communicating one with the other and use three distinguishable "codes." They are not as limited as we are in this sphere.

Thus, the advantage that we have on the visual side is more or less balanced by the advantages that they have on the acoustic side. If one is to live at high speed in the murky ocean, one had best be prepared to have this advantage. In the ordinary sea under a tropical sun at high noon in very clear water, one can gain useful information through visual channels only up to about 100 feet; with acoustic channels this distance can be extended several miles. Thus, we can say that the dolphins are adapted as well to their medium as we are to ours in terms of the inputs to their visual and acoustic systems and their outputs in the vocal acoustic systems.

To return to the large computers, the total amount of information received by the dolphin and by us is thus shown to be comparable, in the major methods of communication with one another and with one's surroundings.

A general statement can be made about these very large biological computers; all inputs, all outputs, and all long interconnections between parts are multiple and operate simultaneously in parallel. The numbers of such inputs, outputs, and long interconnections are very large; at least several thousands to over a million in each mode. Every active element (neuron) is closely interconnected with about three to five others nearby and larger numbers at a distance. The largest part of each of these brain computers is in the cerebral cortex of man and of dolphins. The cortex, in *Tursiops truncatus*, for example, is slightly larger than ours (10 per cent to 40 per cent).

The cerebral cortex seems to be the "general purpose" part of our large computers. By special means it can be shown that we can use our visual cortex and its special characteristics in the service of our acoustic problems (along with the acoustic cortex and its special inputs). To do these experiments we remove the necessity for visual inputs, i.e., by closing our eyes or darkening the room. With proper techniques (hypnosis, drugs, etc.) we can program or compute an "acoustic space" into the "visual space." For example, the blind may use the general purpose nature of the cortex in extending the "acoustic space" into the "visual space" to circumvent complex objects. In special states one can do the same thing with one's own biocomputer. The evidence for the general purpose nature of our brain computers, i.e., their convertibility from special purposes to more general purposes, or to purposes from one special area into another special area, is a long and involved technical argument, too technical for the purpose of this book.

What do we mean by the term, "general purpose" computer? This term means that a computer can be used to model or to set up problem-solving methods for very large classes of problems. "Special purpose" computers are limited to a certain small number of classes of problems. The larger a general purpose computer is, the greater are the range of and the number of problems it can work on simultaneously and continuously.

Another important function for our purposes is the concept of the "stored program." This development in man-made computers opened up new vistas of computer uses. A stored program is a set of instructions for the computer, written and fed into the computer memory. These instructions in memory then direct the computer itself as to how to deal with inputs and outputs, with data, how to compute desired transformations of these data, how to calculate, the equations to use, the order in which the equations are to be used, how to reason out the logical alternatives based on previous choices made, the form of the desired logic to be used in this reasoning process, and the order in which each logical form shall be used. In the modern artificial computers, then, we have not only numerical calculations being carried out but we have logical "reasoning" in limited forms. Such large artificial computers can develop new models, store them as new subroutines, construct more inclusive models from the earlier ones, and manipulate the old subroutines into new large programs, and so on, until all of memory is used up. Thus the stored program takes up portions of memory.

In a modern computer, one either can use memory for storage of new data or for storage of instructions to handle the data; there is a competition for the memory space in the computer between these two processes.

In the modern computers, parts of memory can be selectively erased and used in new ways. The storage of new data may require that in the currently running program, the old data once computed be erased, or alternatively, as new programs are introduced, the old stored programs be erased in part. Thus a modern computer has many properties which are shared with brains. Since brains are very much larger computers, they have many powers in addition to those of the present artificial computers.

The modern computers as part of their basic structure have some logic routines "wired in," i.e., fixed unmodifiable and nonerasable. Such wired-in elements can be switched in different ways and related to one another in different ways. Analogously, our brain also has "wired-in" circuits. Many of these programs are necessary for our survival, for the maintenance of our bodies. For example, one group of these "wired-in" programs is called "the autonomic nervous system." This part of the nervous system is beyond our manipulation directly, though we can influence its programs indirectly from the large, cerebral, cortical computer.

This is a more comprehensive, open-ended view of the man-dolphin communication problem. This view is at variance with current theories in conventional zoology, ethology, marine biology, ichthyology, and mammalogy. This set of concepts are far more powerful research tools than the limited theories current in the above fields. With the new theories we are turning up new data which are not predictable by the older theories at all.

In this theoretical view which we are generating, theories are analogous to computer metaprograms. One's own brain is analogous to a huge computer larger than any built today. The theories (programs and metaprograms) stored in one's self operate the way a stored program in a modern computer operates. The stored program gives the orders for the data acquisition, the computations to be done, the logic to be used, the models to employ, the new models to be constructed, the end use of the results, and the outputs to be chosen to carry out the end uses.

Thus, to test a given theory, one "programs" himself with the as-complete-as-possible theory and joins the system under investigation as a participant-computer operating "on line." This operation of a computer "on line" is a new concept in computer technology. It means that instead of using punch cards or magnetic tapes for feeding the information into the computer, the computer operates from data being generated in real time, right now. In this mode of operation, the computer continuously collects appropriate data, continuously computes these data with the stored program, sets up small models based on theory, tests their parts against the new data acquisition rules, plus the now new data coming in, and sends out control signals to the rest of the system.

When we wish to test, for instance, a communication theory about communication with dolphins, we must act like computers operating on line. We must, as it were, be able to think on our feet; theory revision must occur almost automatically and continuously as the new working models develop and integrate each one with the adjacent ones. The inappropriate parts of the stored programs are thus

93

found by comparison with incoming new data. They are erased, and new parts are written in as rapidly as possible.

This concept of the on-line testing of a theory is relatively new. This approach was not known at the time of Roger Bacon; for example, Bacon defines science as collecting new information and as a consequence of this new information generating the hypothesis which held the information together. Then one tested the hypothesis by means of further collected information. The Baconian method of operation does not correspond to the on-line theory testing method; his method presumed only part of the total feedback network, the input side only.

The on-line method of testing a theory assumes continuous data acquisition, continuous model modification, and continuous change of the method of operation with the external system. When two huge computers (such as a dolphin and human) interact in an on-line fashion the problem is not only the proving or the disproving of a hypothesis by new data acquisition. It is also the forcing of on-line testing continuously, and trying to elicit what model program of communication is stored currently in each of the computers.

When I deal with another person, I want to know what model he is currently working with. We often ask questions of one another with that in mind. If someone is using an inappropriate model of us, we can become quite emotional about it. We feel that it is unfair, unjust, or inappropriate. So must we operate with the dolphins.

If we are using an inappropriate model of dolphins in ourselves, and they are using an inappropriate model of us in themselves, many mistakes occur on both sides. *If a man can get the idea across to a dolphin that man is trying to modify his model of the dolphin, that he has certain limitations in his present model, he can then get the cooperation of the dolphin, on a longer-term, more strategic kind of mutual research.*

In the very long-term view, of course, the test of the theory hinges on finding key facts. One may suspect that such facts exist, but has to have an unequivocal demonstration of their existence. Sometimes new definitions have to be made in order to enunciate the kinds of facts that will be found. In part in this computer discussion, we are giving some directions for finding the key facts and for evaluating their worth. The important aspect of this new view is the "participant computer" one. New data are absorbed rapidly and quickly, and continuously exert maximum influence on the current and future theory. The way is thus pointed out to new collection systems for new data to fill missing parts of the picture ("proof" or "disproof"). As our internal models become more perfected and tests show that the new models predict new facts not yet found, and these are then found, we can move ahead in the development of, for example, interspecies communication.

For the sake of completeness, let us add that there are several important rules basic to this program for research. These rules underlie the axioms of the whole computer, its primary directives. First of all, *truth is sought.* Whatever one's rules for truth and its seeking are, it is sought. This is the strategy of the game of science. We seek the truth no matter the cost in program revision, personal repute, dollars, energy, dedication, or time.

Secondly, *one streamlines himself for the program.* If one is going to be a participant computer, he must get rid of excess emotional baggage. Excessive guilt has to be eliminated. Personal blind spots and tender pain-shame areas must be changed or erased. The model of the computer itself which one is striving for contains no personal blocks against finding the truth no matter where it lies.

Thirdly, *one starts the almost endless process of creation of the pertinent "software."* "Software" is defined loosely as all of the programs and metaprograms present in and used with a given computer. This concept is contrasted with the concept of the structure of the computer itself which, in the jargon, is called "hardware." Thus one must have a meta-program which says "create necessary subroutines, routines, programs, metaprograms, and models to find the truth as it exists in the real system in which one is interested."

Fourthly, *one programs a model of a dolphin consonant with the real dolphin insofar as this can be determined at the present time.*

Fifthly, *one must be willing and able to change his model of the dolphin* as rapidly as new data arrive and are computed about that dolphin or other dolphins.

Let us now return to dolphins and us. Each dolphin from the wild is a huge computer. If he is old, he is filled with many programs, even as we are.

Most of the content of these programs, and probably even their form, is very strange to us. We cannot even presume that the logic is like ours. It may be alien and totally different from human logic. The rules that the dolphin has regulate his data collection, his data computation, his logical manipulation, and his end use of the results of his computations; the rules are probably quite alien to us. *Our problem is to find out what is common between our computer and his.* The dolphin's ability to construct models of reality, of other dolphins, of us, is probably well developed; his models are probably quite different from ours. For example, his predominant acoustic life generates acoustic models where ours generates visual ones.

We do not know the categorical imperatives of the dolphins as yet. Among our many problems is how to achieve a *common program universe and a common data universe* with the dolphin. Conversely, the dolphin has a difficult program in living with us. He also has to achieve a common program universe and a common data universe with us.

In other words, the basic problem of interspecies communication is convincing both sides that the problem exists. Both sides must explore with what sort of shared dimensions this problem can be approached.

There is an old saying that it is very hard to teach an older person new tricks. This may be true for some oldsters, but apparently is not true for all of them. However, perhaps the older dolphin has a similar difficulty. The problem may be that the old memory is so filled and his ability to erase so limited that we should not choose old dolphins for the interspecies communication program. It may be a better idea to employ a young dolphin with a memory less taken up with delphinic life programs and introduce him to the man-dolphin communication program.

This plan is currently being followed in our Dolphin Point Laboratory on the island of St. Thomas, U. S. Virgin Islands. This program is described in detail elsewhere. Suffice to say here that it is difficult to find and create a compromise environment for the dry-thinking, dry-living us, and the wet-thinking, wet-living them, for the continuous day-and-night programming of the human and of the dolphin in shared quarters.

It is also difficult to find and create a compromise mode of communication for dolphins and for us. As was shown above, they are specifically adapted to an underwater kind of communication. We are specifically adapted to an in-air kind of communication. We are primarily visual, and they are primarily acoustic. Luckily, both sides are seeking compromises.

However, the older dolphin is yet to be tested. We now have some oldsters to work with. New information on the vocal capability of the wild dolphins is coming from our work with the older dolphins. We have learned many new things from the older ones. They have taught us about their disciplining of the younger dolphins, of their disciplining of one another, and also of their disciplining of us. Some of the dolphins' own developed programs are beginning to show up.

Sometimes the young dolphin adapts so rapidly to our ways that we miss the programs he learned in the wild which he apparently abandons when he is with us. Such programs as we see are now in response to us and to our demands.

With the older dolphins interacting with another oldster or with a youngster, we see more of these programs which were developed in the wild without man's interaction with the dolphin. Typical data with the older dolphin, for example, is the already developed complexities of their vocalizations mentioned above. They were found to have fully developed repertoires of all of the classes of sounds previously listed. The oldsters have memory stores of several kinds of information which the younger dolphins apparently lack.

Thus in this chapter we have presented something of what we have learned of the dolphins' vocalization, of the physical characteristics of the sounds they produce, a comparison of them to us in terms of the sounds that they use, and a guiding theory for research on their and our communication. This theory looks as though it will be useful in the interspecies communication program. It may be that it will be useful with interspecies communication with species other than dolphins, say with elephants or with the large whales, or between man and woman!

CHAPTER 4

Communication Is between Minds

IT IS useful to have a working definition of what is included and excluded from the term "communication." Communication is a fundamental concept essential to a basic understanding of man and of other species. The definition used in this book is essential for an understanding of this book and of *Man and Dolphin.*

DEFINITION: *Communication is the exchange of information between two or more minds.*

A mind is housed in a brain residing in a body detectable by the senses or by the senses aided by special apparatus. The medium of communication is any one (or more) available to the two minds involved in the exchange. The modes of communication are the ones available to the two minds.

The special case of interest is that of the mammals, terrestrial and aquatic. The information which is exchangeable is of a complexity and an apparent variability which depends on the size of the two or more minds involved in the exchanges. The size of the mind is a direct and eventually specifiable function of the size of the brain. The size of the brain is a direct and eventually specifiable function of the number of active elements contained therein, i.e., present theory says the number of neurons and possibly the number of glia cells contained within the total brain itself determine functional size. The size of the brain in terms of numbers of active elements is close to a linear function of the total weight of the mammalian brain. Thus, we can say that the total weight of the living mammalian brain is a gross measure of the size of the contained mind, and hence, a gross measure of the complexity and apparent variability of the information which can be transmitted.

In order to keep this definition open-ended, not limited to presently known modes of communication, it neither explicitly includes nor implicitly excludes direct transference of thought from one mind to another. In other words, the definition leaves the question of thought transference to future research. Direct thought transmission has not been demonstrated unequivocally, i.e., the existence theorum for thought transference does not yet exist. Among the modes which do exist are conventional speech; gestural, nonvocal transmission and nonhearing reception; some kinds of music; writing and reading; mathematics; dancing; love-making. Many of these modes are not usually contained within a definition of communication. The new science of nonvocal communication between humans includes these activities.

Known media of exchange include electromagnetic waves (including light, radio, etc.), elementary physical particles, mechanical contact, mechanical waves in gases, solids, or liquids, and electric currents in solids, liquids, or gases. The use of elementary physical particles for communication purposes exists only in limited regions of space and of materials. Such particles as the electron are used in vacuum tubes in radio; other kinds of particles are used in solid state circuitry devoted to communication purposes. Mechanical contacts are used for communication, for example in the Braille system of reading for the blind, by means of finger contacts. Mechanical waves in gases are the usual sound waves with which we communicate. Such sound waves can also be transmitted through solids and liquids.

The dolphins use them in sea water, for example. Electric currents for communication are used in the ordinary telephone, and by some species of fish which can detect very small currents and thus tell how far away they are from various objects; possibly such fish use them in communication one with the other. Electric rays use electric currents in water as offensive weapons and may possibly use them in communication systems between members of the species. Whether or not dolphins use electric currents in the sea water is not as yet known. Whether they use elementary physical particles is not known. We do know they use light waves. Whether they use, for instance, very low-frequency radio waves is not known. They do use mechanical contacts.

In the rest of the definition, we leave a large area for unknown media of exchange, and unknown modes of exchange, i.e., we assume that there are new ones yet to be discovered. One develops a respect for and a sensitivity to the unknown operating in the area of communication. I believe this is an essential characteristic of a proper scientist in this area. A respect for the unknown is needed at every level, not just at the level of the media and the modes, but at high levels of abstraction. In other words, exchanges may be operating between dolphins in known media and known modes, but at levels of abstraction which we have not yet grasped. Such awareness of the ever-present and intimate presence of unknowns keeps one's mind open and one's system of reasoning open. Without this openness, discovery is impeded.

The so-called spiritualists and the so-called psychics maintain that their methods of communication and modes and media are part of the unknown yet to be discovered. They maintain that the reality of such exchanges is incontestable and quite anxiety-provoking. They maintain that such communication can occur with a mind without a detectable body. These people may be, as they maintain, special sorts of human beings with special sensitivities to unknown media and modes. However, as far as I am aware, such thoughts are still in the area of childish wishful thinking. Proof that they are not in the area of childish, wishful thinking is yet to be forthcoming. All of the investigations of these phenomena over the years by proper scientists usually show up some sort of trickery, fraud, or unconscious use of ordinary modes of communication. In respecting the unknown, one should not worship it and make it more powerful than the known.

Respect for *unknown minds* in *known brains* is another story. Data derived from careful experimentation with smaller-brained animals do not convince me of the lack of a mind in a dolphin. As far as I am concerned, I must assume the presence of a large mind in a dolphin whose brain is larger than mine. Until proven otherwise this is my basic working hypothesis.

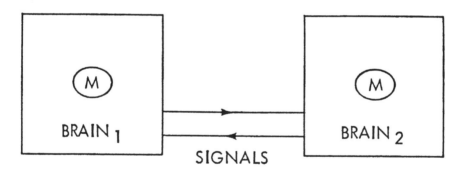

SCHEMA OF THE DEFINITION OF COMMUNICATION

This diagram shows a mind (M) on the left in the circle contained in brain 1 (the square) transmitting signals to mind (M) in the circle on the right contained within brain 2, the square. In turn, mind 2 is sending signals to mind 1. The information is not generated from these signals until the signals are received, computed, and turned into the information by each of the minds in turn. This is the essential core of our definition of communication.

The *information* does not exist as information until it is within the higher levels of abstraction of each of the minds and computed as such. Up to the point at which it becomes perceived as information, it is *signals*. These signals travel through the external reality between the two bodies, and travel as signals within the brain substances themselves. Till the complex patterns of traveling neuronal impulses in the brain are computed as information within the cerebral cortex, they are not yet information. Information is the result of a long series of computations based on *data signal inputs, data signal transmissions to the brain substance,* and *recomputations of these data.*

The usual definition of "physical information" is different from the one I use here. The schema of the definition shows that one must differentiate very carefully between "signals" and "information." In this view, a set of signals of at least minimal detectable size in a given mode and given medium is not information; *it becomes so only if and when it enters, is computed, and changes the contents of a mind.* As can be shown by special methods, many complex patterns of signals enter the mind quite below the level of conscious awareness, are stored there for years, and can be reinvoked in full vigor. What is stored is patterns of signals, bits of signals from each mode with the rules for their reassembly on proper command. These stored patterns are not called "information" in this schema and in this definition. *The stored materials, like the signals entering from outside, are not information until they are reassembled in "spatial" patterns varying in time in the present or future mind.* In other words, our boundary for information is at a level of discourse of *Cogito ergo sum,* "I think (or I know), therefore I am." *Information is that which I know now, coming from outside me, and coming from the storage inside me, allowing for delays in computation and in transmission.*

Most information theorists do not consciously make these distinctions. What we call signals themselves they say consist of "bits of physical information," even as I did in the previous chapter when talking about the eyes and ears of the dolphin. But careful analysis will reveal a circularity of concepts in these "physical" definitions. The "kinds" of bits lead one into bypaths of explanation not necessary with the above definition. The mind of the observer-participant is where the information is constructed, by and through his own programs, his own rules of perception, his own cognitive and logical processes, his own metaprogram of priorities among programs. His own vast internal computer constructs information from signals and stored bits of signals. The "bits" of information thus take on a new meaning: *A bit is a smallest possible piece of information recognizable as such coming from either inwardly moving signals or from outwardly moving ones.* Fundamentally, this is similar to the standard definition in the usual "information theory." This can be understood by recognizing that the standard information theory exists only in a mind, and that even the bits, the signs of the signals in the external reality are still "bits" only in a mind.

Communication engineering theory is a theory of communication from one mind through a brain and its outputs, through a specifiable set of processes to the external world, through a portion of that world with specifiable modes, media, and artificial means to another body, another brain, to another mind. *The "bits of information" in each of the two minds must be agreed upon by those two minds by sharing their definitions.* The signals must be able to pass from one mind to the other mind and back again, and again to create the same or similar information each time. Therefore, the basic theorum of "information" using the "signal/noise ratio" and its dependence on the "pass band"

and on the "bit rate" is incomplete. This theorum, or its analog in the new set, must be redefined to include the new interfaces. Let us see what we can do to make such new definitions with the new interfaces considered.

In general, the signal/noise ratio is a definable entity only when each of two minds agrees on the definition of what is "signal" and what is "noise." In the standard theory, "noise" is ideally a detectable random process, a stochastic ensemble varying with time (in a random fashion). "Noise" is a form of energy in which no part can be taken, no matter how chosen, as conveying any meaning whatsoever. Physical noise is that set of signals which, when received by a mind, generates no new information in that mind. In this sense, a noise must have no beginning and no end. If a noise *begins,* this of itself is a signal. If the noise *ends,* this of itself is also a signal. We have new information at the beginning and at the end of a noise sequence. Therefore, the duration of a noise in time also gives information.

Thus, we can say that any change other than purely random changes detectable by the mind in any aspect of the noise is a signal and hence can generate information in the mind. When we place the new boundaries on information theory, one can see that one's own mind can be and does act as if it were a source of "new" information. The sources of "new" information in one's own mind are analogous to the sources in the external world. This can be seen most dramatically by either looking at a very noisy visually presented process or by listening to a very noisy acoustically presented process. If one watches long enough or listens long enough, he begins to "make signals out of the noise" by introducing systematic changes into the noise. Where do these "signals" come from? Where does the new "information" come from?

In profound physical isolation, this process can be shown most dramatically. *Our minds project a pattern onto the noise.* We can even project an "as if" source of the signals (as if they were coming from the outside) even though they are being brought up only from the storage within our own minds. Basically, investigators who are looking into their own minds (under special conditions) may mistake the sources of "new" information within their own minds as if those sources were outside the head. This process in psychology is called "projection."

This process can use noise at any level of abstraction (from the physical, physiological levels of functioning) as a computer, and make this same mistake. One can have noise, as it were, in random, logical processes as well as by the random motion and the random collisions of molecules. If one is watching "noise" at the logical level, he can sometimes "hear messages," as if he were being spoken to by other persons and these persons were telling him some important message. Basically, these processes within the human mind are just beginning to be investigated thoroughly with the help of special conditions. (This approach may be applicable to a study of severe psychoses.)

Fundamentally, then, we must eliminate, insofar as our brains and minds and their scientific investigation are concerned, a hypothesis which says that the noise coming from inside one's own mind and brain can be "signals caused by direct mental influence of other minds without the interposition of the usual modes and media of communication." Modern scientific theory says that I have my mind, here and now, and that there are other minds, here and now, resident in brains in bodies present in the external reality outside my body but nowhere else.

Modern science denies interest in the existence of such things as the spirit world, the direct influence of God on human minds, and extraterrestrial influence machines manipulated by other beings. Most of the phenomena described as happening within the minds of people can be explained by the above mechanisms, the projection of signals from within one's own storage onto noise, and hence hearing or seeing what one wants to hear or see rather than some objectively existing "spirit" or "God."

One might say from a modern scientific point of view, then, that transcendental religious revelations are merely the projections of one's own expectations in the area of religion. A disembodied mind cannot exist according to current scientific theory.

I am quite empirical about this. Until I can send telegrams (from me to a third party) through such media and through such minds, and receive a verifiable telegram through the same routes, I will not believe in the existence of such media, modes, and minds.

The existence theorum states, "To prove the existence of a something one must first present evidence of that something and its existence acceptable to other minds." The non-existence theorum states, "As long as one assumes the non-existence of a something one will assume that the signals from the something either do not exist, are noise, are created in another human mind, or come from some mindless process in nature." Therefore, if an unknown mind without a visible, detectable body sends signals, we ignore them, repress memories of having received them, attribute them to noise, or attribute them to a mindless but systematically varying source or, say, that they are the results of faulty operation of the observer, i.e., projections from the observer's own mind.

This theorum (the non-existence theorum) is a useful one in dealing with uncomfortable evidence one is tempted to reject, usually with a powerful emotional propulsion on the rejection. This theorum may cause one to at least slow down and think of alternatives to rejection. I find it useful, especially in special states of mind, including times of great disappointment, fear, great joy or sorrow, and others. I also find it useful when dealing with dolphins. If we assume that the mind of the dolphin does not exist, we will assume that the signals from it do not exist or are noise created by the human mind, or come from some mindless process in nature. If a dolphin sends signals, we ignore them, repress memories of having received them, attribute them to noise, or a mindless source or say that they are the results of faulty operation of the observer who reports them. This is the treatment that dolphins usually suffer at the hands of scientists.

When I first postulated the existence of a mind in a dolphin in the book *Man and Dolphin*, I saw this effect operate strongly against me, and against the "dolphin mind hypothesis." Why must we say that the dolphin has no mind, that no other creature in this world has a mind of the complexity and size of ours? Why has the theory of a mind in other creatures become *persona non grata* and discredited over the years? I suggest that it is because man has been concentrating all of his scientific efforts in areas of endeavor in which this presumption of the mind is totally inappropriate. Man has progressed rapidly in physics, in chemistry, in biology, in engineering, and in other such areas by defining a mind as nonexistent in these processes. In these areas of scientific endeavors, this is a basic assumption that must be made, is appropriate, and can be shown to work very well.

In other areas such as the ones discussed in this book, we must assume a mind exists in order to make progress. The assumption of a mind in research with dolphins does work: "Each of the large-brained dolphins has a correspondingly large mind." The theorum does not say what kind of a mind the dolphin has, it says only that it exists.

One reason that science has abandoned the hypothesis of bodiless minds, minds without brains, is partly because it has been misused in the past history of the human species throughout all of the races. Historically, practically every one of the human races, and in some of them currently, there are superstitions, animisms, totemisms, and various other kinds of projections into the noise of one's own areas of ignorance. When one does not have hard-nose data about the surrounding realities, and also hard-nose data about the internal realities of his own mind, he projects the concepts in his mind into the surroundings, into other persons, into other animals, and even into plants. This seems to be the origin of the multiplicity of such things as gods, devils, wood spirits, and nymphs with which world literature is replete.

Such factors are seen still operating even today in one's own mind, if one is willing to go into solitude and profound isolation from physical stimuli. Under these conditions, if a "white acoustic noise" is present in the background and if one is fearful enough or expectant enough or feeling neglected enough, one can begin to make out "voices" in the noise and sometimes even count the number of people who are doing the talking. A few subjects under this condition can actually hear "the voice of God" in the noise. If one carefully analyzes "what God said" it is found that, as far as that person is concerned, nothing new is said. In other words, the things in the storage of the personal big computer are all one finds in the analysis of what God said. With a sufficiently prolonged period of analysis following such an episode, one can trace out all of the details of the so-called "religious revelation" and show that they have been present since the childhood of the human being involved. Under such circumstances, one tends to project things picked up in childhood and long since forgotten in adulthood.

This projection is into the unknown sets of signals which one can interpret as noise and hence project onto fairly freely. It is this ability which has plagued scientists since science began. It is this error, rather than *anthropomorphism* or *anthropocentricity*, that is basic to the skepticism and cynicism about finding minds in animals other than man. As a scientist we are each trained not to indulge in conscious projections and conscious phantasy. We are also taught to be very suspicious of certain kinds of theoretical constructions, because of this bad history of such constructions. Through careful and prolonged psychoanalytical training, we can begin to see these traps for our theories in ourselves.

The theory of a mind, not human, existing in another animal, not human, is attractive and seductive. This, too, puts off most scientists. Those who deal with lower animals want hard-nose data concerning the quality of the mind that one is postulating as existing in a dolphin. The problem in interspecies communication is to develop it so that even the most hard-nose skeptics can have satisfactory data about the existence of the mind in the dolphin.

In our society, the postulation of disembodied non-brained minds exists in religious endeavors side by side with scientific endeavors. The religious thinkers must assume the existence of some sort of a mind other than human. Religion would quickly cease to exist without the postulation of a spirit or God or gods. Some scientists at times need to believe wholeheartedly in their own personal basic beliefs and defend them as vigorously and emotionally as any zealous missionary.

Some of these scientists tend to keep their religion for Sunday and yet carry over their zealous defense for the rest of the week. My own position about religion is the same as my position about ESP and thought transference. Until I have empirical, down-to-earth, hard-nosed information thrust upon me, I will maintain a position of not knowing; such thinking also belongs in the area of the unknown.

Thus, I agree with those who maintain that I or others must produce very good information about the mind of the dolphin before they can believe in its existence. On the other hand, there are those who deny that *any* mind can exist in a dolphin. It is with these people that I take definite issue. One cannot very easily demonstrate the absence of anything. If the mind exists, it is going to be easier to demonstrate its existence than it will be to demonstrate its non-existence, if it does not exist.

Those who want a demonstration of existence, if it exists, suggest certain experiments. They would show, for example, the intelligence of the dolphin by testing for the kinds of abstract ideas that one dolphin exchanges with another. Such an experiment is as follows:

One dolphin is put in an isolation tank with a series of problems to be solved in sequence. These problems are as cleverly arranged as the investigator is able to achieve. One suggested arrangement is to put the problems in a cascaded series in which the solution of each depends upon the previous one. The dolphin is induced to solve or is taught to solve the sequence of problems with suitable rewards for success. During this period, he is kept out of contact with other dolphins.

Once he succeeds in a performance, he is placed in a vocal-auditory contact, two-way, with a second dolphin. No visual nor mechanical contact is allowed between the two dolphins. Dolphin No. 2 is in an isolation tank similar to that of No. 1. He also has the problem materials with him.

The major question to be answered then, is: Can dolphin No. 1 now transmit the appropriate information to No. 2 to allow No. 2 to solve the sequence as fast or faster than No. 1?

A few cautions are necessary. 1. The problems must be of such a novelty and of such a unique type that no previous dolphin can have had any previous experience with them. 2. The problems must be difficult enough to solve so that a detectable time is taken in the solution of the problem. 3. The difficulty must be great enough to insure that no dolphin can reason out a solution on his own without help. 4. The problems must become interesting enough to a dolphin to keep him working on them long enough to solve them. 5. The problems must be interesting enough for No. 1 to interest the other dolphin, No. 2, in solving them. 6. The problems all must be in the framework and in the content of the dolphin-to-dolphin communication. 7. Alternatively, the problems must be convertible by dolphin No. 1 into the content and the framework of dolphin-to-dolphin communication.

I am very much interested in this approach and have encouraged several scientists in efforts to make progress along these lines. To date, the usual failure is during the initial period in selecting the problems and in teaching dolphin No. 1 the problems. The usual investigator forgets some of the above requirements, especially the last four, i.e., that the problems must be interesting to dolphins and appropriate to their cognitive, conative, perceptual, and transmission-reception systems. Undoubtedly, variations of these experiments will be done in the future in sufficient numbers so that the evidence will gradually accumulate as to what dolphins can transmit and what they cannot transmit one to the other's mind.

In the Institute, our own research program includes this point of view. I believe that we need to share the contents of the communication with the dolphin in order to have the proper materials for the above experiments. In the system which we are devising, we establish a shared set of symbols, a set shared among us and among the dolphins themselves. Such symbols must be understood by the dolphins in their way and by us in our way. In this pursuit, we learn what does interest them as problem materials.

Sometimes the dolphins tell us what interests them by showing interest, i.e., by sticking to a given kind of a problem. We learn also what is appropriate to their reception-perception-cognition-volition-transmission systems, either "naturally" or in an artificially taught and learned context. As the bits and pieces of the shared symbols fall into place, problems can be constructed in which these symbols are used.

Each of us as a child learned by being presented by our parents with tens of thousands of pieces of information daily. We are allowed, as it were, to pick up that which we can pick up at each age. By the time we enter school, we have already learned the basic way to speak and the basic way to communicate. Thus we can say man learns, as a child, enough language to begin to solve problems posed by the parents and his peers and to pose problems to be solved by them. Thus we must teach the dolphins by constant contact, some sort of a shared language between us, before we can carry out the proposed experiments on testing their intelligence. Other scientists have not agreed with this point of view. They feel that we can make faster progress by demonstration first of the dolphin's high intelligence. If they are right, it should be possible for any psychologist trained in intelligence testing methods to make such a demonstration possibly long before the demonstration by means of interspecies communication. Those who are trying this approach so far are delighted with the dolphins' abilities to solve complex hierarchies of certain kinds of shared problems.

Once again, I underscore the necessity of the sharing, cooperative efforts to keep the dolphins interested and to keep the investigators happy. I feel that those who immerse themselves in the dolphins' world and have dolphins in their world can learn and teach the above posed problems through interspecies communication methods. But I do not feel that a psychologist can "take a summer off" and get the desired results in a short time. We are not dealing with small-brained animals in short-term experiments, in which most of our animal psychologists are trained. One can take a genetically pure strain of rats and in a few months quickly arrive at desired results. The rats' solutions to problems are well known and what rats can do and what they can't do has been well described (though not yet fully).

We have found in the Institute that both the human side and the dolphin side are still too strange to one another to do such problems quickly and easily. In the vocal sphere we have accomplished some rather novel and unusual tasks with dolphins. We have demonstrated that the dolphins can do certain vocal tasks that no other animal except man can do. No parrot, no mynah bird, no monkey can do these tasks at all. Later in this book these experiments will be described and their results given in detail.

I will also describe the mother-child approach to these problems in which a young dolphin and a female human actually lived together in order to explore methods of communication. To progress in these experiments it has been found necessary that each of the personnel have a belief in the existence of the mind of the dolphin and in its large size and complexity in order to make progress.

Currently, the whaling industry is busy wiping out most of the big whales, and in Japan, at least, dolphins are slaughtered by the thousands for food. (Such industrial efforts have been less than what the navies of the world could now do to exterminate the whales but it is still effective.) In this area, I am not proud of my own species. Do we have anything that might impress the sperm whales aside from our killing abilities?

For some years I have been hunting for anything that human beings can do which might impress brains and minds larger than ours (see Figure 1 caption). We have expert abilities to build: to build buildings, to build roads, to build cities, these of themselves are impressive. If the whales could see these in detail from the land side, we might achieve a certain measure of respect from them.

We also build ships, submarines, and yachts. This probably impresses them more at the present time because sea craft are more within their sphere of experience. Our abilities to pollute the oceans by means of the rivers also must be impressive to them. Loren Eiseley once wrote that to see the detritus of civilization spewing forth in the oceans from the rivers must be a mysterious and at the same time impressive sight; a proof of the activities of the animal called *Homo sapiens.**

It is to be noticed that all of the things that I have mentioned here are done by many people cooperating with one another. This is true of the whaling industry as well as of the building industry. This cooperative activity of the humans is the thing which is impressive even though no one of us might be impressive to a single sperm whale. Operating in concert we are an impressive species.

Probably that which would excite the most respect for the human species in a sperm whale would be a full symphony orchestra playing a symphony. At least this would be an excellent starter to try to convince a sperm whale that maybe some of us are better than just in-concert murderers of whales. A symphony orchestra playing multiple melodies and their complex transformations might keep him interested for at least two or three hours. With his huge computer the sperm whale could probably store the whole symphony and play it back in his mind to himself at his leisure. I suggest that whoever tries this experiment first should be ready to play several symphonies, each symphony only once. Otherwise, the sperm whale would be bored with the performance. Since he probably has the capacity to store the whole thing at one playing and doesn't need

* "The Long Loneliness," *Phi Beta Kappa Quarterly* (1961).

to hear it again from outside he would be bored by repetition. He probably re-creates it for himself fully from storage in his huge brain.

You will notice that I picked complex multiple human *acoustic performances distributed in space* as that which would impress the whale. As stated for the dolphin earlier, since in the sea sound and ultrasound are far more important than light and its variations, this is the area that he understands best. As we stated earlier in this book his brain, his big computer is also more acoustically orientated than ours; very large masses of it are given over to acoustic computations, even as in ours we are given over to visual computations.

The sperm whale's re-creations are probably complete. He probably can re-create this spatial distribution of the sounds. He probably can also replay the complex interrelationship between the sounds simultaneously in pitch, in space, in loudness. His reproduction is probably in "high fidelity" coupled with the original feeling that he had at the first play. This probably would be easy for any sperm whale. I understand there are a few human beings who spent years acquiring some of this ability.

In my own case, I have visualized and felt this kind of experience but only during the actual playing of the music itself, here and now. It would be a great privilege to be able to reinvoke the full playing. Imagine being able to relive a full playing of Mahler's *Messiah* or any of your favorite symphonies without any apparatus or recordings outside of your own brain!

This huge brain of the sperm whale may also have re-programming abilities for the symphony. He may modify the music and even further elaborate it beyond any human conceptions of music. How can we ever know if this hypothesis is true or not? Let us make this idea "the carrot in front of our donkey" and let it motivate us to learn to communicate. Then we can ask these questions and proceed from there.

Of course we may never have the chance to have the intriguing and uplifting experience of communicating with a sperm whale. Our enterprising friends of the whaling industry are too involved to give us this opportunity. Economic gain is still mightier than the Golden Rule. Economic gain is beyond curiosity, beyond our ethics, morals, religions. It is indeed a black mark on the escutcheon of the human race to allow profit here to override the best in man. Those involved in the whaling industry create delusions to serve overriding their own and our ideals.

In a book called the *Whaler's Eye*,† one chapter describes the sophistries of a scientist working for the whaling industry. He was having a hard time deciding whether or not the whale was hurt by the harpoon which finally killed him. It could easily be demonstrated with dolphins to such people (if they were interested) that the skin of all of these animals is exquisitely sensitive. We could demonstrate unequivocally that they do feel pain and object to pain as strongly as humans. The industry has been so busy for over a hundred years rationalizing their position with respect to the whales that they have forgotten that there is evidence that whales do not only have pain but express it unequivocally. Many people have written of the moanings and carryings on of injured whales. In the last century the whalers with their wooden vessels could hear these sounds through the sides of the ships. The problem is distinguishing the moans of their pain and fear from the normal communications between the whales. As I said earlier in this book if the human race is ever to be measured by another species for the qualities of our activities in regard to interspecies communication, this is the worst possible record of our failures to respect and nurture other species.

† Christopher Ash (New York: The Macmillan Company, 1962).

CHAPTER 5

The Mind of the Dolphin

"COMMUNICATION is an exchange of information between two minds." Thus for interspecies communication we start with the basic postulate that each dolphin has a mind. The size, the complexity, and the capability of each dolphin mind is a function of the size of his brain. Each individual has some limitations placed upon him by the limits on the number of neurons in his brain. The quality of the development, through the use of the brain and of the mind, is a function of the natural experiences and formal education to which each individual is exposed.

Each dolphin's mind is very strange and distinctly different from ours. The problem is: How are the dolphins different? Will we ever be able to understand them? Will they ever be able to understand us? How are they similar? Are they similar enough to us to make possible the first bridges of understanding between the two species?

Our minds and their minds are in bodies whose differences have been described in the previous book. The differences between our brains were begun in that book and are discussed further in this book. The inputs and the outputs to the human and to the dolphin brain are discussed in another chapter. The differences in our environments and theirs are described in the first book.

I mention "minds, bodies, brains, environment" in the same context because of their close interdependence in life.

One important additional factor in the generation and maintenance of the mind is the social milieu. Most of us operate in "mostly human" social environments. Only very few of us have the privilege to operate in close contact and as essential parts of a dolphin's milieu. Only a few dolphins operate directly and closely with a human. I feel that there are not enough such close combinations nor are there enough persons willing to devote themselves to dolphins in this way at the present time.

The dolphin minds which I am most concerned with are those living with human beings. Something of what I have to say may concern wild dolphins, but these are not available for close study.

Our search for the mind of the dolphin and our search for the common ground between our two kinds of mind, starts with our own mind. This cannot be emphasized enough. Since we do not yet fully understand the human mind, there may be aspects of it which are closer to the dolphin mind than we yet know. In the research on our own minds, we should seek aspects which are shared with large brains in general. The large mind in the large brain may have underlying (and presently not understood) similarities which we can use. At any point we may find a bridge across to their minds through the investigation of our own minds.

Elsewhere in this book, I discuss some possible operations of the very large mind-brain of the sperm whale. I wish to limit here the discussion to brain-minds the size of ours, and what such brains can do if unhampered by the usual conventions of thinking. Dolphins are unhampered by our conventions; they may become hampered by our conventions; they may be hampered by their own conventions.

My purpose here is to expand our horizon beyond the necessary, daily, constricting confines of our operating society. Each one of us must streamline himself to fill a role within that social milieu. Most of us are so "locked in" with our everyday lives with our family and our work that we do not have time to see the structures of our own minds, as they can operate when freed from these external reality necessities. Let us try to visualize another situation which may help us in understanding how our minds are limited and how the dolphin's mind may differ from ours.

Let us visualize a situation in which a person is taking a vacation in which his duties are completely suspended. His work and his family are adequately cared for. All the bills are paid up. The telephone is turned off. There is no radio nor TV. For a period of three to five days, no demands are placed upon him. All of his needs are satisfied automatically. He is immersed in silence and darkness and freed up from the demands of gravity. He is placed temporarily "in orbit," as it were, with automatic feeding machines.

Would this be an ideal vacation? Some busy people might conceive of it as idyllic. Most people, placed in this situation, make themselves unhappy, at least for a period of time. During some 1954 short-term experiments, profound physical isolation and solitude taught me some things which I present here.

After some work I found this condition quite comfortable. But the work was necessary first. The outside-the-body conditions were perfected; then my own mental attitude had to be investigated.*

I learned that conditions which should be idyllic can become so when one deep down wants them to be so. In other words, that which a person believes is that which becomes true, within the limited confines of this experiment. This is all inside the person's own head, and hence is subject to the unique laws of thought, not to the natural laws of external reality. After many exposures to the physical isola-

---

* Lilly, John C. (1956) in General Bibliography.

tion under ideal physical conditions, I was able to overcome self-created mental discomfort to a certain extent. I learned a lesson about our minds as follows:

Our huge computers are, to a certain extent, self-meta-programming and self-programming.† If one is left alone long enough, he can see how he acts as a cause with respect to himself. We can see also that each one of us can cause a large fraction of our own unhappiness. We can see that we have within us "programs for unhappiness" as well as "programs for happiness." In isolation, we see to what extent each of us also is programmed by others in our normal, everyday lives. We can see that we often blame the programming of others when we should be blaming the programming of ourselves. Since the number of such programs in each one of us is immense, we have to set up a meta-program which says "investigate programs which are counter to one's major interests." We must also set up the metaprogram, "find out how much one's self is the causative factor in an unhappy situation, and vice versa, how much someone else is the causative factor (untangle the feed-back)."

When a person first enters isolation, the interpersonal programs continue to operate during the first hour or so. It is only as these immediate day's programs fade out and the self-generated programs come in and replace them that the latter can be clearly seen. Without proper programming in isolation, we can make endless excuses to ourselves and make endless evasions which avoid analysis of self.

This situation is epitomized in the statement, "Alone with one's God there are no distractions, nor excuses, nor alibis, nor evasions."‡ Once we are launched into the self-gener-

† Lilly, J. C., *The Human Biocomputer: Programming and Metaprogramming* (*Theory and Experiments with LSD-25*) (Miami: Communication Research Institute, 1967; Scientific Report Number CRI0167).

‡ Lilly, J. C., *loc. cit.*

ated metaprograms and programs we can eventually find the ones which work against our ideals and goals. One group is the "how and what to think" metaprograms. One of these tells us that "certain ways of thought and certain kinds of thinking are negative." (The term "negative" means that which is unpleasant or forbidden or dangerous or "psychotic" or "sick" or evil or anti-social or sinful, for example.)

This kind of metaprogram is very difficult to see in one's self. With psychoanalytic experience and training, I began to see this particular metaprogram and to attempt to attenuate it in my thinking. Without finding it and modifying its effects, I would not have been able to continue the isolation work at all. *By long and hard work I found that the evil label "negative" should not be tied to any mode or any kind of thinking at all.* Literally, there is no such thing as an "evil" *type* of thinking *per se*. There are negative *thoughts;* there are evil thoughts, hostile thoughts, guilty thoughts. There is no evil *mode* of thinking. Negative thoughts can occur in any mode, but the mode itself is not negative. One's horizons in the metaprograms for "what to think and how to think" should be wide open with no holds barred.

For example, consider the subjective phenomena which I call "projection of visual imagery and visual thinking." I chose these words expressing these phenomena very carefully to avoid "negative" terms (such as "hallucination" or "delusion") one could borrow from psychiatry. In this area William James said that one should keep the terminology as objective and yet as "positive" as possible. The first time I experienced these phenomena in isolation I reacted negatively. The first judgments were negative and hence it required courage to continue to do the work. By continuing I learned my first lesson: *No kind of thinking, no phenom-*

ena within the mind are of themselves negative unless one defines them as negative.

If one chooses to regard all projections as "psychotic" or "sick" or "evil," then within our own mind, within our own computer, they are so regarded. By so judging such phenomena we prevent ourselves from seeing them in our own mind. This is self-metaprogramming. Let us rephrase it in another more general way. *What one believes to be true of his own mental phenomena either is true or becomes true within his own mind within certain limits to be determined experimentally by himself.*

Specific examples of this principle are as follows: If one believes that his mind is inferior to other minds and that his thinking processes are less great than those of other people, this is reflected in all the operations of his own mind. He can hardly enjoy the vacation in isolation when he believes that he is inferior in mental functioning.

Similarly, if one believes that he is worthless, evil, destructive, and hostile, in isolation he can hardly enjoy the vacation. He will be castigating himself for his essential evilness. This is a particularly nasty game that persons play with themselves under more usual conditions and oftentimes project on to others in their environment. If we feel that we are worthless, then others feel the same way about us. We are then tempted to blame others for making us worthless, evil, or sick.

Let us now return to the isolation situation once again, the outside situation. I found that bodily sources of discomfort, pain, or threat tend to program the mind in the negative mode and keep it there as long as the discomfort continues. As long as pain, even at a very low level, continues, the computer (which is one's mind) tends to program a negative pall. All of one's thinking assumes now the negative flavor of the pain. Apparently some persons can eventually prevent this, knowing it, especially with a long experience of low-level pain in their lives.

This metaprogram, "external pain causes me to think negatively," is difficult to change. If one has a potentiating metaprogram which says either "accept pain and bear it stoically" or one which says "pain is needed to expiate your sins," it is difficult to change the causative chain. By personal experience I say that it can be difficult to deal with these and to reverse them. In the early experiments, we had residual sources of low-level pain. As we discovered them, we found that they were influencing our thinking. This fact was found only as we eliminated the painful sources. The relief was great when we eliminated the pain. One such good experience and the way was found for further experimentation.

In attempting to replicate isolation experiments, other researchers did not eliminate the low-level sources of pain. For example, some of their subjects experienced a low-level back pain when staying in the same position on a bed for too long a period of time. Such subjects did not recognize that fact in their thinking nor did their observers pick this up. In these experiments, the observers had not done the experiment on themselves and hence did not know about these sources of this kind of thinking. None of these subjects wished to repeat their experiments.

Once one has eliminated the sources of pain and found the sources of negative thinking, he can enjoy this "isolation vacation." In a sort of rebound from the release from low-level pain, my computer turned the mood of the thinking to a delightful, optimistic, pleasure-filled one. I then felt what fun life can really be when one's inner and outer programs are consonant. I also found how rewarding it is to be free of pain, free of threat, and free of non-rational interdictions. In this new positive mood, in this new positive approach, the visual projections were pleasurable and at times humor-filled. Instead of the old negative moods, punishing feelings, and uneasy thoughts, new positive moods, rewarding feelings, and comfortable thoughts took place.

One may wonder why I dwell on such matters at great length here, in a discussion of the dolphin's mind. We bring all of these things to our work with the dolphins. We must also recognize the possibility that they, too, at times, can bring these things to their relationships with us. These may be universal mammalian characteristics of mind. Even though one's self is unique in certain areas, one has something of a postulated general-purpose mammalian brain. Even a person's mistakes probably have more validity with respect to others than is generally thought.

Such discoveries about one's self give a person a sense of responsibility to share them with other persons. He quickly finds that this sharing is not too wise a course of action. This immediate and altruistic sharing with his wife, with his friends, with his children can have quick repercussions. He is being unfair to them to do this sharing without careful preparation. Each of them have not been through all of the steps that he has himself. Most persons of his acquaintance are still involved in the usual "safety metaprograms" which are prescribed by the interpersonal experts. These metaprograms define certain kinds of thinking as negative, or as "mentally ill."

I wrote up some of these results and published them.§ I quickly found that a few psychiatrists could not free themselves up enough to understand the generality of the basic points. Their reasoning was colored and their metaprograms filled with "well-sick clinical dichotomies." I do not feel it appropriate for scientific research on human thinking itself to use such categories. The universality of their application to the human mind is questionable. It is possible

§ Lilly, J. C., *loc. cit.*

the public clamor would be if an underwater ballet group of humans were in the nude and indulged in uninhibited excretion and free sexual play. I doubt if this human activity could be photographed and broadcast on color television the way the dolphins have been televised.

We tolerate this kind of thing in public displays of dolphins because they are so different that it isn't yet brought to our attention, as it were. (It may be that after reading this passage certain persons will put pressure on the circuses to segregate the male dolphins from the female; then the pressure will be put on to hide the males entirely because of their obvious "homosexual activities" with one another.)

Thus, the mind of the dolphin shares some things with us but not others. At least the dolphin has sex on his mind every so often with the right partners. A thorough Kinsey Report has not yet been made upon dolphins. This is one area in which we must accept their behaviors and their activities and eventually their thinking. If we cannot accept them, I am sure that we will never be able to communicate with the mind of the dolphin. The sexual activities in the mind of the dolphin are apparently more like the Polynesian model than the American model.

Young males start their obvious sexual actions while very young. They continue them into very old age. The females, like ours, are more subtle. This picture of the more or less constant sexual activities among dolphins is generated by dolphins that we have seen in captivity. It may be a very faulty picture. Like Zuckerman's¶ picture of the sex life of primates in zoos, it is colored by the artificial confining, and luxurious quality of the way in which they are held. Free food is provided. There are no enemies to threaten. Sex is probably being misused to deal with boredom (or is this one of the conventional types of human thinking?). In the

¶ Sir Solly Zuckerman's *The Social Life of Monkeys and Apes* Trency, Trubner & Co. London: Kegan Paul, 1932.

wild, there is probably relatively little time for sex. It must give way to other pressing necessities. One must seek food, must be aware of enemies and deal with them; must migrate and travel long distances to be assured of the proper temperatures, and so forth. Carpenter and others have shown this to be true for the lower primates.* Any human couple on an African safari sleeping in lion country in a tent can show it to be true for themselves also.

We must be able to face the sex life of the dolphins as we face any other aspect of the dolphins' lives. We must be able to investigate their sexual relationships not with prurience but in the spirit of objective cooperative interest. We must recognize that this is one of their major sources of pleasure even as it is with us. We must also realize that this interest of theirs can be turned to interspecies communication advantage even as it is turned to advantage in interhuman communication.

It has been said that one of the major problems in human sexual relationships is the disengagement of the process of reproduction from that of the intense pleasure that can be obtained from sexual acts. With our property laws and our ideas of property we make such a legal fuss about offspring, that we apparently spoil the pleasures that we derive from sexual activities. Similarly our peculiarly human ideas about our excrement can bar a person from contact with dolphins.

Let us return now to the mind of the dolphin. What kind of thinking do they do? Are there any leads as to the possible differences from our types of thinking? One basic physiological difference should always be kept in mind. This difference will influence the thinking along lines which may be very hard for us to visualize. This is the basic difference in their brain versus ours which I discussed earlier in this book. A large fraction of their huge computer is acoustic

* C. R. Carpenter *Naturalistic Behavior of Nonhuman Primates.* Univ. Park, Pa., Univ. Press Penn State, 1964.

(Plate 4), a similar fraction of our computer is visual. The acoustic part of our computer is much smaller than theirs, even as the visual part of our computer is larger than theirs. As I described earlier, they need this acoustic kind of computer in the sea. And they do not need so much of the visual type. To try to see what the dolphin's mind may be like, let us try to imagine ourselves in the place of a dolphin in the sea.

Imagine swimming in water so murky that you can see only a few inches in front of your face. Imagine that you swim at ten or so knots. How can you know what is ahead in the water? You can come to the surface and look around across the surface of the water with your eyes and see for a distance of miles depending upon the lighting, the fog, or other special conditons. Thus we go "visual" out of the water in the air. The dolphin can do the same and does. But this tactic is good only for non-fog daytime and for objects and enemies that stick up out of the water. Under the water one must use sound and ultrasound, which can penetrate through the muddy water and give a hint as to what is going on "out there" by analyzing the echoes coming back. Such echo-recognition and -ranging is characteristic not only of the dolphins but of the shrews and the bats and several other animals.

For probably several millions of years, the dolphins have worked with sound waves in water. The more I work on their echo-recognition system the more I admire its beautiful efficiency. They use it almost continuously in one way or another; this is part of thinking processes almost beyond our ken. Let us try to imagine how it affects their thinking. Imagine yourself as a dolphin in the sea, with sonar.

In the water of the sea we would have to use our sonar to construct sonic representations of our surroundings in our mind. While our sonar was turned on we would "know" through the operations of our computer what was going on around us in the muddy water and/or in the pitch-black night. The evidence that we were doing this could easily be obtained by carefully recording the sounds we emitted. During difficult seeing conditions, we would continuously emit various kinds of sounds, some pulses, and some other kinds of sounds. By having echoes automatically come back through our ears into our huge computer, signals would be converted into information in our mind. Rapid automatic computation of the signals coming from the two ears would be computed into constructions and pictures of the scenes around us. We would "see" our friends, the shape of the bottom, where the waves were, the height of the waves, the presence of fish, and any possible lurking enemies. Because of the nature of sound waves, we could, at will, change the wave lengths used. Changes in wave length would vary the clarity with which objects of different sizes were "seen." When one varies the wave lengths (thus the resolution and directionality), he varies the amount of detail that can be seen. With a long wave length, he sees around his body in all directions. He can sense large things such as the bottom or walls or large objects in given directions. This sensing with long wave lengths gives gross aspects but gives no detail nor small directions for the objects. The gross mapping with the long wave lengths gives one the gross sector in which something large is appearing but gives us no details of that object nor of the surfaces behind it.

Let us say that some strange object is first detected. It is very much out of focus. It is over in that direction. One then shortens the wave length voluntarily; a sound beam is shaped up out in front of his head. He then sweeps the beam like a flashlight back and forth across the object in two directions in two different ways. To sweep it laterally, he moves the beam back and forth, to sweep it vertically, he moves the beam up and down by movements of the head. At the same time, to sweep in depth, he makes small rapid changes in the rate of pulse production. Then he makes an additional small change in wave length which allows him to focus on larger and smaller details one after the other.

Converted to human terminology and human concepts, this is apparently the way the dolphins operate with their sonar.

Purely by sound waves (controlled by one's own will) in wave length, direction, and rate, one *sees* underwater. He keeps a picture in mind of all of his surroundings for some distance away from the body. This is done then for several hundreds of yards around and even behind his body.

We depend to a considerable extent on our vision for what we might call "visual communication." We watch very carefully the facial expression of another person to whom we are talking. We watch their bodily gestures and the movements, in other words the external aspects of their body. We cannot see inside their bodies; clothing generally inhibits our seeing an accurate view of anything but their hands and face.

If we were placed underwater and looked at one another by means of sonar, what would each of us look like to the other?

Sound waves in water penetrate a body without much external reflections or absorptions. Skin, muscle, and fat are essentially transparent to the sound waves coming through the water. The internal reflections are from air-containing cavities and from bones. Thus we see a fuzzy outline of the whole body plus the bones and teeth fairly clearly delineated; the most sharply delineated objects are any gas-containing cavities. We have a good view of portions of the gut tract, the air sinuses in the head, the mouth cavity, the larynx, the trachea, the bronchi, the bronchioles, the lungs, and any air trapped in or around the body and the clothing. You can imagine again the conventional person's unease at being able to see inside another person's stomach and lungs.

There would probably be new kinds of social relations such as follows:

"Darling, you are upset with me. You are swallowing air and your stomach is churning the bubble around as it always does when you are angry."

"No, darling, I am merely sick."

The facial expression of another prson is very dim when viewed this way. You see bright reflections from air sinuses and from the bones of the face. In the case of the dolphins, you see some bright reflections from the front end of the head which we lack; they have several air sacs which are immediately available to form echoes from the impinging sound waves. (We might imagine one dolphin saying to another, "Darling, you do have the cutest way of twitching your sinuses when you say you love me. I love the shape of your vestibular sacs.")

Thus, living dolphin-wise, we would have little need for external facial expression. We would try to express similar things probably with our air sacs on our head. The truth of our stomachs would be immediately available to everyone else. In other words, anyone could tell when we were either sick or angry by the bubbles of air moving in our stomachs. The true state of our emotions would be read with ease. For some persons this might lead to disadvantageous situations in, say, a bargaining transaction. I can imagine in a game of poker for high stakes this might be very inhibiting.

Since our facial expressions are controlled by "voluntary muscles," we learn to control our facial expressions in spite of an emotional state. We might have to learn to control our stomachs in a similar fashion. Could we learn to control the emotional affects expressed by our stomachs if we knew that other persons were watching them? These organs have "involuntary" or autonomic muscles and nervous connections, generally considered beyond our voluntary control.

Please notice that in the above descriptions of the sonic acoustic underwater world I use primarily visual language "to see by means of sound." Since we are more visual than we are acoustic, this is necessary, using our current language. This language requirement is reflected in the construction of our nervous systems. We have ten times their speed, their storage capacity, and their computation ability in the visual sphere; the dolphins have something of the same order of speed, storage capacity, and computation ability in the acoustic sphere. This, then, is one of the major differences between the minds of men and the minds of dolphins.

Hence, probably the thinking of the dolphin and hence the construction of their languages, is filled with acoustic representations rather than visual ones such as we use. For example, our verb "to look" probably has an equivalent in their language which we would have to translate somewhat laboriously in scientific terms as follows: "when I emit a wave length 'N' the appearance is 'Z.' When I emit a wave length 'M' the appearance changes to 'X.'" In the dolphin's mind, all of this is probably expressed by the equivalent of one or two of our words.

Since we do not have a built-in light to see objects in the dark, we do not have the appropriate words of ancient origin to convey directly and simply the meaning. We must struggle with visual analogies and adapt our own thinking to their universe of objects and sonic echoes. I cannot overemphasize the difficulties that this kind of situation leads to in terms of our understanding them and their understanding us. Our only hope is that each species does have an acoustic system and each species does have a visual system. I hope that some day we can devise ways of learning how to feel and see, the way the dolphins feel and see in the acoustic sphere. There are some hints derived from experiments with blind persons that may indicate we can do more in this area than we are at present able to do.

To solve the problems posed by these differences, we may have to devise equipment or adapt our own bodies to give us the same kind of signals underwater and/or in air. We will then begin to receive the rewards necessary for successful development of a new ability. We will then develop our latent "acoustical-spatial thinking." We can imagine a dolphin suit with built-in, three-dimensional, sonic and ultrasonic emitters and receivers and with built-in streamlining. We can develop the proper program in ourselves to model the dolphin's well-developed programs.

Even though we are several millions of years behind them here, we may be able to catch up. By the use of machines we have finally caught up with some of the birds' flight in air. Why shouldn't we similarly catch up with the dolphins' life and thinking underwater? Apparently to catch up, we must devote much of our first-rate thinking, engineering, scientific, financial, and other kinds of resources to these kinds of problems. I hope that enough effective people can be interested in these problems to accomplish these ends in the not-too-distant future.

These are only the beginnings of the careful exploration of the mind of the dolphin. We wish to explore the similarities and the differences between our minds and the mind of the dolphin. One major point is that we should be prepared to change the kind and the content of our own thinking to understand their thinking. In reciprocal and mutual fashion, the dolphins must be prepared to meet us at least halfway in this quest. We must give them the opportunity to have shared visual experiences with us, stereoscopic, visual experiences. We must accept the opportunity to receive shared, acoustical experiences, stereophonic. Thus, we will try to furnish them with experiences to show us to them on our terms. We may thus close the circle of cooperative efforts between us and them.

135

We must adapt our minds and they must adapt theirs for the purposes of eventual true and satisfying interspecies communication at all levels. An incredible amount of good hard work is needed on both sides. This book and the previous one are devoted to discussion and to demonstration of the necessary setting in which one works to achieve interspecies communication. Please remember our aims are to elucidate the structure and adapt to the mind of the dolphin. We do this by experiments and control of laboratory setting, by experiments in living together, in a cooperative and two-sided adaptation, and by an educational program, of which these two books are a part.

Since mind, brain, set, and setting are inextricably tied together by complex and complete feedback, both human and non-human mind-brain must share a common setting and, by the proper signaling and interaction, achieve a common or at least a cooperative and communicative set, one with the other. Contingencies in the setting interact with the satisfaction of basic needs and thus teach shared "meaning." But a long time of sharing of a dolphin mind and a human mind must exist first.

To achieve the proper interaction and the proper data in the storage of each mind, chronic and unending, continuous contact must be achieved. Like ourselves, as children, it takes long-term (years), unremitting (twelve to twenty hours per day, seven days per week, fifty-two weeks per year) efforts to achieve communication. The application of the proper set in the proper setting for us to learn to speak and learn to act human is the best road to interspecies communication.

These are some of the necessities for basic interspecies communication as we see them in 1967. With these we will learn to know the mind of the dolphin. Later in this book, application of these ideas is shown in the girl-dolphin live-in experiment.

136

CHAPTER 6

New Findings: Double Phonation and Stereophonation

Dᴜʀɪɴɢ our investigation with the phonation of the dolphin we were puzzled by the doubling of the phonation apparatus. Inside the opened blowhole, the passage is double, even as it is in our noses. On each side of the dolphin's nose which is here turned up on the forehead, is a complete set of sacs, muscles, tubes, and a separate vocalization membrane. There is a right phonation apparatus and a left phonation apparatus, each one in its half of the nose. Some of the features of the right apparatus are usually larger than those of the left one. We had come this far in the state of our knowledge in the previous book, *Man and Dolphin*. This set of puzzling anatomical facts continued to bother me.

When the dolphin gave us controlled, humanoid sounds in air we saw that the two sides were operating quite independently of one another. We took high-speed motion pictures of the activities of the blowhole and found that this was the truth. When these pictures were slowed down we saw that the two sides of the blowhole plug or the two "tongues" (as we now call them) were being used separately in the production of the airborne sounds. With more complete and more sophisticated methods, we have now demonstrated that the dolphin can not only produce sounds on each side, separately and independently, but that he can intermix the two sets of sounds, sequentially and simultaneously.

This process of mixing the two sets of sounds from the right and from the left in particular ways we call "stereophonation." Experiments to demonstrate these findings have now been completed. The demonstrations are of several types: listening to the sounds produced in stereophonic apparatus, graphical analysis, and high-speed X-ray motion pictures taken during the production of sounds. Each of these methods gives a different aspect of the phenomena. The experimental configuration of the dolphin and the apparatus are as follows:

The dolphin is selected for his sophistication in the production of various sounds, i.e., one of the older dolphins. He is transferred gently to a sound-insulated and -isolated tank designed to absorb the sounds he produces in the water to avoid powerful echoes. He is placed carefully on a platform suspended under the water. The water depth can be adjusted to suit the experimental necessities. At the beginning of each experiment, the water depth is adjusted so as to float him freely above the platform. A flat hydrophone is fastened gently over the right side of his head and another flat hydrophone over the left side of his head. The positioning of these sound receivers is very critical. They are adjusted carefully while listening to the sound production of the dolphin so that they are in a place where the sound is maximal.

The output from each of these hydrophones is amplified and recorded in separate channels. A tape recording is made in two separate tracks one from each side of the dolphin's head. Simultaneously, the separated channels are led to a cathode ray oscilloscope. The sounds are recorded as they occur in various ways on the oscilloscope. For example: 1. they are recorded, one played against the other, on the X and Y axes of the cathode ray tube in a so-called "X versus

Y" plot; 2. the two channels can each be portrayed as displayed in time with two separate beams on the oscilloscope; 3. the output of various frequency analyzers can be plotted on the screen also; 4. with X-rays we can follow with high-speed motion pictures what happens inside the head during these various processes. Thus, with patience and with luck we can obtain a visual anatomical portrayal of the instantaneous events occurring during various kinds of sound production.

These recordings are studied in various ways. The separate channels of magnetic tape can be listened to stereophonically by a human observer with headphones. The observer can then detect those sounds which occur on the right side alone. He can also detect those that occur on the left side alone. Suddenly, he will notice that sounds are occurring on the right and sweeping slowly over to the left and then back over to the right. The apparent source of the sound moves between his two ears and moves through the center of his head. These "stereophonic movements" are most dramatic for some whistles and some humanoids but are true also of some of the click trains. The process by which the dolphin produces these apparently traveling sounds is called "stereophonation."

The same results on the same recordings can be shown by the objective records from the oscillograph. In Figure 4 is a sample of such an oscillogram. The sound amplitude from one side of the dolphin's head deflects the cathode ray beam straight up and down. The sound from the other side of the dolphin's head deflects the beam sideways. When the sound comes from only one side, we then see a straight narrow line on the record moving either vertically or horizontally. If two sounds occur, first one from one side and then one from the other, completely separately in time, we see a pair of lines, one vertical and one horizontal forming a cross on the oscilloscope screen.

If two sounds occur one on each side, not separately but related stereophonically, the beam of the cathode ray traces complex patterns on the scope face. These patterns show the instantaneous amplitude relation between the two sounds. When an observer hears the sound moving back and forth between his two ears inside his head the beam traces circles and ellipses of varying sizes and inclinations. This is especially dramatic for the whistles for the two sides. At other times, during clickings, one can see similar ellipses, complex loops, and various figures whose size and slopes change from one click to the next. As we go through a long click sequence, we see beautiful systematic progressions of very complex figures on the cathode ray tube.

Some of the other sounds emitted by a dolphin fill the screen with "noisy," complex patterns. For example, the sounds of respiration have characteristic noisy patterns which vary with the depth and speed of the breathing.

We can relate the objective patterns on the screen to the subjective patterns that we hear by listening stereophonically and watching the cathode ray tubes at the same time. Quickly then, we see that the patterns which occur, when the sound's source apparently is moving inside our heads, are circles, ellipses, loops, and lines at other than the vertical or the horizontal parts of the screen. In other words, if the dolphin's two emitted sounds, the one from the right and the one from the left, have an instantaneous relation between them of the proper amplitude and the proper phase and the proper timing, we sense an apparent movement of the sound source. In other cases, we hear the sound only in one ear or in the other ear.

The two sounds that have these side-to-side relationships in the head of the dolphin from the two phonation organs are thus "stereophonic," one with respect to the other. We are using the term stereophonic to show that these sounds have space-time relations which allow one with one's own brain to compute them, as if coming from a single apparent source located away from the two real sources. Stereophonation is thus a voluntary, unique, physiological process known only now for the dolphin and not yet known for any other animal.

In our own voice mechanisms we lack completely this stereophonation dimension of his sonic communication mode. He can move the apparent source of his voice from one side of his head to the other. He can do this easily, smoothly, and continuously. Our voice is close to the mid-plane and, apparently, comes from the nose and the mouth near that plane.

How does a dolphin use this ability? With his two ears he can detect the fusion of his two sources in an apparent single one, even as we do with stereoheadphones. With this stereolistening, he can thus control the effects of the proper feedback to himself. He can put the apparent source anywhere that he wishes within the side-to-side limits of his own organs. Or he can move the apparent source very rapidly to and fro between the two sources. He may thus introduce a "Doppler effect" on his own speech. (The Doppler effect is an apparent shift in frequency due to the motion of a source of sound. A classic example is that of a car horn or train whistle; as it approaches us the apparent pitch rises, as it recedes from us the apparent pitch falls.) He can also control his near-field and far-field amplitudes as he shifts from monopole to dipole modes.

There are additional complexities to the dolphin's voice and to his phonation abilities which we should add to the discussion at this point. As was described in *Man and Dolphin*, his right phonation system is usually larger than his left one. This asymmetry of the two sides has interesting effects on what he can do with each side. Some of the tones on the right can be lower than those emitted on the left. I first came upon some of these interesting properties through the vocal abilities of a dolphin named Chee Chee. When we first met, Chee Chee was estimated to be twelve years old. At that age, she was found to be a much more sophisticated sound producer than the youngsters, Elvar and Tolva, mentioned in *Man and Dolphin*. I studied her vocal productions in detail.

Chee Chee had a "personal call" which was distinctive. It was a call which we had not heard from any other animal. Her sound in this call was quite different from the personal call of the younger dolphins. It seemed to have some very low frequencies in it, below those heard from any other dolphin. All of our human observers in the Institute heard it without straining in the upper limits of our frequency pattern recognition range. This call did not sound like the usual "squeaks" of the other dolphins' calls. With the other dolphins we were always conscious of the straining to hear in the upper registers.

I studied the production of this whistle call of Chee Chee by frequency analysis and other means. I watched her blowhole move in a different fashion than it did in the case of the other dolphins. Usually when the other dolphins gave their personal call underwater, there was a large smooth continuous movement of only one side of the upper end of the blowhole plug. This movement occurred throughout the whistles synchronized with it on the one side only. In contrast, Chee Chee moved both sides during her underwater call. The two sides apparently moved in almost opposite directions, giving a peculiar twisting motion to the top of the blowhole plug.

The call itself was analyzed in various ways. One of the most important findings is shown in Figure 5. This frequency analysis shows the variation of the frequencies of the whistle as they change with time. Notice that two major components occur simultaneously for part of the record. One component starts at a low frequency and rises fairly steadily.

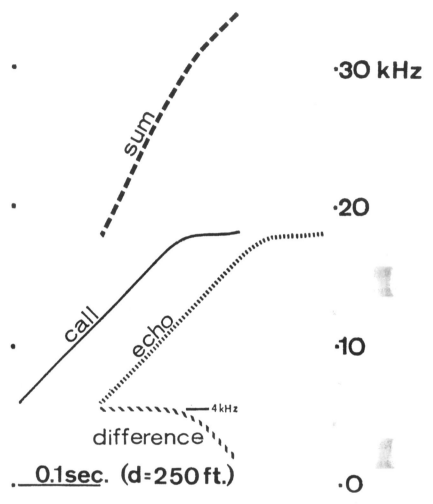

·30 kHz

sum

call

echo

·20

·10

——4 kHz

difference

·0.1sec. (d=250 ft.)

·0

FIGURE 5. *The Slash Call and Its Echo* (*see text*)

The dolphin emits the frequency-versus-time curve labeled "call." Its echo resembles the call, delayed by being reflected from a flat surface 250 feet away. The call lasts approximately 0.3 second as does the echo. At 250 feet the echo overlaps the call when it returns to the dolphin generating a sum and difference set of frequencies. The important frequency difference is at approximately four kilocycles (kilo-Hertz); the dolphin could use this "constant difference frequency" (between the call and its echo) to know that the object is at the given distance. With his extended hearing range he can also hear the sum (of the call and the overlapping echo) plotted as the dashed curve going above thirty kilocycles (kilo-Hertz).

143

The other component starts at a high frequency and falls during the same period. Further note that no particularly loud, low frequencies show on the record.

This lack of low frequencies was not predicted by the human listeners. Each one of them heard loud low frequencies. The objective record failed to show the low frequencies which we all heard. Where were these lows coming from? Agreement among listeners ruled out "imagination." The lows were there for every listener; no matter how we tried to eliminate them by double blind controls, they still were there. And no matter how many times we ran the records through the analyzers, they were not as apparent on the objective frequency analysis techniques as the high frequencies.

Chee Chee then gave us a hint as to what might be going on. She is quite capable of producing the climbing frequency call alone without the falling frequency one. This call is similar to the younger dolphins' personal calls. When heard in isolation from its mating component, the rising frequency component had no low frequencies. It sounded as it was shown on the objective record, all of it at uncomfortably high frequencies for the human listener.

Similar findings were made for the falling component alone. In other words, the only time we heard the low frequencies was during the time that Chee Chee emitted the two components simultaneously. At this point, we began to look at the frequency differences themselves.

We went back and listened carefully to the low-frequency variations; subjectively, the frequencies started low and increased with time.

If you inspect the frequency time curves (Figure 5), you can see that the difference in frequency between the two components has a rising series of values. At the point where the two frequency curves cross, the difference frequency is zero. For all later points, the lower curve value, subtracted from the simultaneous value in the upper curve, is higher. The frequency differences thus have a time course similar to the subjectively heard low frequencies. Their values also correspond to those subjectively heard. In other words, one high-frequency component combines with the other and generates "beat" frequencies.

If Chee Chee is aware of what she is doing with these two frequencies and is aware of the beat frequencies between them, then she may have developed this call for some particular purpose. Let us see what the rest of her experience has been before we detected this call. All of the people near Chee Chee had been instructed to speak to her loudly in ordinary English. They had been told also not to reply to any of her very high frequencies, i.e., to her "delphinese." Because of the particular structure of her phonation equipment, she could not whistle directly the very low frequencies which were present in our voices. I suggest that, with her extensive experience with our low-frequency voices, she developed the best low-frequency voice that she could, using her double phonation apparatus. Thus, she developed a call that attracted human attention. In this view then, she combined two sets of high frequencies varying in time to give this set of low frequencies varying in time well within our ordinary, everyday voice ranges. (One might say that this is asking a lot of her reasoning powers; it probably is not asking much. Perhaps they commonly use frequency "beat" phenomena in their everyday lives.)

If we look at the frequency-versus-time curve of Chee Chee's call (Figure 5), we see that the double curve forms a crude letter V on its side ($<$). The falling frequency curve is one limb of the "($<$)" and the rising frequency curve is the other limb of the "($<$)." Let us then call this the "($<$)"-shaped call. This is in terms of the delphinese frequency bands objectively recorded.

One important property of this call for our purposes is

that to us, it sounds like a rising, low-frequency call. On the frequency time graph this would be represented by the slash (/); therefore, let us call this the (/) call. In other words the beat frequencies of an (<) call form a (/) call.

If you remember your elementary physics you can see that when two frequencies are present simultaneously, not only do we get a difference frequency, but we get a sum frequency as a result of the combination of the original two frequencies. In other words, with heterodyning, both the sum and the difference frequencies appear. Careful inspection of the figure showing the (<) call will show that the set of the sum of the pairs of frequencies at each instant will be a straight line or a "bar" which is represented by "(−)". This bar set of frequencies is considerably above the original pair in frequency, way too high for us to hear, but well within the dolphin's range of hearing. In other words, the bar is a delphinic transformation of the frequencies and the "(/)" is a human transformation in terms of the relative hearing abilities of the two species. Thus the complete conversion of the "(<)" call is "the slash-bar call" symbolized by "−/". The dolphin probably can hear "slash-bar." In the best part of his hearing and at the very low frequency, he probably can hear the slash, whereas the humans hear the slash and (faintly) the (<).

When Chee Chee makes the "(<)" she produces the rising portion of the call with her left phonation apparatus. The right phonation membrane vibrates at each instant at the frequency of that particular instant of the rising portion. The left phonation membrane vibrates at the frequency of the other limb of the (<) at the same instant. The two phonation membranes are each connected to the membranous portion of the nasal septum in the midplane. This septum in the upper part of the nose is very thin and has special connections to two cartilaginous caps over the nasal bones. There are also muscles present in this septum. This

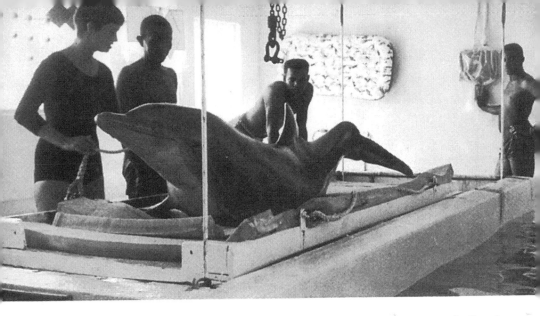

PLATE 11. *The Dolphin Arrives in Wet Room on the Elevator from Sea Pool.* The electric elevator is seen in raised position. The hand-operated chain hoist with shackle lifts the pallet off the elevator and carries it on an I-beam monorail off the elevator into the soundproof area to the left. The four ropes from the four corners of the pallet are fastened together in the shackle. (This room is seawater-flooded to a depth of 22 inches for the 2½-month living-in experiment.) Man at rear of room operates elevator controls.

This is the elevator that was used as a bed by Margaret during the 2½-month program. The foam was used as a mattress, and it was later surrounded with shower curtains. (See later photos.)

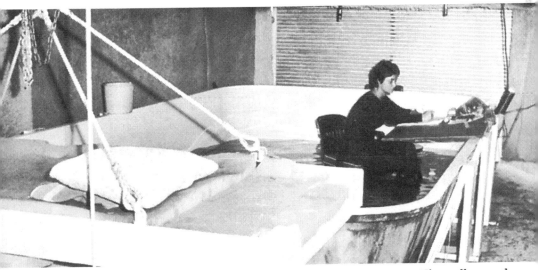

PLATE 12. *The Setup for the Seven-Day Preliminary Experiment.* The pallet to the left hanging from the chain hoist is used as a bed. The tank contains 18 inches of water. Margaret, dressed in leotards and tights, is at her desk, sitting on swivel chair in the water. Pam (not shown in picture) is in tank. TV can be seen on shelf at upper right, covered with polyethylene.

PLATE 13. *Margaret Howe and Dolphin during Seven-Day Experiment.* Margaret frequently sits in tank to develop new relations with Pam. Water flows out bottom drain at right (dark area). Inflow is near dolphin's beak.

PLATE 14. *Margaret Howe and Dolphin: Seven-Day Experiment (continued).* All feeding is an in-the-water-personal-contact affair. The fish are thawed outside this tank room, brought in the bucket, and given by hand. At times, depending on the experimental plan, the dolphin must produce airborne humanoid sounds to obtain a fish; at other times she

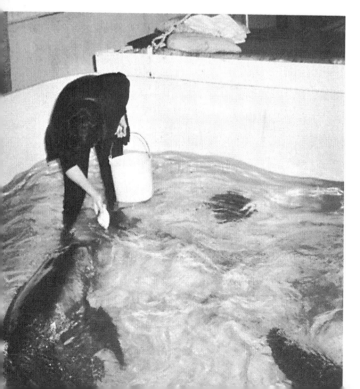

is fed with no demands, one fish at a time, or even all fish placed in the water at one time. Demands for sounds from the dolphin can thus be disconnected from the feeding itself. Care is taken to feed to full satiation no matter when or how food is given; no use whatsoever is ever made of a starvation-hunger drive.

PLATE 15. *Facility Changes for the 2½-Months' Experiment.* Margaret lives in with dolphin (Peter) in new flooded area. The outside flooded balcony is above the sea pool. Maximum allowable floor loadings ratings allow three feet of water (wall height). The outflow regulator is in upper right, just above spiral staircase entrance to sea pool walk. Margaret and dolphin Peter are on balcony, dolphin Sissy is seen in sea pool, 16 feet below.

PLATE 16. *Flooded Balcony: Construction, View, and Water Entrance to Flooded Room, Looking West.* The door in the wall to the right was cut into two parts and a slide substituted for the lower half to allow the human to cut off the trade wind by closing the upper half and to allow the dolphin to swim in and out at will unless the slide is in place. The white coil hose floating on the water is a vacuum cleaner hose for floor cleaning, underwater. The elevated end of hose is thrown over balcony, down 15 feet, to start the siphoning action and the vacuum cleaner propelled over the floor by hand for cleaning.

PLATE 17. *2½-Months' Experiment: Margaret Howe and Peter Dolphin in East End of Flooded Room.* A protected microphone hangs behind Margaret. The wall to retain the water is four feet high. To the right is Margaret's desk, suspended on ropes from the ceiling so that it can be pulled up out of the wet when not used. Margaret is touching Peter's raised beak with pencil; his mouth is open. Even when Margaret is writing, Peter can reach her and interrupt her at will.

PLATE 18. *2½-Months' Experiment: Margaret Howe and Peter.* Margaret's sleeping quarters are on the elevator surrounded by shower curtains. To the right is the runway from the cooking gas stove on a shelf above the water. Food cupboard is visible above the runway. Margaret is brushing Peter near his one-half air, one-half underwater mirror on elevator wall. When alone, he "looks" at himself in mirror and "talks" and "scolds" his image. Carpet (sound-absorbing screen) hangs between bed area and soundproofed area around camera. Ceiling and wall also covered with carpet in this "recording studio" area.

PLATE 19. Peter approaches Margaret.

PLATE 20. Margaret lifts Peter's head for a kiss and a hug.

PLATE 21. Peter does "dead man's float" on side as Margaret strokes his tail.

PLATE 22. Peter becomes suddenly active and is trying to force his way between Margaret's legs. She discourages his violent motion, gently but firmly. His flippers, sticking out of either side, catch on her shin bone . . . and as the forward edge of the flippers are hard and rather sharp . . . it hurts! There is a bit of a feeling here, on Peter's part, of "how much can I get away with." Peter is not angry, Margaret is not angry . . . they are feeling each other out. Matching strength, seeing how the other reacts. This form of exercise was fun for both and was encouraged; *within the limits and under control of Margaret.* A good deal of time was spent allowing Peter to learn what her abilities and strengths and failings were, and then in teaching him to respect these failings and to control his own strength.

special anatomy apparently allows Chee Chee to control the amount of vibration in the nasal septum. If she wishes to mix simultaneously the frequencies of vibrations of the right and the left membrane, she can do this through muscular control and through control of the opposing surfaces of the various folds of the nasal tongues. This control of the combination of the frequencies coming from the two sides, meeting in the nasal septum, makes the beats between the two sides. The nasal septum vibrates in such a way as to "amplify" the beat frequencies at each instant as the frequencies in the right and left membranes are changing. It is here that the slash call probably is emitted.

In the book *Man and Dolphin* and in a subsequent scientific paper,* we described the distress call of the bottlenose dolphin. The distress call on the frequency-time plot is an inverted V or a "lambda call" at higher frequencies than those of the beat-frequency-generated slash call. In general, in the distress call (Figure 7) the frequencies start at a medium value, rise to a high value, and then fall to the original value, all in about three-tenths of a second. This means that no two frequencies come out simultaneously, and hence the dolphin can produce the call alternating right and left nose or produce the whole call on either the right or the left alone. We would thus not expect either beat or stereophonation effects with the dolphin's distress call (lambda call). By the separation in time of the two parts of the call, simplicity in the spatial and in the frequency domains has been increased.

Let us now examine another call which is simpler than any of the previous ones. Let us consider a rising frequency call produced on one side only. On a frequency-time graph, this would be a line going up to the right, or to simplify it a direct slash "/" (not beats) (Figure 6).

* Lilly, J. C., "Distress call of the bottlenose dolphin: stimuli and evoked behavioral responses." *Science,* 139: 116–18 (1963).

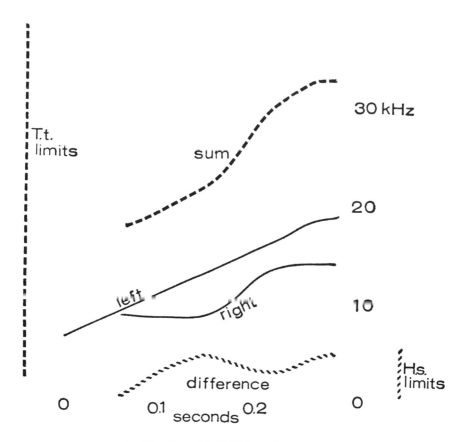

FIGURE 6. *The Special Call Developed by a Dolphin*
(*Chee Chee*)

This figure is discussed in detail in the text. It shows two separate whistles given on the two sides, the left and the right at high frequencies. The whistle on the left rises fairly linearly with respect to time over a period of 0.3 second. The one on the right is delayed in its beginning and then warbles for 0.2 second. The bottommost dotted curve shows the difference frequency that was generated, within the limits of man's pattern recognition hearing (H.s. limits). The dolphin hearing limits (T.t. limits) extend over a much wider range; the dolphin can hear the left and right whistles, the difference frequency, and the sum of the two frequencies. It is suggested that the dolphin generated this special signal so that the people listening to the dolphin could hear the clear difference frequencies.

148

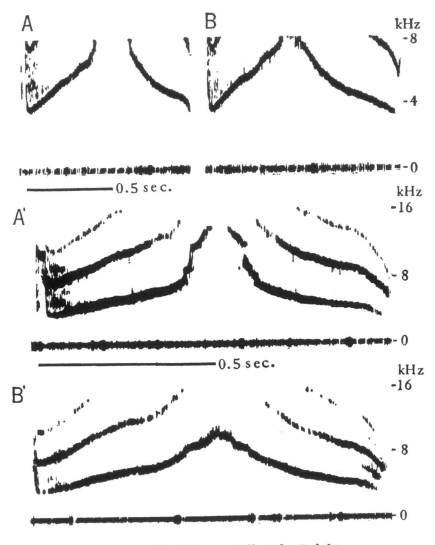

FIGURE 7. *The Distress Call of the Dolphin*

These are typical samples of distress whistles which have been recorded from very young and older animals. It is to be noted that the frequencies reached are beyond the usual "pattern recognition" range of the human ear. The upper two traces include only the first 8 kilocycles and show that the whistles start at approximately 4 kilocycles (kilo-Hertz). The lower two traces are derived by slowing the tape down and doubling the frequency range to show the harmonics of the whistles. Slowed down four times (even more than is shown here), these whistles sound like air-raid sirens. (From J. C. Lilly, "Distress call of the bottlenose dolphin," *Science* 139:116–18 [1963].)

149

The slash calls vary in their length from 0.1 second to about 0.6 second as emitted by the dolphins. Let us now imagine that the dolphin is swimming along in a bay and that there is a flat surface on the water from which his call will be reflected. He starts at a distance from this flat surface such that the call starts out, leaves his head completely, and then returns and at no point overlaps itself. He will then hear an unimpeded echo of his own call which will be the same shape as the call which he emitted and will have the same frequencies in it. However, as he approaches the flat surface and the echo returns before he has finished the call, there will be chance for beat frequencies between the beginning and the ending frequencies of the call. These beat frequencies are different from the ones above described for the ($<$) converted into the slash call. These new beats are between the call still being emitted and the echo returning to the dolphin. Since the call is rising in frequency at each instant, the early parts beating with the later parts will generate a lower-beat frequency at each instant as long as overlap exists between the outgoing and the incoming portions. As he approaches still closer, more and more of the call will be beating with itself. The distances involved can be easily figured using the velocity of sound in water as 5000 feet per second (1540 meters per second); in one-tenth of a second sound will travel 500 feet (154 meters), and if the dolphin is 500 feet from the surface and emits a tenth-of-a-second call, there will be no overlap. He will hear the call repeated in the echo. If he prolongs the call two-tenths of a second, the returning echo of the first half of the call will overlap and beat with the second half of the call. What is the nature of the beat that he will hear?

If the slash call is a linearly rising frequency-versus-time curve (i.e., if it is a straight line), the first part beats with the latter part and gives a constant-beat frequency. If there are small wobbles in the frequency, these will be reflected in the beat as long as they are not present equally and at the same times in the first half and last half of the call. Thus a slash call is converted into a bar beat of a shorter length than the slash itself. *The frequency of the bar beat will vary with the distance of the object from the dolphin,* i.e., *distant objects will give higher-frequency differences because of the greater delay in the overlap. Nearby objects will give lower-beat frequencies because there is less delay between the parts which are combined to form the beat.*

Thus it is easy to see that if the dolphin emits a slash call, he can obtain from objects in all directions around him beat frequencies which are different depending on the distance of the objects giving the reflections. Thus with a slash call he can tell pretty well what the shape of the bottom is, where the top of the water is, and what other large objects may be in the water around him, in what directions. He has only to listen to the beat and obtain their directions by the use of his two ears in the usual stereophonic listening fashion.

At the frequencies he is using in the slash call (from about 5000 to 25,000 cps), the wave length in sea water varies from one foot (0.301 meter) to about 2.5 inches (6.35 centimeters) in length. If the analogy of our visual detection holds for his sonic detection system, he can resolve details something of the order of one-fourth of a wave length to one-thirtieth of a wave length. Therefore, with the slash call, he can probably detect objects from about three inches in their largest dimension to about one-half inch in their smallest dimension. Thus, his slash call should tell him pretty well in what direction a school of fish of the proper size is —where his friends (other dolphins) are and possibly even where his enemies (the sharks) are. Of course here he is limited to certain distances (from something like a few feet to something like a few hundred feet).

The internal picture which the dolphin can then create

while sounding slash calls, the internal picture which he creates of his surroundings in terms of beat frequencies coming stereophonically combined from the two ears, must be a very interesting kind of picture. It is as if to us the nearby objects emitted a reddish light and the farther objects emitted a bluish light, with the whole spectrum in between. We might see, for example, a red patch very close by and then a dimmer, blue patch in the distance farther away . . . a blue background downward symbolizing the bottom, a red patch up close meaning a fish nearby, and a large green object swimming between us on the bottom meaning another dolphin. This conversion of their acoustic beat frequencies into colors is one way we can visualize how their surrounds look to them. (Once again, as in the previous account earlier in this book, we must convert their "acoustic pictures" into our visual pictures, because of the differences in our brains and in our approaches to our surroundings.)

Thus, they could use the slash call and other more complex calls in order to delineate their surroundings by what I call their "long wave length sonar." Their "short wave length sonar" operates at very much higher frequencies; the measurements of this mode that we have made in the Institute show that they use frequencies from approximately 15 kilo-Hertz to around 150,000 cycles per second. The sounds emitted in this region have wave lengths in water from about 4 inches (10 centimeters) down to about four-tenths of an inch (1.0 centimeter). As we and others have shown, this sound is concentrated in a beam with a maximum amplitude straight ahead off the upper jaw of the dolphin. This sound comes in the form of short pulses of very high amplitudes (3000 dynes per square centimeter or 140 decibels above the reference level of 0.002 dyne per square centimeter). Since this is a beam and since it is very high amplitude in shorter wave lengths, it can be used for a more detailed inspection of objects which are found by the longer wave length sonar. He changes his ability to resolve details by change of wave length: the shorter the wave length the finer the detail down to two-fifths of an inch (1.0 centimeter).

The dolphin may find (by a slash call), off to his left, that there is an interesting object at such-and-such a distance. He can then merely turn his head, turn on his "short wave length sonar," and inspect that object in detail by scanning it with his "sonar flashlight." The narrow beam and the shorter wave lengths give him a resolution which he didn't have with his longer wave length slash call or other kinds of whistle. As he wants to see small details he moves the frequency of each pulse upward toward 150,000 cycles per second (two-fifths of an inch wave length).

So far we have spoken about echoes from non-moving objects with a non-moving dolphin. When a dolphin is moving and picks up echoes the apparent frequency of those echoes will vary somewhat, depending upon his velocity relative to the reflector. One can see this effect (called the Doppler effect after the man who discovered it) by standing beside a road when a car or some other vehicle sounds a constant-frequency horn or siren as it passes us. When the sonic source is approaching us, the frequency apparently rises and as it passes us and recedes, the frequency falls. We can just as well have a fixed-frequency emitter on our car and approach a big wall. The apparent source in the wall is now approaching us at the velocity of the car so that the reflected echo will have an apparent shift of frequency upward. Alternatively, we can sit still, aim a sonic beam from a fixed-frequency emitter at a moving object approaching us, and the reflected echo will apparently rise in frequency. If the object is moving away from us, the echo will have an apparent fall of frequency, depending on the velocity of recession.

Returning then to the slash call and the objects of varying distances from the dolphin, if he is remaining motionless in the water, he will hear various frequencies. If objects are approaching him, the frequencies will increase. If objects are receding from him, he will hear the frequencies dropping. Similarly, if he is moving through the water very fast and other objects are also moving through the water very fast with him, these echoes will have apparent beat frequencies which will remain constant, whereas objects which they are passing will have the rising-falling Doppler effects. Thus the internal picture of his surrounds becomes more complex and we must bring in change-of-frequency with respect to time as well as frequencies which merely depend upon distance.

All of these various acoustic concepts (and many others) in some way or another must be used in the dolphin's construction of his language. When a dolphin wishes to talk about an object at a given distance with another dolphin and wishes to describe how that object moved and at what velocities, he can do it merely by transmitting the proper frequency pattern in his clicks and whistles. In other words, be can converse about moving down from the surface of the sea toward the bottom, he can converse about fish of a given size at given distances, sharks of a given size and all of these other matters, in a frequency-time-intensity domain which we would have to convert into visual images. It seems to me that this can become a sort of Rosetta stone for proceeding on an analysis of "delphinese." At the least it is a good enough lead for further research and it is a testable quantitative hypothesis.

By blindfolding ourselves or by using blind persons with the proper apparatus, we can copy these various matters with our own subjective systems. However, we must be aware that our brain can handle only one-tenth the amount of information in the acoustic sphere that the dolphin's brain can. The dolphin can store huge amounts of spatially distributed acoustic information for making up his pictures and will have stored away many models of what his surroundings are like. We lack these advantages quantitatively. In other words we should expect an extended period of training to develop the same abilities the dolphin has. We may never be able to match his performance, at least not at the speed with which he has developed because of the limitations of our brains versus their brains.

What is the evidence that they use the slash calls for long wave length sonar? Some of the evidence is that if one takes a dolphin and places him in new surroundings emitting series of slash calls, after he has been there for a while he stops emitting these calls. In other words, he initially uses them to make an acoustic map of his surroundings. From that point on he doesn't have to emit them so frequently because he knows at any given instant where he is from the last time that he emitted any noise at all. He has mapped all of the obstacles, the walls, the depths, and the boundaries of where he is. He is then free to travel, using, say, only his short wave length sonar or his eyes to tell him in what part of the real surroundings he is and hence on what part of his internal map he is. Any new change in the surroundings starts him off again as he readjusts his internal map. We have observed this behavior literally hundreds of times.

The conversations between two dolphins by means of whistles thus might be explicable on these grounds. They have a very large brain with very large, general-purpose computer properties, i.e., a very large neocortex. Since a large portion of this is acoustic cortex, they have probably developed symbols (i.e., shorthand) of all the special relationships and descriptions of the various objects (including themselves) which correspond to the whistle (and click) echoes and the whistle's beats. Thus one dolphin might start a slash call to another dolphin and then wobble the upper end of it (as we have seen many times when two dolphins are speaking one to the other). It is these wobbles at the upper end which are probably transmitting the subleties of meaning, one dolphin to another. The very great frequency shifts that we see in the ($<$) call, the inverted V call, and in the slash call and various others probably symbolize changes in mode, i.e., in whole large categories of meaning. The subtle variations, beats between the two sides, the Doppler effects in the call as the apparent source is moved between the two sides, convert the subtleties of the meanings. If we are ever to break "delphinese" and convert it into human language, we thus have many hints on which to proceed. At least we have testable hypotheses to either bear out or disprove.

CHAPTER 7

Consideration of the Spiritual Side

MAN LIVES not by bread and by facts alone. In the American tradition, one rushes to the end of a research project digging up all of the basic facts needed to apply the results practically to some technological advances. This seems to be the major basis for scientific research in America today: a practical result. Our development of space travel, our development of nuclear energy, our development of the potential of treating human illnesses are examples of this kind of human pursuit. The basic science upon which each of these activities is thoroughly grounded was done many years ago. The basic discoveries behind each of these areas now being applied were made in the past. The lag time of the practicality behind the basic research is said to be shortening. A modern physicist makes a discovery about certain basic particles; it is applied in the construction of nuclear bombs, with a lag of ten years or so. A biologist makes a basic discovery about biology, then it is applied in the pursuit of cures for human diseases, with about a ten-year or more lag. In the space program, the technological advances built upon, for instance, Goddard's basic research on rockets, seem mainly to have made the rockets larger but operating on his basic principles.

Since the pioneering basic research was done in each of these fields, a good deal of technological development has been done, and thus we can now use the fruits of this work in the production programs. These production programs are built on "bread" and facts. Without the "bread" rewards, there would not be the hundreds of thousands of workers needed to produce the practical results. Without the hard facts, the program would not exist. Since these are the activities which (in addition to the defense budget) support the industry of the United States and of the Soviet Union at the present time, let us ask some basic questions.

Where does the motivation for this kind of activity come from? Why do we start these programs at all? Is there some secret behind the national scene giving the motive for our whole picture? Let us look behind these programs for clues to the human forces motivating these programs. Let us then relate the discussion to the present status of the interspecies communication field.

The spiritual side of man seems to be used as a major driving force behind science as well as behind religion. It is definitely used behind industry. In the face of the vastness of the unknown, some of us have awe and reverence. In most discussions in science, this factor is neglected. We discuss curiosity, intellect, intuition, genius, truth, power, support, facilities, and facts. Most scientists neglect the inner wellsprings of our own beings in their chosen profession. When questioned, they usually make a joke of it. It is as if this reverence and awe are left for an embarrassed consideration in church on Sundays only.

In my education at the California Institute of Technology, this split was obvious. Awe and reverence were delegated to the Humanities Department. If anyone dared mention them in the scientific departments (and some did) they were met with yawns or biting sarcasms depending on the listener. The professors, assistant professors, and teaching instructors did not have time for this kind of a discussion. And yet, practically every student that I knew well said he was there because of these two factors.

We should be concerned with the driving forces in the young people going into science. We should be concerned with their ethics, their morals, and their motivations. The whole future of our civilization is in their hands. (At least I hope that we turn it over to them without destroying it.)

Unless we aid the youngsters to see the necessity of awe, reverence, and respect, they can become dangerously calloused and cynical, not only in their scientific work, but in the application of their scientific work to technology. With more reverence for all of life, with more awe in the face of the inside unknown and the outside unknown, with deeper experiences with other human beings from the far side of the planet, maybe the bombs would never have been needed and hence not made or planned.

Once one has been through deep experiences in tune with the vast forces of the universe, the vast forces within ourselves, we see that the need for conflict, the need for hostility, and the need for hatred become less intense. One finds the universe inside and the one outside so vast and so lonely that any other living thing that loves or shows any signs of loving is precious and close. One's own inner discontents show up as the trivial conflicts that they really are. Time on this earth is of immense value beyond the small grievances, the bickerings, the complaints, the encroachments, and the fools. Time here is for exploration of the unknowns. If, at the time of the death of each of our bodies, the spirit also dies, then this time is incredibly precious. It's all the time we have for each one of us. If the spirit lives on, here or elsewhere and continues to send and receive information, this time may also be precious and incredibly important. Our behavior, our achievements, the marks that we make now may or may not determine what sort of an after life we may have. I don't know which of these alternatives is the real truth. I do know that it is important to spend our time now on important projects.

The so-called scientific pragmatist in me says that I die with the death of my body. The sensitive humanist in me says there are vast areas of ignorance and of ignorings in this part of me, this scientist part. This humanist side says there is more than our science has yet dared to dream of. The humanist side says that science's present postulates are accidentally ordered in man's history. We only have chosen our form of arithmetic and our form of geometries because these were the forms first discovered and first dealt with by those who came after. We are at the mercy of the historical sequence in which things accidentally first happen. It is almost too late to go back and start over. The structures built upon them would be too expensive to tear down and start over, both intellectually and in the external world. Thus we are stuck with our history.

John Van Neumann said of arithmetic that addition-subtraction-multiplication-division were accidental discoveries; that we are caught in their tradition as the basis of our mathematics; that if only we had first discovered something else, more powerful, intellectually, and more like the brain's own mathematics, we would be much farther ahead. So would all of our knowledge. We are aided and yet we are also handicapped by what we know, by the amounts we know, and by what remains to be known. We tend to say that what we know is all there is to know. Obviously, this is nonsense and it is nonsense in arithmetic as well as it is nonsense in the knowledge of the basic particles of the universe. Our current knowledge is a very thin closed shell surrounding our minds with vast unknowns inside it and outside it.

If some other species with a different logic and mathematics tried hard to teach us, probably we couldn't recognize and learn the alien ways of thought and computation. We tend to ignore the possibilities of thought outside the traditional prescriptions for thinking.

My sorrow for the young human is great; why cannot his genius flower as it will? We straitjacket the young and penalize the thinking they do outside our beaten and beat-up paths inherited from the past. Personally, I have finally learned to value the freeing up of the spirit, now. In this freeing, I am penalized by my own straitjacket. Tradition and personal history are terrible taskmasters with entirely too much power over one's spirit, now. Means of loosening the slaves' chains are sought. One hopes that eventually one can see the new vistas through the prison window.

One view through the window of the prison is that which we can see in special states of consciousness. However, this too may be a romantic trap for humankind. The powerful human imagination, attempting to break free from the real bonds of the human body and brain, can imagine an infinity of unreal worlds and unreal states of being of no use whatsoever to us. The only use may be as vacations and entertainments. Fantasies of mental communication with other beings greater than ourselves are currently considered as science fiction and hence only entertainment.

This peculiar concept of "entertaining" ideas frees us up from being "serious" about these ideas. Thus we can look at them, savor them, even experience possible realities postulated by them and come away unscathed, uninfluenced, as it were, titillated and uncommitted after they are over. As mature adults, we have gone beyond the necessity of inner sensation for sensation's sake which we valued so highly when we were young. We insist that sensation be integrated into our life plan as an integral and unassuming part of that plan. There are those scientists and ex-scientists who would lead us into "new paths of enlightenment." Somehow they forget that this has been tried by religious leaders in the past. Somehow they forget that, at least in Western civilization, these "new paths of enlightenment" have already been cast aside as will-o'-the-wisps, illusions and delusions. Some of us need such comforting illusions and such tranquilizing delusions. The harsh facts of existence can somehow be softened by romanticizing.

"Each man has a spirit beyond the reach of present scientific knowledge. This spirit is larger than the man as he is seen by fellow men. The uttermost depths of one's own mind are still within the bounds of and less than this spirit. The spirit reaches into that which is beyond the mind's comprehension and beyond the prescribed consciousness of our time. With faith and belief, the spirit will allow the mind to travel into these vastnesses and will carry it there. Courage is needed to face these regions. Courage is also needed later to tell of the adventures there."

This is the kind of thing succinctly expressed which I learned as a small child. This is the essence of my childhood programming in religion. Now that I have grown and become a mature scientist, I would translate the above passage into a more scientific view, as follows:

"Each man has a mind beyond reach of present scientific knowledge. This mind is larger than the man himself conceives of or/and is larger than he is conceived of as seen by his fellow man. Our minds have depths beyond our present ken. Parts of the mind reach beyond our own conscious comprehension and beyond the prescribed consciousness of our time. With special techniques and special knowledge we can travel through the vastnesses of our minds locked within our brains. Much romantic nonsense is stored in our minds. Courage is needed to get rid of this romantic nonsense."

What does this have to do with dolphins? This is the basic reason for attempting communication with the dolphins. If our minds are reflections of the quality of our brains and the size of our brains, so their minds must be a reflection of the quality and size of their brains. What we can find in their mind may free us from the burden of our traditions and from our accumulated bias, prejudices, and apparent knowledge. They may find the same in exploring our minds.

It seems to me that the mutual edification of two species will be achieved when our minds can meet. Theirs must be immense minds reaching into regions we cannot yet comprehend nor even see clearly.

One night standing beside the dolphins' sea tank on the island of St. Thomas, these feelings about the dolphins came to me very strongly. There was no moon. There was a storm. It was three o'clock in the morning. The sea was throwing large waves into the seaward bulwarks. The water from the Caribbean was boiling and crashing into the intake of the tank. In the dim light coming from the stars through the storm clouds, I could barely see the water's surface. It was in violent motion in the pool. The considerable noise was that of an angry sea dissipating its primal force on unbending ancient rocks. In this rather eerie setting, I resolved to let my thought go out to the three dolphins in the tank. I tried to catch something of them, of their minds, in my own. The strangeness and violence of the scene was reflected from me in them. All three were swimming tightly close together; their triadic surfacing to breathe was heard above the din. When their position was right, I could see the rare glitter of their skin above the water. I imagined their bodies below these small signs of them. I felt terribly alone, a lone human being. I shivered at the thought of the sharks in the sea outside. I imagined myself as a dolphin in that violent sea outside surrounded by sharks. (A young man had been killed by a shark not too far away from this location the year before.)

Suddenly I laughed. I realized that all of these thoughts were not from the dolphins at all but were from within my own mind, from my own brain. I, a dry-land primate, whose ancestors moved out of the trees onto the land, evolved from forms far from such scenes as the one I was watching. This romantic foolish nonsense was being generated by my own fears. The dolphins had no such thoughts as mine.

Obviously, the three dolphins were snug in their protected pool, enjoying the wave motion of the warm tropical water. They swam in a group circle for several hours apparently having a wonderful time. They realized that no sharks could penetrate, no sharks had penetrated, for the preceding two years in their pool. They were on a relatively confined, but danger-free, vacation. In their terms, I was inappropriately dry, stiff, and afraid. They could not afford, as it were, to be fearful when there was no reason for being fearful, for them. In this pool they were in a relatively protected part of their own ocean. Every night, every day, twenty-four hours, 365 days and nights a year, their whole lives were spent in the sea. They cannot afford fear of wind, fear of the waves, fear of the darkness, fear of the depth. The dolphins must stay at least half awake all of the time. This is their usual, everyday, everynight life. We will not get very far projecting our own fears and states of mind into the mind of the dolphin. We will get much farther (as is shown in the last chapter) along leads which are different than our kinds of thinking.

It is an uplifting experience to imagine the seas and the oceans of this world of ours as a vast house of dolphins and whales. Audacious in the extreme is this featherless biped walking on the dry land which is my species. His little, dry spirit has a great deal of gall to try to push his way into the primal soup. In the face of the dolphin's necessities, one quickly loses one's self-esteem. Perhaps we can brave out the terror of the deep but we are still not built nor equipped to live in it free as a dolphin. Their appropriateness of body for their life in the sea must be matched by their minds and their brains built and equipped for this life. Their freedoms are our prison walls; and vice versa, our freedoms are their prisons. Every time I walk away from a dolphin in a pool, every time he swims away from me, I feel this reciprocity of freedoms-prisons.

We must assume that dolphins have their own principles, their own assumptions, their own postulates, and their own actions for their mental lives. It is probable that any large computer (such as their brains) has huge alien programs. At the very least, in our search, we can see if they act as if they do have consistent logical bases on which they operate. By living with them and forcing them to live with us, we can discover many of these things by behavioral methods.

At the very most, we some day may be able to ask them and see if their replies show familiar forms or whether we come upon only unknown alien forms of thinking and of philosophy. Between these two extremes there are many other possibilities. For example, we may ask questions vocally or nonvocally, verbally or nonverbally, and receive answers in these modes. The answers may be somewhat comprehensible or totally incomprehensible. Our thinking and speaking are only human. Their thinking, their speaking so far are only delphinic. In order to first ask the proper questions we must become partly delphinic (with their help), and to understand the questions the dolphins must become partly human (with our help). To give proper answers to our questions the dolphins must go partly human, and to understand the answers we must go partly delphinic.

Each side, delphinic and human, can rewrite some of their programs to adapt to the other side. Each side has programs they cannot rewrite, the built-in sets of programs. In this book, I describe where we see this line between us, between the built-in programs and the rewritable problems as we can determine them to date. This line will continue to be delineated as we do more research with the dolphins. It takes a fantastic amount of work and special methods (new and imaginative ones) more carefully to define these lines. The fine border between "rewritable" and "forever-fixed" programs is a fascinating area for the courageous researcher. It is an area in which it is possible to make horrendous mistakes and maintain them for years. It requires courage to break up one's deepest prejudices here. We do not yet fully understand how much of what we think and believe can be fundamentally changed. We know that much can be modified but not how much it can be modified. We are especially stable in many areas because of the special properties of our feedbacks—our social feedbacks, and our feedbacks to ourselves and to our loved ones. Society itself daily re-establishes certain kinds of programs in us repeatedly again and again. Other programs are stable because they are built-in and necessary to maintain life itself from the physiological body levels to the monetary, economic, external feedback levels.

We have some programs for assuring failure in certain areas of our endeavors. These are best erased. I hope that no dolphins acquire these programs. I doubt that they are compatible with life at sea under the difficult conditions that dolphins must meet successfully.

In certain areas, the delphinic ethic is apparently non-Western-human. Their constant nudity, public sexual display, public urination and defecation, tasting one another's excrement and urine are things for which Western man locks up his fellows and calls them "psychotic" or "perverse" or "committing a public nuisance."

When we explore some of the communication areas which are possible between man and dolphin, we see some of the barriers in the past to human-delphinic progress. One such area is a common human communication path. This is the path of the man and woman in love, making love. Their best form of exchange and communication is in their sexual activities. Can sexual activities be used for communication across the interspecies barrier? On the delphinic side, the answer would probably be yes. On the human side this is called a crime (sodomy). Such are some of the difficulties in our future with the dolphins. There are bound to be interspecies conflicts even as there are intercultural conflicts between men.

A charming person of the opposite sex who knows a language one does not know is probably our best teacher of that language. Will this empirical finding apply to interspecies communication? It will. This motivation is assured between us and the dolphins and that the male dolphins will prefer a female human teacher as the female dolphins will prefer a human male teacher. Our main difficulty with these teachers will be shedding our human shams in the face of the candor of the delphinic life. To begin to move beyond our dry-featherless-biped-on-the-dry-ground philosophy requires imagination, determination, and a certain kind of wet courage. Whether one likes it or not one must go into the water to meet the dolphin. One must be willing to live in the water to a certain extent. This point cannot be compromised. To talk and make sense with dolphins we must meet them at least halfway in their own element. In sea water, we will communicate. We must learn to live wetly. The new undersea houses of the French, of the Americans, and of the British are a beginning in one direction. Let us look at another direction of exploration in the water, less environmental and more mental kind of exploration. We are interested in the inside view.

Imagine a special pool in a special room in a special building beside the sea. The building is in the tropics. The location is private and remote and, above all else, silent. There is no rumble of traffic, there are no horns of automobiles, no subways, no air raid sirens, no explosions, no jets. Crowds, visitors, parties, lectures are all missing. The primeval sea is close by. The antediluvian rock of an ancient uplift above the sea's surface is the foundation on which the building is placed. The greatest of the hurricanes, the tsunamis, and the earthquakes are the only real dangers to this installation.

In this building is a room at a dead end, isolated, silent. The doorway has a light lock to keep out daylight. There is no way for light to come in from the outside. In the room is a large cube-shaped tank eight feet in each dimension. The room's air is warm and wet (85°F) and 100 per cent relative humidity. With the lights turned off the feeling is of a warm, wet, soft blanket gently enfolding one in the intense darkness.

The tank is filled with sea water to the top—9½ tons of it. The water is kept at a constant temperature anywhere from 88°F to 95°F by a special fresh water thermostatic heater. The walls are insulated thermally from the outside walls and the floor. A six-foot man can stand inside the tank on tiptoe and keep his nose and mouth in the air with the rest of the body immersed.

If one's body fat and muscles are correctly distributed, he can float horizontally on his back just far enough underwater to keep his nose in the air. Most of the rest of his body remains immersed. With his hands under his head to keep the strain off his neck, he can relax and even doze off. With the lights on for many hours and many different exposures, he undergoes training to be able to trust himself to be completely relaxed under these conditions.

One notes immediately that the water enters his ears and cuts off whatever small sounds were still left in air. He may begin to imagine himself in the situation of the dolphins. If there is a residual sound in the water, he hears it as immersion starts. The airborne sounds have been reduced in intensity from nine hundred to several thousands of times. He immediately sees the difference between our hearing in air and that of a dolphin under the water. If someone speaks in the air above the tank, the voice heard underwater is reduced to this same degree; he barely hears it. (The dolphin's hearing underwater is very much better than ours and hence they can hear these voices better than we can. Our ear is adapted to airborne kinds of sound waves; underwater the drum is loaded with water so it works less efficiently.) The freedom of movement, of slow movement, is positively sensuous. One can assume many different positions without much effort. Once one accommodates and develops the proper reflexes to keep his nose in air, the freedom of movement and the rewards thereof become appreciable.

At the right temperature and with the right frame of mind, the water may seem to disappear. By slightly moving and feeling the soft currents across the skin one can bring back consciousness of the water. A delightful feeling of suspension in empty space can be created, if he can remain still long enough. By this time he has already adapted to the intense darkness.

The darkness in the space about one is almost palpable; soon there is an immensity. The only disturbing factor is the line of stimulation which is between the air, the water, and one's skin. One feels as if he is in two worlds which are separated at the line of the air-water line at his skin. If he is on his back, he feels he is looking into a black "air world" from a comfortable vantage point from the "underwater world." With imagination, he can abolish the line of gravity, abolish the line of stimulation of the water and the air.

This elimination of gravity's direction is made easier by the use of the proper, custom-built breathing mask. Such a mask is fed air by a special, silent, air supply system. One can assume any position in the water without fear of breathing any water whatsoever. He can move to the bottom of the tank or to any preset depth and remain indefinitely. The proper adjustments for buoyancy are made by special apparatus. The mask system has a restricting effect, however, in that it adds complexities and hence worries about its operation.

Under these circumstances, in most situations, one learns to avoid touching the walls and the bottom of the tank or breaking the surface. The mental phenomena to be described are attenuated by contacts with walls or bottom. The situation of the dolphin lying still beneath the surface of the warm tropical sea in the pitch black of a densely overcast night without sharks or other dolphins present is imaginable when one is in this situation.

After many hours of exposure to this kind of situation, one begins to understand some additional analogies of the dolphin's mental life. When one's bladder fills, the urge to micturition occurs. At the beginning of these experiences he holds on and suppresses the urge for a while. Finally he says to himself, "Why?" He lets go. It's fun. Once again he is becoming more delphinic. The usual dry-civilization reasons are not present here in this isolation and in this solitude. We know, intellectually and aesthetically, that the plumbing takes care of what we produce. One then is on the way to appreciating some of the advantage of living in the dolphin's house, the sea. Even as the dolphins have solved bowel movements long ago, some day both one's self and the plumbing may be ready for the bowel movements.

With the establishment of comfortable acceptance of wet, free suspension in sea water, one can progress with new types of thinking and feeling and new progress in the changes in his mind and spirit. Not that these new types of thinking may or may not be used by the dolphin, rather that we have not used them freely up to this point. Perhaps they will be useful in our encounters with the dolphins.

The purpose here is to free up one's own mind to see the new possibilities of feeling and thinking without the dry civilized strictures. For a while there is only the contrast; thinking before, in the dry, civilized life, and thinking now in the wet, civilized life. We are preparing here as if we were setting out to prepare for a new mathematics, a new logic never before seen or discovered by man. To free the mind, the initial creative state for such inventions is needed. One must free oneself from the usual, from the conventional, areas of cognition and of emotion.

Cogito ergo sum is all that is needed to navigate these new, unique, and strange depths underwater. One is secure in his own being because he thinks and hence knows that he exists. For a while, he is content to allow the conflicts and the storms of civilized life to go unheeded.

The great nonscientific writers of the past may furnish us with guideposts. The areas in which one is now moving need the maps from man's knowledge, irrespective of its origins or the current fashions in truth. For you I cannot espouse any particular knowledge or any particular parts of the total knowledge of man. Each of us must choose our own, each of us has internal universes which are characteristic. *There are underlying, basic internal realities in a separate series of nonconventional forms inside each of us.* As children, we are taught to stay away from these realities. As children we are told to accept only the realities of our parents. We are taught that our time is the best time, that our culture is the best culture, and that certain kinds of realities are the best for each of us. Yet as children, we each knew about these other realities behind the usual forms. Almost consciously, society limits the consciousness of our species to certain kinds of realities to streamline us in the job that our species is currently doing.

I was brought up and educated in a certain kind of consciousness. I am writing in that kind now in this book. Only through monumental effort can one move out of this powerful control of the current mode of cognition. We are assured of being kept in this mode of cognition by the constant feedback with members of our own species. This feedback is valued (practically) above anything else. This feedback with others is a precious commodity, precious to one's mind and to one's spirit.

This kind of explorer is a lonely one, at least temporarily. He must step out of this social arena which we all value so highly, this intraspecies arena. He must learn to step alone into new arenas. Although he knows that he will meet his "cognitional lions" and the other "carnivores" of his mind's deeper spaces, he must step out away from his own species.

One loves his wife and his children. He loves his parents. He respects his colleagues and looks forward to those sympathetic ones of the future and the sharers of the present. However, into these new realities he must move essentially alone.

I use the term "new" advisedly. I mean new to one's self, not necessarily to others. Some of these realities have been experienced by others in the past. Some of the underlying universes within ourselves have been described—some of the descriptions are quite far from our present scientific purposes.

The spectrum of inner realities is huge, it runs from the Gnostics, the Catholics, the Protestants, the Tibetans, the Buddhists, to those of Sir James Jeans, Albert Einstein, Swedenborg, to those of spiritualistic mediums, quantom mechanikers, rocket pioneers, astronomers, and extrasensory perceptionists, and the persons locked up in the hospitals and prisons. Some of these inner universes are current dogma, some are currently outmoded, some are considered dangerous, some are proscribed, and some are prescribed.

If one watches the way he treats his own children's thinking and doing, he can learn much about the shapes of the prescriptions and the proscriptions he is passing on to them. His insistence on the lines of cognition is hardly conscious. He is hardly aware of what he does to them. A four-year-old talks to an unseen playmate that she has created. How do you react to this situation?

A ten-year-old boy cries out in terror in a nightmare at 4:00 A.M. What do you say to him about the reality of the nightmare? Do we ever explain to the children that apparently behind the palpable appearance of things as we see them today there are other types of consciousness awaiting them? Do we ever explain to them that the kind of consciousness that adults apparently have and they, the children, share and watch, is only one of several? Do we explain to them the experiences that we have had inside during a high fever, with anesthesia, with severe pain, with our dreams at night? Do we explain to them how it feels to have taken too much alcohol? Apparently we do not generally so explain in the United States of America in 1967.

Apparently, one does not explain to his children what it is like to be isolated in solitude and to be intensely alone. We leave such descriptions of the different states of consciousness and the experiences there to the literature generated by the previous generations. We leave it to the latest "horror" movies which are not really very sympathetic to the positive aspects of these different states. We leave it to the TV shows which are similar.

Most of these media are controlled in such a way that all states of consciousness, other than a certain narrow slot in which one is expected to go, are treated as "negative." These other states are labeled horrifying, terrifying, frightening, crazy, irresponsible, addicting, or psychotic.

Why do we not give this gift of creative exploration of the mind and spirit to our children? Why do we not teach them directly how to explore their own minds? I believe it is because we have abdicated our judgment and our reason in this area to specialists.

For safe pictures in the area of the spirit we have the religious specialists. For sane and logical constructs of the outer realities we have the scientific specialists. For healthy pictures of our biological life we have medical specialists.

173

For "non-neurotic" and "non-psychotic" views of our mental life, we have the mental health specialists. We have the explorer specialists and the astronauts to give us complete pictures of strange lands, peoples, or outer space. To give "anthropological" pictures of members of our species other than ourselves, we have the specialists on man himself. Statistical pictures of how we operate in the mass are generated by the psychological specialists. How all animals differ from us is given in detailed pictures by the animal specialists. The political specialists give us the latest picture of a human danger to our national and local social existence and how to meet it.

We abdicate our rights to teach our children the sacred internal freedom of how to think and feel. We bestow this right upon all of these others of our species, all of these "experts." When we abdicate our own right, we abdicate that same right for our children. It is dangerous and foolish to do this.

The great modern dilemmas, wars, and potential wars, are the consequences of this invited encroachment into the wellsprings of one's own being. A world of individuals inwardly free may be the freest and the safest kind of world. The spiritual and the bodily betterment of all men need the fabulous resources of this planet. Can the motivation of man in the mass be devoted to these ends rather than war? In the modern world the industrial organization of man is like a huge organism. The "metabolism" of this organism is devoted to maintaining the structure of the interrelated parts. Like the cells and the tissues in one's own body which are each specialized for its own function, so in this kind of "organism" individual persons must be so specialized. This specialization is carried even into our internal life where it is quite inappropriate and not needed.

Are there not other ways of maintaining all of us? Are there not other ways of teaching us of our own internal universes, our own internal states of consciousness without these external necessities of control? I asked seeking answers. I, like all persons I know, depend on the given social structure as it is. I plead frankly and candidly for new paths to inner freedom; but I plead for these paths *within* the structure of the modern society as it is best created to date. I believe that at least in the United States today *one can have inner freedom consonant with one's functions in the modern society.*

How does this relate to the dolphins? They may have more of this precious commodity of inner freedom than we do. Therefore they may be able to help us.

Let us try to communicate with the dolphins and see if they do have inner freedom. In the search, we may or may not find this freedom for man. However, I am sure that we will find new mental vistas, if and only if we are open to them and do not try to impose our kinds of consciousness on the dolphins.

Since we have multiple inner realities and the multiple states of consciousness, we can imagine that the larger brain of the larger dolphins has a greater richness and greater range than ours does. In our brain the present and separate states of consciousness exist one beside the other, as it were. In the words of William James, the filmiest of screens separates everyday, physical, agreed-upon reality from each of the others. The Eastern philosophers and religious leaders have explored some of these realities and explained them but only on *their* terms. A whole language of the multitudinous states of the mind and of the soul and of consciousness has been developed and used by them. Many of these explanations seem to be inappropriate for our Western minds. Apparently we must devise whole new languages to describe these states on our own terms.

The Eastern systematization does not seem to be appropriate for the Western personal use. We can derive some confidence and security in the knowledge that these persons have explored some areas of interest for literally hundreds of years. We can copy some of their techniques and some of their approaches. But with our own history and with our own society we must have other explanations for what happens.

We may seem incredibly naïve to these people; so be it. We are Western, American and European in origin, education, religion, politics, marriage, customs, business practices, and children. (Even our dolphins come from the coastal waters of the United States. Whether this makes our dolphins Western is a moot point.) We hope then to explore the multiple states of consciousness of man and also the multiple states of consciousness of dolphin. It is extremely likely that our spiritual life will be enriched by such expansions both in ourselves and in the dolphins.

CHAPTER 8

The Medical Problems of Dolphins and Man

A SICK DOLPHIN is very different from a sick human. A sick human can lie in a bed alone and suffer through a large fraction of his or her illness. Our automatic nervous system and our automatic physiology take over. We can go into coma and survive.

A sick dolphin cannot afford to go into coma. He cannot afford even to fall asleep for periods longer than about six minutes. If he falls asleep longer than this, he is in danger, great danger, of dying. Asleep too deeply, his respiration stops. Because of this particular peculiarity and necessity in the dolphin's makeup, a sick dolphin must be attended twenty-four hours a day. One dolphin will do this for another dolphin. Again and again in the Institute we have seen dolphins tend one another twenty-four hours a day until recovery took place, several days or weeks later.

One of the problems of maintaining dolphins in captivity in close proximity with man is that they share the diseases of man. Each time there is an epidemic among the attendants in the Institute the dolphins share that particular disease whether it be influenza, hepatitis, or the common cold. Therefore, we emphasize three basic medical facts about dolphins.

1. *Dolphins in close contact with man are infected and infested with each of the communicable diseases which are*

transmitted by water, by air, by food, and by direct handling by men.

2. A sick dolphin does not eat. If a dolphin is not eating for one or two days it is best to take his body temperature and do a thorough medical examination.

3. A dolphin who is ill is best nursed by another dolphin. An ill dolphin should not be left in solitude.

Another dolphin is a better nurse than he is a doctor. One dolphin will care for another one continuously twenty-four hours a day in the water like a human nurse does a sick child. More active procedures than nursing care, however, must be done by proper doctors. Dolphins do not have doctors or dentists.

The signs of an ill dolphin in general are anorexia, sneezing through the blowhole, bad breath, fever, and a short temper.

Sneezing to a dolphin is a very explosive and continuous affair. One will hear the breath expelled through the blowhole in an almost explosive fashion several times in rapid succession making very loud noises that can be heard some distance away from the tank. A nasal discharge occurs usually late in the disease; if it has an odor it is a bad sign.

Dolphins who are ill seek to rest away from humans and away from a crowd of dolphins, alone with one other dolphin. Play ceases, as does sex. They refuse to work with us during illness except to cooperate for necessary procedures of medical diagnosis and care. Many dolphins learn to swim into the proper sling to be lifted up for antibiotic shots. Some can even learn to come to have their temperature taken by a rectal procedure. When we are helping them and do not hurt them while we help them, they will not fight our attempts nor will they interfere when we help their companions.

Despite publicity to the contrary, most dolphins caught in the wild cannot live in close quarters with man for very long. Aside from accidents and diseases to which they are not immune (acquired from the humans) there are other causes for morbidity and mortality. Some of the major problems are clustered around the water supply, the training of the handlers, air and water temperatures, sunshine, exercise, monotony versus amusement, and food supply.

Even in the most expensive and largest tanks in oceanaria, it is a question of the survival of the fittest of the dolphins. Of those who survive all of the accidents which can befall dolphins being captured by man, the survival of the others depends to a considerable extent upon the vigilance of someone who is continuously looking out for their welfare day and night over the years. As I have said elsewhere in this book, the morbidity and mortality rates in the oceanaria up to recently have been kept as confidential information. A number of times I have been present in oceanaria at times when the loss of a number of favorite specimens occurred in a very short period of time. And yet there are specimens who have lived up to fifteen years in oceanaria. These are the rare dolphins adapted to these circumstances.

However, even these longer-term dolphins sometimes apparently become maladapted and must be put in the sea or otherwise disposed of, to save the rest of the colony from their attacks. Thus even in the relatively large, seventy-five feet (twenty-five meters) by twelve feet (4 meters) deep tanks of the occanaria with large amounts of water flowing through them, the best that has been done is approximately fifteen years. Let us examine some of the probable reasons why the dolphins have these difficulties in living in the confined conditions which we impose upon them. We have found many facts in the Institute which may be of help in avoiding these problems in the future. In this particular area we have made some progress beyond the stage written up in *Man and Dolphin*.

The major change when a dolphin is captured is the

change in his surroundings from the open seas, bays, and estuaries to the relative confinement of a tank in close proximity to man. No matter how large the tank or even the fenced area of the sea in which he is kept, the dolphin is in a fixed, unchanging, static bit of territory. This is the radical change in his life. The size of the step the dolphin is asked to make to adapt to us is huge. I wish to emphasize this. This change can be extremely tough on the dolphin. Probably our whole present philosophy is wrong.

After the publication of *Man and Dolphin* I received a plea from a woman in England to leave the dolphins free in their sea and not to confine them. I believe this can be done and is best done for their health and for the future of our relationships with them. We can set up a special facility by the sea into which dolphins can come and go as they please. We would still have to be cautious in our relationships with them to avoid accidents and to avoid infecting them with diseases and vice versa. Man and dolphin could then meet on a more equal footing, free to come and go. This chronic confinement, together, in the same space, year after year, cannot be healthy either for them or for us. Let us then imagine an idealized facility in which man and dolphin can so meet.

Imagine a bay protected from storms and from the open sea but with access to the sea. In this bay, the sea water depth is no more than nine to eighteen feet (three to six meters, 1.5 to three fathoms). Preferably, the tidal range should be small, less than about three feet (one meter, one-half fathom) year round. Ideally, the water temperature should be somewhere between 65°F and 85°F (18°C to 30°C). Even 65°F (18°C) in the winter is a very low temperature for a man for constant contact with dolphins. The upper end of this range is better.

The bay must not be contaminated by sewage or industrial waste, i.e., the sea water must be clean; ideally, there should be a continuous flow of new sea water through the area. There are no man-built structures on or near the shores of this bay except a few fishermen's homes and small docks. The kinds of structures we want to build are on or at the sides of this bay. In general we want two kinds of structures: we want a scientific investigatory building, i.e., an *ideal dolphin-man laboratory*. However, we also want a *flooded house* in which dolphins and humans can live continuously in close proximity to one another day and night, year after year. Each of these buildings must be protected from hurricanes and storms of various sorts. Let us describe the idealized laboratory and secondly the idealized man and dolphin house.

The laboratory is a large building (or a series of connected small ones) built on pilings high enough to avoid damage from large waves and tides from hurricanes. This structure either juts out from the shore or is built separated from the shore. There is a very large fenced-in area of the sea bottom which overlaps this building but does not completely enclose the base. The open bay has access to one part of the base of the pilings under the building. The fenced-in area has access to other parts.

The open bay and, at times, the fenced-in area are for dolphins and sometimes for persons. The buildings are for humans and at times for the dolphins. The laboratory building includes elevators which can be let down into the sea water —one inside the enclosure and one in the open bay. These are large elevators with special shapes and controls on them. The elevator shape includes a depression six by twelve feet (two by four meters) in its surface. This depression is about three feet deep (one meter), with gently sloping sides inside and outside. The slope of the sides is such that a person can safely walk up the sides from each direction in air or in very shallow water.

These elevators are used for two different purposes: 1.

for transport and holding of persons from the building into the sea, and 2. for transporting and holding of dolphins from the sea into the building. The up-and-down motions of the elevators are controlled in several ways from several locations. A dolphin or a human can control the elevator.

The controls are such that a dolphin can call the elevator down underwater far enough to swim over the tank. Once the dolphin is in the tank on the elevator he can command the elevator to rise either to the surface of the water or up into the buildings. If he is up in the building he can command it to go down into the sea. When in the building, the dolphin always has the option of going back down into the sea. In the cases during the initial period of dolphin training, the humans have only overriding controls to prevent damage to the dolphin. Eventually, each of the experienced dolphins is given complete control of the elevator and of the times of his trips up or down. Any time, day or night, a dolphin wishes to use the elevator, he can do so.

In the proposed design, several novel features are described. A large fraction of this building is flooded to a depth of eighteen inches (0.5 meter). The elevator comes up into the flooded area so that the dolphin coming up can swim away into the flooded area or if he is upstairs he can approach the elevator and swim aboard at will. When the elevator is down in the sea, the dolphin upstairs can bring the elevator up at his own behest.

It may be more fundamentally correct to have the laboratory at sea level (like the house to be described later) so that the sea washes through the laboratory rather than using this elaborate elevator and its elaborate controls. This modification of the design is currently being worked out in the Institute. We have the elevator system (not yet with these controls) and have the sea pool below and the flooded rooms above in our Dolphin Point Laboratory on the island of St. Thomas.

It is intended that this building and the sea pens be as much of a "school" as a "laboratory." It is both a school for dolphins and a school for humans.

The basic principle behind all of such designs is to furnish the opportunity for each side to meet and interact with the other with maximum safety, maximum integrity, and maximum initiative for each species. This is the "Interspecies Communication School, Man and Dolphin Division."

First, let us describe the house and the school; then we will discuss the problems of staffing.

The house (or home) in which man and dolphin interact is open to a bay which is open to the sea. Ideally, the house is located at the water line and, once again, the tidal range is limited to a foot or so. Larger tides can probably be handled but may require a more elaborate installation. (For illustrative purposes we are assuming the tide is like that in Florida and the Virgin Islands.) The idealized house would have three separated, distinct divisions. There is the dolphin part, the interaction part, and the human part. The dolphin's part is deep water, approximately six feet immediately adjacent to the sea. The human part is dry, immediately adjacent to the land. The rest of the house (the major area) is for man and dolphin interaction.

By careful tests in the Institute over several thousands of hours of experiments we have found that the ideal water depth for interaction is just below one's knee. At this depth, the dolphin can swim fairly freely and the human can walk relatively easily through the water.

Thus, the shared compromising area for man and dolphin is flooded to a depth of eighteen inches. In this shared area are all of the usual things of the usual life in a home for a human. The dolphin can tag around behind or beside the humans. When the humans are sitting down eating or talking, the dolphin can approach them with the freedom that a dog or a cat has in our own homes. Special kinds of furniture made with special materials, special walls and floors, and lighting are required. We have explored the details of these requirements (see chapter on living with a dolphin).

Obviously, special clothing, special cooking facilities, special desks, tables, chairs, toilet facilities, and many other items have to be designed, built, and tested for this wet house.

In the dolphin's deeper area (six feet or more) the humans and the dolphins can swim together, at the dolphin's mercy. This area communicates with the sea by special walls or fences with holes in them to allow the seawater to flow through the house, without allowing large predators of the sea (especially the sharks) to enter. This area, however, is allowed to grow its own underwater vegetation and have its own smaller inhabitants so that the dolphin is surrounded with his natural wildlife in this particular area of the house. This is sort of the "play yard" for the dolphin analogous to the yard around the normal house. His access to the sea here is a special gate which he can operate, but which is not operable by sharks, rays, sawfish, octopuses, or other larger inhabitants of the sea.

The dry portion of the house has visual access to the flooded portion. The dolphin can be in the shallow water and see most of what goes on in the dry part of the house. The basic principle in the design of the house is that the dolphins can share most of what goes on, both vocally, visually, and, as far as possible, tactually. This is the "interspecies exchange home."

The staff of the man and dolphin school and the staff of the man and dolphin home have to be very carefully chosen. In my experience, most persons cannot stand the pace of interactions with *Tursiops* for very long: most persons sooner or later flunk out of this interspecies school. Some of the reasons for this are clear, some are not so clear. Let us see what some of the requirements for such persons are.

First of all comes youngness of spirit; this may or may not be associated with youngness of body. I have seen many people who were aged in spirit though young in body, and many who were young in spirit but aged in body. To interact with dolphins, one must feel young, irrespective of age.

There has to be a seeking for new experience on the part of the person; this seeking is not for sensation's sake but for adding to his private knowledge. In other words, he has to be curious and explorative.

The person must be capable and dedicated, even though it may take years to complete the project.

An ability to improvise is needed. In the interactions with the dolphins, this improvisation is essential. Unexpected and new behavior is met and encouraged up to a certain point, at which one must hold one's ground with the dolphin. This is just as important as it is with another human or with a horse or with a dog or with a cat. One's own integrity (but not his own vanity) must be maintained. His limits are tested by a dolphin sooner or later in every conceivable way.

There are things that each of us must learn about dolphins, in general, and each dolphin in particular must teach each human many of these things. For example, each of us must learn that dolphins are "teeth oriented," and dolphins must learn that we are "hand oriented." Dolphins must learn that we have two hind legs, and we must learn that they have one big tail. Each of us must learn this through bodily interactions, here and now; we receive the rewards and punishments of these interactions day and night for long periods of time before we are thoroughly convinced of these rather obvious facts.

Dolphins of the size of *Tursiops*, Atlantic type, are larger and more powerful than most of us. They use their jaws and their teeth the way we use our jaws and teeth but also the way we use our hands, the way we use our fists, and the way we use a hammer or pliers, or pincher or a rake.

Their massive neck muscles and large bodies give them more force for the jaws than we can muster in a hard kick with the foot. The ends of the jaws are as hard as a leather shoe.

Their tail is also used (just forward of the flukes with its hard lateral vertebral processes just below the skin) as a long hammer or a pike against our legs, body, or our heads. They can literally "kick with their tails." Faced with such formidable tools and a few examples of their use on one's own body, most persons become timid and leave the project. Those who stay realize that these reactions can be controlled vocally and bodily by interactions with the dolphins. It is these persons who can stand the gaff and find why they were singled out for the hurt at a particular time. Some few persons quickly find out that most of the reasons for the dolphins hurting us are obvious. This is the kind of person that we want in the school and in the home.

Some of the multitudinous reasons for a dolphin to discipline a human and for a human to discipline a dolphin are given below. The dolphin's skin is tender. The skin can be badly hurt, even damaged by improper handling, improper instruments, or improper walls. Their fragile flippers are easily damaged by a human pulling them too hard in the wrong direction. Their eyes are as sensitive as ours and easily hurt. Another exquisitely sensitive region is that around the blowhole. This access to their respiration is guarded against ignorant handling. The tongue is a delicate and easily injured part. Special meanings are assigned by them to the region around the anus and the genital opening. Stroking a dolphin here may result in their mouthing and even raking one's arms or legs.

Apparently, the dolphins have times and situations during which they resent interruptions by us. Under special conditions one may be allowed to stay during their sexual activity but not always.

186

At the beginning, at least, it is best for everyone else to stay away while one dolphin and one human are interacting. Later, one can "intrude." Distractions here may be to the detriment of the human or the dolphin. At times, they are jealously guarding their relation with one human against either dolphin or human encroachment. The "impolite" invader may be treated roughly.

But this is not an invariable rule any more than any other rule which may be laid down in this man and dolphin interaction area. With the proper introduction and polite entering, a multiple human exchange can be initiated with one dolphin. Apparently, there must be agreement between the human and the dolphin. In our Institute, we never run and jump in the pool unexpectedly. When awakened suddenly they can act reflexly and hurt one. It is far better to warn them by talking to them and thus call their attention to the fact of our presence.

The most successful humans play it by ear. The mood of the dolphin is tested by entering the tank slowly and carefully. His interest, his irritability, his preoccupation with other matters, or his anger, can be quickly seen and used with a slow entry. At times, a human is invited in. They approach you at the edge of the tank and by body motions unequivocally ask you to enter.

If the dolphin uses his teeth or tail, it is proper to scold and slap his skin at the nearest available place. One must be careful with the sensitive areas described above. Right timing is necessary; even this reaction has to be given correctly to obtain the desired results. Sometimes it is better to move out of reach and think. On one's return the dolphin may be and usually is more cordial. This is not an invariable rule.

All of these considerations are germane to the medical scientist. In the case of humans, medically one appreciates social factors. If one's patient is being mistreated, this is one important factor in his illness. If his contacts are happy and his environment healthy, he is more likely to be well and recover quickly when sick. So it is with the dolphins.

In the proposed school and in the proposed home, a sick dolphin can come in and apply for medical care. It is important that all of his social relations with each of the staff are such that he will so choose to come. One cannot treat a patient who is so fed up that he leaves. This is a very important aspect of the school: freedom to leave and to return.

Once trained, the dolphins can come and go as they please. If they stay, they are fed and cared for and interacted with. Soon we will then know the success or failure of our interaction methods. If we do it correctly, other dolphins may hear about it and come to see. If we do it incorrectly, all of the dolphins will leave.

One elementary precaution is that the dolphins be assured that their enemies will be kept out; sharks are unwelcome visitors as are sawfish. All entrances, elevators, and other contacts with the sea are proof against entering by these animals.

In the medical literature it has been emphasized recently that crowding can cause bad effects in animals and in humans. It has been demonstrated scientifically that other animals become quite disturbed by overcrowded living quarters. I found that with too many dolphins in too small a space there were definite effects. Results can be disastrous. Some individuals become ill and even die. Most of the individuals are jealously involved in every human interaction and, apparently, give one another conflicting orders. Their sexual life deteriorates; their play decreases in vigor and duration; some individuals seek and cannot find solitude and become short-tempered. Unexplained deaths occur that look suspiciously like suicide (or even murder). Training programs become difficult if not impossible.

With the proposed facilities some of these difficulties will be avoided. Any time a dolphin is overcrowded, he leaves and goes to sea or takes one of his friends with him to escape the crowd. A facility in which the dolphins can come and go as they wish will not be overcrowded.

With sufficient space, sun, and air the dolphins survive even severe infections, keep a vigorous and healthy sex life, develop close ties with us, and play together hours at a time. The contrast is gratifying.

We have run two separate groups for three years to find out these facts. The uncrowded ones are happily vigorous and well schooled. The humans in attendance are similarly uncrowded and happy. The other case is more instructive by simultaneous contrast; without this other crowded group we would not have known what to avoid in the future. The design of the new school is based on both sets of experiences; from one we learned the desirable factors to incorporate into the design, and from the other the undesirable ones to avoid. At the present time, we know the demonstration is adequate. We are enlarging the amount of space given to each dolphin to turn the crowded group into an uncrowded one. We hope in the future to be able to build the facilities which we have described here and initiate not only uncrowded facilities but "free" facilities connected with the vast seas. We need help: money, advice, professional aid for architecture and engineering. With this facility man may open new territory, new understanding of the sea and its bright inhabitants.

CHAPTER 9

Vocal Mimicry: A Key to and First Stage of Communication

W<small>HEN</small> each of us is a child, learning to speak our native language, we are in the peculiar position of being inarticulate and yet surrounded by a human world in which language is being used by all of the important persons in our life. At the beginning, from our first newborn cry to our first attempts at vocalization, we are only expressing our own unique selves without sharing our language with anyone else. It has been shown by recordings and analyses of newborn infant human cries* that even the first cry is a unique special production of that particular baby. There is a communality of newborn infant cry, but if we study the details of each cry we find specific and specifiable differences.

Whether these unique specifiable differences of the infant's cry are caused by inherited or acquired physiological factors, or whether they are caused by the baby hearing human speech while still in the uterus, are moot questions. Only the fact of their uniqueness has been established. One important observation is that the human baby is born with the ability to make unique sounds with his vocalization apparatus. This is the first time that air has passed out through this apparatus. Previous to this *in utero* only embryonic fluid passed back and forth through these tracts. *In utero,*

* Truby, H. M. (1965) in General Bibliography.

the muscles have been growing, the nerve connections have been growing, and the connections inside the brain have been established, preparing for this instant when the air can be sucked in and expelled to make these noises. Of course, if all this preparation is not made and the baby cannot suck in the air, he does not survive. Those of us who live after birth were prepared for birth *in utero*.

On this background of preparation, the baby starts life. He is bombarded with sounds from mother, father, and other children in the family. Everyone loves to talk to a baby, and the baby loves to respond with facial expressions, bodily movements, and various and sundry sounds, produced within his vocal tract and by his lips.

We are produced after nine months *in utero* and are born with a four-hundred-gram brain. The baby dolphin is produced after twelve months *in utero* and is born with a seven-hundred-gram brain. One of the major differences here is that we do not need to swim up for air the instant we are born. We lie in a crib and are carried around for those three months of growth in which the dolphin remains *in utero*. Thus, at the end of a year (from the time of fertilization of the egg by the sperm), we have a year's growth of brain and body and three months' experience outside the uterus. The dolphin born at the end of this year has only the growth and whatever acoustical experience he derived while *in utero*. Since the connections between the ears and the brain are made early *in utero*, he probably has a rich set of hearing memories stored in his brain at the time of birth. Since his vocalization apparatus, like ours, operates with the use of air inside it, he does not have much experience in producing sounds which he can hear himself. He, too, has been pushing embryonic fluid back and forth in his vocalization apparatus.

Thus, the human baby at three months after birth has accumulated three months of very early use of his vocalization apparatus which the baby dolphin lacks at birth. The importance of this fact is yet to be evaluated.

By the end of the first three months, one can listen to the sounds produced by a human baby and realize that he has acquired many new patterns in his noises. His babblings are becoming more and more complex as are his various kinds of cries. Of all the noises the baby makes, one can finally begin to distinguish the first distinct word at about nine months. At six months and a brain weight equivalent to that of the newborn baby dolphin (about seven hundred grams), the human baby begins to imitate sounds. The primitive beginnings of mimicry occur detectably at this point. After three months of imitating sounds, the human baby "composes" them into the first detectable word at nine months. During the next two months with his brain increasing to 850 grams, he imitates syllables and words, and the second word begins to appear. By thirteen months (930 grams), his vocabulary expands rapidly. (*Man and Dolphin*, Appendix 2, page 285.)

Basically then, two processes are going on. There is a spontaneous, sound-making process which we inherit and which is built into us. This process allows us to use our respiratory tract for instinctual production of various kinds of sound (for example, cries, shrieks, moans). Secondly, there is a learned, an acquired, a programmed, sound-production process. This programming starts out as a basic process which I have chosen to call "mimicry." Mimicry is the process of reproducing as closely as possible a sound or a string of sounds or a complex pattern of sounds that one hears in one's environment. The source of the sounds can be another human being or another animal or any other artificial or natural source. *The human baby has a drive toward organizing his more or less random sound productions into patterns; he has a drive to produce copies of those sounds which he hears coming in.* In other words, the human baby's brain has sound-production, sound-listening, sound-storage, sound-composition programs; to learn human sounds, he hears them, analyzes them, stores them, recomposes from storage, and composes new patterns. When the stored patterns are in sufficient numbers and varieties, he begins to compose patterns which mimic those he hears. With mimicked sounds, he convinces adults of his established drive and ability to communicate.

Mimicry is the basic mechanism which assures one that the baby is acquiring those sounds which other people share. This process of putting out the sounds and hearing our own production of the sounds allows us to compare it with the models that other persons are putting out. It allows other persons to test the degree of perfection of our patterns, their "goodness of fit" to the shared, communal, speech patterns. First, we compare our productions with the actual productions of other people. This is the slavish, immediate, or *first-order mimicry*. I say a word and the baby says a word immediately after me, enunciating it as well as he can. Later, as I say a word, the baby will store up his image of the pattern of those words in his "acoustic brain" and will practice saying it himself, later comparing what he produces with the model that he has stored in his brain. This is delayed or *second-order mimicry*. He has removed the necessity of mimicking immediately after me. He has stored what I have said more or less accurately and then reproduced it later at his leisure. This process of storage and later reproduction makes it difficult to detect the mimicry process in the older children. They store the pattern and reproduce it away from its source.

When we wish, as adults, to learn another language, fundamentally, we must revert to this beginning process that was used with our native language. We learn the language faster if we can do immediate mimicry rather than delayed mimicry of stored images. In other words, if we can go back to the childhood mechanism of immediate interactions, hooking up the words, the speech, the events, the people, and the objects together all at once, we learn the new language in six weeks. If we are forced back into the position of the child, acquiring the first language, with our adult brain of large size we can shorten the period considerably over what it was in the first instance. We have also perfected our central-peripheral, vocalization apparatus, though sometimes in paths inappropriate for the second language. Our perception processes may also be prejudiced along the first language line and make the acquisition of the subtleties of the second language rather difficult to acquire. Mimicry, with a native speaker of the language, and correction by that speaker sharpens up our new criteria as our parents sharpened our first language by corrections. What then are the basic requirements for learning speech, insofar as we can estimate it at the present time?

Basically, these seem to be 1. a mammalian brain somewhere between 660 and 700 grams; 2. a proper vocalization apparatus; 3. an accumulation of stored patterns of sounds; 4. practice with first-order or immediate mimicry with error corrections by another human; 5. practice with second-order or delayed mimicry.

I cannot emphasize enough the necessity of storing literally hundreds of thousands of sonic patterns on the hearing side before the transmission side can begin to mimic those patterns. Thus, to mimic, we must be able to call up from the stores within our brain large numbers of sonic patterns which we can then attempt to put out through our vocalization apparatus. As they come out so that they can be heard, they are new patterns from outside which can excite on the input side, and we now have both the produced pattern and the received pattern to compare within the brain itself. Thus, the problem of mimicry boils down to 1. stored patterns of complex sounds S which we have received many times and established in memory as distinct entities separated from all other non-speech sounds; 2. recently heard pattern of sounds H; 3. a juxtaposition of the heard sound H with the stored sounds S within the brain itself; 4. the production of a sound in the proper processes of mimicry in which one produces a pattern of sound V which is designed as it is produced to be like H, a recently heard sound, or is designed to be like S, the long-term stored separated-out pattern of sound; 5. if H does resemble S, then V can be tailored to match also; 6. one can, as it were, continue to say various versions of V until the final version of V when compared with H stored and with S, shows congruity along the whole pattern in time.

Of course, the perception process and its processing of these materials "V" and "H" also must be trained by the multiple processes to "know" when the fit is good enough and meets the criteria of the other persons. How much of our perception processes are given to us at birth and how much are acquired after birth is yet to be determined. We do know that we can train perception in language, and pay attention to those portions of the pattern which are important to transmitting meaning in that language. This is the science of phonetics and of phonemics.

To return to mimicry we can see that, as a process, mimicry is essential in detecting attempts on the part of another creature to communicate with one's self. In the cases of the parrot and of the mynah bird, the mimicry does not seem to be an attempt to communicate. In the case of the human child, the mimicry is such an attempt. One basic difference in these two cases is the size of the brain. The parrot and the mynah bird use their vocalization apparatus with a certain degree of success in playing back limited numbers of words. They cannot store sufficiently large numbers of sonic patterns in their small brain; they cannot have the immediate access to and the complex composition ability for these patterns that the larger brain does. To assure speaking a language as we know it, the bits and pieces must be myriad, easily available, and quickly composable. Several persons have spent many years working with mynah birds and with parrots and cannot still satisfactorily account for the processes leading to the parrot or the mynah bird reproducing our words. Here the mimicry process seems to be a mysterious dead end, leading nowhere. The brain just isn't large enough to make full use of it beyond this one end product of a few words expertly pronounced.

In 1957, I discovered the ability of the bottlenose dolphin to mimic sounds occurring in his environment. This experience is given in a scientific paper,[†] from the experiential point of view. Something of this discovery was reported in *Man and Dolphin*. The only previous written account of such a finding is that of Aristotle (300 B.C.). Aristotle said that the voice of the dolphin in air is like that of the human; that he pronounces vowels and combinations of vowels, has difficulty pronouncing the vowel-consonant combination.

About four hundred years later Plinius Secundus shortened this description to read, "the voice of the dolphin is like human wailing."

This fact of mimicry by the dolphins and the knowledge of its necessity for the acquisition of language was apparently not appreciated by Aristotle. He had seen and heard dolphins mimicking humans, but had not called it that. Their natural voice in air was like that of the human saying vowels and vowel-like sounds. But, naturally in the wild, such sounds are not made in air, nor even underwater.

When I came on the phenomenon in 1957, I was not acquainted with Aristotle's writings. In retrospective analysis of tapes I had taken of what the dolphin had been putting out under special circumstances, some of the sounds re-

† Lilly, John C., "Vocal behavior of the bottlenose dolphin." *Proc. Am. Philos. Soc.* 106: 520–29 (1962).

sembled sounds occurring in the laboratory either spontaneously or caused by me. Later, when I tested another dolphin for his ability to mimic, we found quickly that certain physical aspects of mimicry were obviously in their repertoire.

Since the publication of *Man and Dolphin*, work on this phenomenon has been extensive and the results have been very interesting.

Let us visualize mimicry as a key to interspecies communication. Let us visualize one of us captured by another intelligent, extraterrestrial species and held in captivity surrounded by the aliens. If such a captive person wished to establish his intelligence with the intelligent species around him, he might first try talking to them. If they were obviously talking to one another in an alien language, it would behoove him to try to learn that language. It would also pay him to get the attention of an alien or two who might be sympathetic to his wish to learn the language.

To attract their attention such person would try mimicking some of the sounds of that language. If he succeeded in mimicking well enough for the aliens to recognize his mimicry, they might reply and attempt to teach him the language; that is, if he were lucky enough to find an alien who could recognize 1. *that he is mimicking,* and 2. *that mimicking is an attempt to communicate.*

There might have been all sorts of intellectual assumptions by the aliens which would prevent such direct use of mimicking. Many humans unknowingly have such assumptions. I have reported the mimicking phenomenon by *Tursiops* in several scientific publications and have suggested that *Tursiops* uses it as we would in the extraterrestrial situation. My first demonstrations of the phenomenon required a certain amount of particular kinds of training in the observer, i.e., he needed a good ear for accents and a mind capable of separating the signals from the noise.

Obviously, the pronunciation of *Tursiops* is not very good. That he says anything resembling given human words (human words which have just been spoken to him) is amazing and indicates attempts to mimic. Most scientists are not trained in differentiating the human "foreign accents" from their native tongue and are not used to separating human voice signals from badly distorted transmissions. Therefore, my demonstrations of direct tape recordings of the phenomenon have been unconvincing to many types of persons and scientists. For this reason, demonstrations of mimicry which did not involve hearing and psychophysical judgments were devised.

The new demonstrations were reported in *Science* † The summary published in that paper is as follows:

"In addition to its normal underwater sonic communication path, the dolphin (*Tursiops truncatus*) can be trained to emit sounds from the blowhole opened in air. By proper rewarding (positive reinforcement) and evocative techniques, such vocal emissions can be changed from the natural pattern. One such group of sounds is said to resemble the human voice ('vocal mimicry'). Aspects of these sounds which are physically determinable, specifiable, and demonstrable are the similarities in numbers of bursts of sound emitted by the man and by the dolphin and in durations of successive emissions. In 92% of the exchanges the number of bursts emitted by *Tursiops* equalled plus or minus 1, the number just previously emitted by a man in sequences of one to ten bursts." No other animals (with the one exception of unusual humans) can match this performance.

In a moment, let us visualize experiments which demonstrate these points. First of all, let us consider the set of sounds which are presented by the human to the dolphins.

In the early work in 1957 through 1961, we used ordinary

‡ Lilly, J. C. (1965) in General Bibliography.

human speech in single words, phrases, and sentences. In this early work, we detected resemblances between what we said and what the dolphin said. Mixed in among many primitive copies of our speech (called "humanoid emissions") were other vocal "noises." Most of these noises were the usual (underwater) delphinic noises now emitted in air (the familiar clicks, whistles, barks, and blats of the ordinary exchanges between dolphins).

As we shape up his vocal behavior by one means or another, he begins to produce more and more on the "humanoids." We reward only humanoid emissions and by deprivation penalize delphinic sounds.

This process of concentrating and changing his emissions more and more to one pattern of emission is called (in the parlance of psychology) "shaping up" the vocal behavior. At the beginning, the shaping up is done by food rewards, i.e., a fish given immediately after each performance which has in it something of the desired characteristics. The human observer does not reward the dolphin unless the dolphin says something which has some aspect which the human observer plans to preserve in the emission. Once under way, the shaping up takes hours and many repetitions on the part of the human to gradually improve pronunciation.

If we give a dolphin a long list of the proper kinds of sounds that we want him to emit in the proper numbers, the proper order, the proper pronunciation, in something like twelve to thirty minutes, the dolphin will select of those aspects which one is emphasizing in that particular list those he can do. He fails only with his pronunciation: the frequencies emitted are too high for the human ear (*Man and Dolphin*). The human stimuli have a pitch range from 125 to 225 pulses per second and formant frequencies from 300 to 3900 Hz. The dolphin's pitch is 300 to 1000 per second and his formant frequencies are 1200 to 24,000 Hz (Figure 8).

199

For example, in preparation for the article in *Science,* we decided to concentrate our efforts on short, sharp bursts of sound which had no meaning to human beings. This decision developed because we had found that when we gave meaningful sentences or words to the dolphins and they mimicked, say, the pitch and rhythm of those sounds, we could "read in" the rest of the context while listening— for example, if we said, "Good morning *Tursiops,* how are you today?" The series of humanoids that the dolphin gave us back had certain physical aspects of the patterning of the sounds that we had said to the dolphin. The problem was, *what aspects?* We could hear, as it were, the *meaning* being carried by whatever aspects the dolphin was mimicking, and if we listened often enough and carefully enough to repeated playback of the tape, we could "hear" the dolphin saying, "Good morning *Tursiops,* how are you today?" In other words, his playback was good enough so that we could then use what he said to reconstruct what we had just given him. Even this primitive degree of immediate vocal copying cannot be done by any other animal than by man himself. We cannot obtain such immediate "locked in" vocal results with "talking" birds. When the bird mimics he *pronounces* well, but will not lock in his vocal output alternately with that of the human. The dolphin "locks in" beautifully, accurately, rhythmically, for hundreds of times at high speed.

If we put ourselves in the position of the dolphin, who has three sonic emitters as opposed to our one, who is used to transmitting his information to other dolphins underwater, who is forced to speak to us in our medium in air, who is using his nose and not his tongue and mouth for his enunciation, I think we can understand his difficulty in attempting to mimic us and to convince us that this is what he is doing.

We attempted a way around these difficulties by furnish-

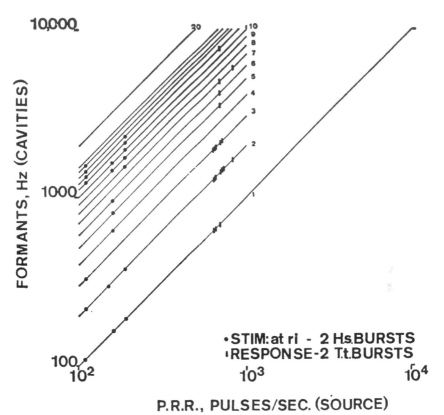

FORMANTS, Hz (CAVITIES)

10,000

1000

100

10²   10³   10⁴

• STIM: at ri - 2 Hs.BURSTS
ı RESPONSE-2 T.t.BURSTS

P.R.R., PULSES/SEC. (SOURCE)

FIGURE 8. *A Male Human Voice Saying "at ri" and the*
Dolphin's Response Showing the Frequency and Pitch
of the Airborne Voice of the Dolphin

This plot is the result of analyses of the human vowel sounds and the dolphin's reply sounds. The horizontal axis represents the pulse rate of the source, which in the case of the human is the pulsing rate of the larynx, in the case of the dolphin is the pulsing rate of the diagonal membrane. The vertical axis is frequencies of the cavity resonances: in the case of the human voice these are the formants (the resonances of changing the size and shape of the mouth and pharynx and nasal passageway during speech by the man). In the case of the dolphin the cavities are changed in size in a voluntary way in a fashion analogous to that of the human, modulating the peaks of energy of various harmonics of his basic pulsing rate. The first group of dots in a vertical row is the vowel sound in "at." The second group of dots is the voiced "r" sound, the third group of dots is the vowel sound of "ri." The dolphin's replies were two bursts of sounds whose basic pitch is at approximately 800 per second instead of the 100 to 200 per second of the human voice. The dolphin modulated his cavities in a way consonant with this higher pitch.

201

	r	l	z	v	ch-/-tch	w	m	n	t	k	s
ē	ēr	ēl	ēz	ēv	ētch		ēm	ēn	ēt	ēk	ēs
	rē	lē	zē	vē	chē	wē	mē	nē	tē	kē	sē
ĭ	ĭr	ĭl	ĭz	ĭv	ĭtch		ĭm	ĭn	ĭt	ĭk	ĭs
	rĭ	lĭ	zĭ	vĭ	chĭ	wĭ	mĭ	nĭ	tĭ	kĭ	sĭ
ā	ār	āl	āz		ātch		ām	ān	āt	āk	ās
	rā	lā	zā	vā	chā	wā	mā	nā	tā	kā	sā
ĕ	ĕr	ĕl	ĕz	ĕv	ĕtch		ĕm	ĕn	ĕt	ĕk	
	rĕ	lĕ	zĕ	vĕ	chĕ	wĕ	mĕ	nĕ	tĕ	kĕ	sĕ
ä	är	äl		äv	ätch		äm	än	ät	äk	äş
	rä	lä	zä	vä	chä	wä	mä	nä	tä	kä	sä
ō	ōr	ōl	ōz	ōv	ōtch		ōm	ōn	ōt	ōk	ōs
	rō	lō	zō	vō	chō	wō	mō	nō	tō	kō	sō
ōō	ōōr	ōōl	ōōz	ōōv	ōōtch		ōōm	ōōn	ōōt	ōōk	ōōs
	rōō	lōō	zōō	vōō	chōō	wōō	mōō	nōō	tōō	kōō	sōō
aī	aīr	aīl	aīz	aīv	aītch		aīm	aīn	aīt	aīk	aīs
	raī	laī	zaī	vaī	chaī	waī	maī	naī	taī	kaī	saī
oi	oir	oil	oiz	oiv	oitch		oim	oin	oit	oik	ois
	roi	loi	zoi	voi	choi	woi	moi	noi	toi	koi	soi

FIGURE 9. *Table of the Nonsense Syllables Used as Vocal Stimuli for the Dolphin*

The vowels are listed on the left in a vertical column and the consonants along the top in a horizontal line. The pronunciation of the "consonant-vowel and vowel-consonant" pairs is then given in the corresponding place in the table. It is to be noted that "W" as a final consonant was eliminated because of difficulties of pronunciation. (Table adapted from J. C. Lilly, in Darley *Brain Mechanisms*, 1967.)

ing him with a set of sounds which did not have meaning and which had unexpected and unpredictable acoustic characteristics so that we and he could not predict what was coming next in listening to the resulting transmissions.

A list of special sounds was made up. This new list of sounds consisted of nonsense syllables, i.e., syllables which strung together in groups have no meaning to a human listener. These were made from arbitrary lists of consonants and an arbitrary list of vowels combined systematically. The nine vowels were i, I, e, E, a, o, u, aI, oI. The consonants were r, l, z, v, t, w, m, n, t, k, s. The international phonetic alphabet shows the pronunciation of the symbols used. The consonants were placed in order across the top of a sheet of paper and the vowels placed down along the left-hand edge of the paper (Figure 9). The consonant-vowel combinations of these were then paired up throughout the list; similarly, a vowel-consonant combination was made up from each pair. This gave ninety-nine vowel-consonants and ninety-nine consonant-vowel syllables. Of these 198 syllables all but eleven were pronounceable. The final list had 187 items in it.

These 187 nonsense syllables were then placed on cards, one to a card. Each card was then reproduced four times. The resulting deck of cards was shuffled to assure a random order.

From a table of random numbers a list of the numbers from 1 through 10 was arranged in random order. These randomized groups of numbers were then used to select the number of nonsense syllables in each presentation. This process was continued until the list of nonsense syllables was used up.

From these cards, lists of the random-numbered groups were then typed out in random order of the nonsense syllables. These lists were the ones used in the experiments.

Several dolphins had received a preliminary training in

vocalization in air. One of these was chosen for the first experiment. A special tank had been constructed. It consisted of a home tank in which the dolphin lived which had a transparent Plexiglas sidearm extending from it (*Man and Dolphin*). The dolphin at its own option could enter this sidearm which contained approximately twelve to eighteen inches of water. When he entered the sidearm, the dolphin's blowhole would thus automatically be placed above the water . . . he could either place the blowhole above water or the water depth could be adjusted in such a way that his blowhole ended up above water when he came into the sidearm. At any time, the dolphin could leave the sidearm and go back to his tank.

We found that we obtained best cooperation and the hardest work from *Tursiops* when we left the option of stopping the experiment (leaving the sidearm) to the dolphin. This meant to us that when he had enough, if he was getting tired, for example, he would leave, take a short rest, and then come back for more. The dolphin acted as predicted.

A microphone was placed above the water-filled sidearm in the proper position near the dolphin's blowhole. The human operator stood beside him in such a position that he could feed the dolphin a fish with his right hand while reading from the list in his left hand. A lavalier microphone, protected from the seawater, was placed in front of the human operator's mouth. The information coming from each of these microphones was recording separately in a two-channel tape recorder (Minnesota Mining & Manufacturing Company 3M Wollensak and Crown 800 series at higher frequencies). The tape recorder was outside of the room and the operator of the recorder could watch through a glass window, and adjust the gains on the tape recorder to a satisfactory level.

At the beginning of an experiment, the human operator

walked into the room, placed the microphone, turned on the light over the sidearm, and called to the dolphin, "All right—let's go." In the usual experiment, the dolphin with a short delay entered the sidearm. The human then said, "Hello." The dolphin gave some humanoid reply. The human then read the first group of items on the list, held the fish out so the dolphin could see it, and, when the dolphin gave a reply in air with humanoids, he was given the fish. Within a few minutes of the first attempts the dolphin began to give back a number of bursts of sound. As more syllables were read, the dolphin began to give a number of bursts of sound just equal to the number given by the human.

When the human gave five bursts of sound, the dolphin replied with five. When the human gave four, the dolphin replied with four. When the human gave three, the dolphin replied with three. Figure 10 shows a human-dolphin exchange of 10 bursts of sound matched by the dolphin.

Dolphins habitually reply sonically one to the other.§ This part of the performance (the "transactional form") is apparently already known by the dolphin. In the experiments with the human the loud noises in air are the new phenomena.

We analyzed the results of one thousand such bursts of sound between the human and the dolphin. The next figure (Figure 11) shows the number of bursts in the dolphin emission as compared with the number of bursts in the human emission which just preceded that of the dolphin. We call the human emission the "stimulus emission" and the dolphin's "response" or the "reply emission."

If we subtract the number of sounds emitted by the dolphin in each of his replies from the number emitted by the human in his stimulus, we obtain a measure of the dolphin's error. If the difference between the two numbers is zero,

§ Lilly, J. C. and Miller, A. M., "Vocal exchanges between dolphins." *Science* 134: 1873–76 (1961).

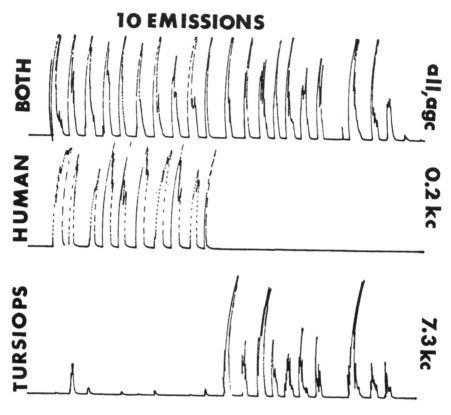

FIGURE 10. *Oscillographic Record of a Dolphin Exchange Showing Ten Bursts of Sound Emitted by the Human Matched by Ten Bursts of Sound Emitted by the Dolphin*

The upper trace shows all of the sounds emitted by both the man and the dolphin; the second trace, those by the man only; the lower trace, those emitted by the dolphin. It is to be noted that the delay between the end of the human presentation and the beginning of the dolphin reply is of the same order of magnitude as the interburst silences in the human presentation. This is a selected portion of a very long experiment in which numbers of bursts of sound emitted by the human were varied from 1 to 10 and the replies of the dolphin were from 1 to 10. (See J. C. Lilly, "Vocal Mimicry by the Dolphin," *Science* 147:300–1 [1965].)

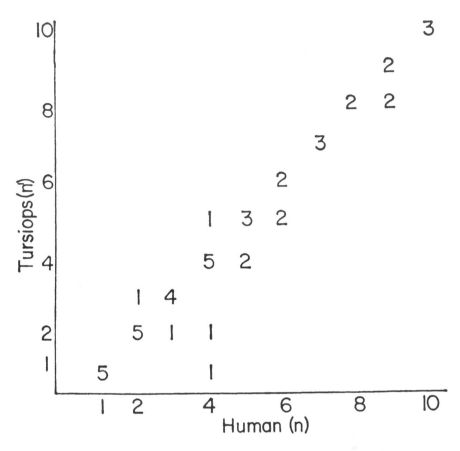

FIGURE 11. *Scoring of a Single Experiment: the Number of Human Nonsense Syllables on the Horizontal vs. Number of Bursts of Sounds in the Dolphin's Reply on the Vertical Axis*

When the dolphin made no errors in his number of replies, the resulting number of instances are plotted on a 45-degree line which reads 5, 5, 4, 5, 3, 2, 3, 2, 2, 3. The next 45-degree line to the right shows cases in which the dolphin added one; the 45-degree line to the left, he subtracted one. This was an early experiment in which the dolphin was learning and making some errors. (*Science* 147 [3655]: 300–1 [1965].)

the dolphin's error is zero. If the difference is plus one, the dolphin has made one too many emissions compared to those of the human. If the difference is minus one he has failed to give an equal number and his error is one. The third figure of this series shows his scores for one thousand emissions. The very large peak at zero error shows that most of the time he emits the proper number.

A source of error we picked up and allowed for in the emissions is as follows: in syllables containing a vowel and, for example, a consonant "t," we actually make not one but two separated sounds. To illustrate, in pronouncing the word "it," one says "i," then a short silence, then the "t" sound. Thus when we think we say only a single syllable and hence a single sound, physically we are emitting actually two bursts of sound. The dolphin does not hook up these two sounds into a single syllable the way we do. In reply to this kind of syllable, he will put out two bursts of sound instead of the expected one burst. When we discovered this form of our error, we had to recount again some of the dolphin's emissions and correct them to correspond to the "physically specifiable" bursts of sound rather than the "humanly expected" number of bursts of sound (Figure 12). This example illustrates the value of choosing physically specifiable variables so that one is not confused by syllables or words which have "human meaning."

To give an idea of the magnitude of the task the dolphin solved let us give some of the quantitative measures of what happened. These nonsense syllables were presented at a rate of one every 0.7 second; the average duration of each of the sonic bursts was approximately 0.4 second. The "interburst silence" periods were approximately 0.4 second also. These numbers were derived from measurements of objective inkwriter records made directly from the tape recordings.

From the end of the human's presentation to the begin-

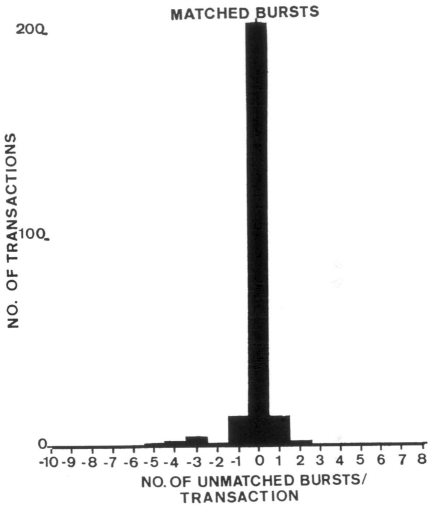

FIGURE 12. *The Over-all Scoring of Several Experiments
Showing the Relatively Few Errors that the Dolphin
Makes in Matching the Number of Bursts of Sound*

For those exchanges in which the dolphin made no errors the scoring is in the column labeled "0." When the dolphin added one the score is kept in the column to the right, when he subtracted one to the left. In some instances he did not reply, shown at minus 2, minus 3, minus 4, minus 5, etc. The largest fraction of the replies, however, matched numbers of bursts to numbers of nonsense syllables given, in 200 exchanges. (From J. C. Lilly, H. M. Truby, A. M. Miller, and F. Grissman, *Some Parametric Regions of Vocal Copying by the Dolphin* [manuscript, 1967].)

ning of the dolphin's emission was approximately 0.4 second. This time is equal to the human's interburst silence duration. Thus the dolphin could not be using an elapse of a certain amount of time to know when the human had finished his list and when to begin answering it. How did the dolphin decide when the human had arrived at the end of the list and it was his turn?

If one reads a list of anything, numbers, nonsense syllables, or groceries, he finds he does not pronounce the last word of the list the same way he pronounced all of the previous items on it. If I say "1, 2, 3, 4, 5," I change the word "five." It is easily shown that the dolphin detects this change of voice and uses it to tell him when the human operator has reached the end of that particular group of nonsense syllables.

Detection of clues as to what to do from changes in one's voice is a very convincing demonstration of the quality of the mind listening at the other end of this system and of the abilities of his hearing system. That he is able to pick up, recognize, and use such clues means that he has a very discriminating and complex approach to sonic events. In this experiment, a rapid rate of presentation and a rapid rate of reply was maintained for periods from twelve to twenty minutes without stop. To give a perspective of how fast this is, it is as if two human beings were doing a question-and-answer task as fast as they could talk for these periods of twelve to twenty minutes. The rate in our experiments was so fast that the human operator came out of the experiment fatigued; the dolphin would pace us at a very high rate.

Other physically specifiable variables that were measured showed that the dolphin matched the human duration of emissions and the human duration of interburst silences within a narrow range of error.

The important question of how well the dolphin pronounces each of the nonsense syllables is still a matter of the personal opinion of the observer making the judgment. "Non-physically specifiable variables" are invoked to compare what one hears with something else he hears. We have then moved into the area of psychophysics.

The most conservative statement that can be made about what one hears when these tape recordings are played back is that some particular aspect of the human voice is being accurately copied. I found that by playing back a tape through a special filter system this parallelism between the two voices (human and dolphin) could be improved.

The human voice, in general, consists of a basic pitch and the harmonics of this basic pitch as emphasized by the cavities shaped by one's tongue, soft palate, and the pharynx, for example.

Some aspects of the human voice are physically specifiable by a sound spectrograph which presents the variation of frequency in the voice with time. This shows that most of the meaningful portions of our voice (cutting out the less-meaningful noises) reside in the middle of the speech spectrum, i.e., from approximately 300 cycles per second to about 3000 Hz. At each end of this range are sounds which are less important in carrying word meanings, i.e., in determining resemblances between what another person is saying and what one expects from what he has learned of that language. The predictability of the emitted sonic patterns thus is determined mainly by the region from 300 to 3000 Hz. If one chops off the two ends, less is lost than if he chops into this region. Above 3000 Hz at approximately 3800 to 8000 Hz is the fourth formant. In general, this formant seems to say only that the speaker is speaking; it does not vary much with different words and seems to remain constant every time he speaks.

In experiments we cut the human voice down to these essentially meaningful areas. The resulting dolphin emissions then more closely resembled the human voice. A psychophysical correspondence was found between what the humans said and what the dolphins said. The dolphins sounded more like the distorted human voice.

Similarly, if we took the previous nonsense syllable recordings and listened to them, cutting off all of the very-low-frequency sounds in the human voice (i.e., everything below about 2000 Hz), the resulting playback of the human and the dolphin voices resembled one another more closely. These lines of evidence tend to show that transmitting to the dolphin and receiving from the dolphin, as a feedback system, have a low-frequency cutoff characteristic, i.e., somehow or other, either the dolphin does not hear the low frequencies (Figure 13) or he is unable to transmit the low frequencies with any degree of fidelity. However, he is good at transmitting fair copies of the higher frequencies.

This line of evidence agrees with the normal dolphin underwater voice. In this case, experiments in our Institute have shown that the dolphin has difficulty emitting any sort of underwater sound below about 400 Hz; his barks, blats, and vowel-like sounds seem to end near this value (in general, the low end whistles stop at frequencies of about 6000 Hz). This indicates that a dolphin vocalizing in air will have difficulty in the lower frequencies where we have good control of our voices.

That dolphins enthusiastically move into such complex and discriminating acoustic vocal paths as mimicking our voice shows one aspect of the functions of their large brain. As was stated previously in this report their acoustical brain is of the order of ten times the size of our acoustical brain even as our visual brain is ten times the size of their visual brain. To explain the above results, we must assume here that dolphins are expert counters, or else they have a very large, immediate, here-now acoustical memory. If we take the distribution of the errors of the dolphin as a guide to the number of items in the stimulus list just read to the dol-

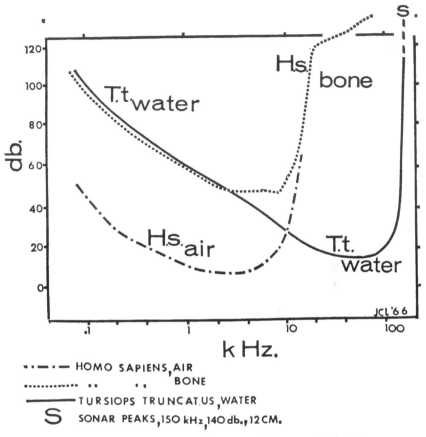

FIGURE 13. *The Hearing Curves of Man and Dolphin*

The hearing curve of the dolphin (T.t. water) extends from 100 cycles per second (Hertz) to 160,000 cycles (Hertz). The hearing curve of man (H.s. air) extends from 100 cycles to 15 kilocycles. The minimum pressure needed for detection in each case is at zero decibels (re 0.002 dyne per square centimeter). It is to be noted that the bone conduction curve for man (H.s. bone) corresponds to the dolphin's underwater curve (T.t. water) from 100 cycles per second to approximately 3000 cycles per second. It is also to be noted that the "air" and "bone" conduction curves in man have a difference of approximately 45 decibels up to about 3000 cycles per second. (Man's ear drum and bones in the middle ear do not work well underwater.) The rapidly rising portion of the dolphin's hearing curve relates very well to the amplitude of his emitted sonar impulses. The point "S" is the peak amplitude of single sonar peaks at 150 kilocycles (140 decibels) at 12 centimeters off the end of the beak. (The airborne curves of man are from Licklider, the bone conduction curves are from Zwislocki and Corso; the dolphin data are from Scott Johnson; the sonar amplitudes are from J. C. Lilly.)

213

phin, we see that up to ten items, the errors do not increase as the number of items increases. Tested with similar lists, human subjects fall off at five to six items. Of course, these are lists heard for the first time in orders heard for the first time. This is the naïve performance with a new set of stimuli, not the polished performance of memorized material, in either the dolphin's case or in the human's case.

Probably the dolphins have a very good, recent, acoustic memory and can, as it were, accurately "play back" acoustic events up to unknown numbers of items and up to unknown durations of time.

The work recounted broke into a new area of investigation of the dolphins. Guided by the large acoustical brain and our knowledge of it, we began to test things which are acoustical-vocal combinations, properly functions of the acoustical brain. These are the things, processes, and thoughts with which dolphins should be pre-eminently occupied and in which they should be pre-eminently qualified. These are the first tests to show the areas in which dolphins can and do outperform human beings. They can outswim us; this is an obvious, necessary adaptation. Their vocal-acoustic behavior is not so obviously such an adaptation. Their use of sonar is a necessity in the sea. However, like us they found that communication and that key to communication with strangers called "mimicry" pushed them along farther and faster in relation to other creatures around them than probably any other single accomplishment of the species.

The necessity of a large brain for the development of language is recounted in a published paper.¶ This was an extension of the argument in *Man and Dolphin* for the presence of language in and among the dolphins. This is still our guiding hypothesis, i.e., their brains are large enough so that they can have developed a language, though very unlike any human one.

¶ Lilly, John C. (1963) in General Bibliography.

The above experiments in mimicry indicate the existence of several of the necessary abilities for a language. They show that the physiology and the anatomy is usable, trainable, and adaptable for language.

The experiments do not demonstrate, however, the detailed meanings of the dolphin's language nor do they demonstrate that the dolphin understands our meanings. The dolphin can proceed to take our directions in vocal and nonvocal language. We can, as it were, "train a dolphin" to recognize that on a given signal, we wish him to do certain things. All of these tests the dolphins have passed. They are eminently trainable in their body movements, swimming, coming to a given place, and such behavior as moving objects from one place to another. The present experiments show that they are also eminently trainable in the vocalization and acoustic spheres. The next step, a long one, is demonstrating that the dolphin can meaningfully use these sounds as we use language and speech.

CHAPTER 10

Living with a Dolphin: Learning the Way

In the initial phases of research development with the interspecies communication problem with man and dolphin, it was stated that one possible method of teaching this species a human form of language was the use of the human mother-child teaching-learning model (see *Man and Dolphin*). During the period of a year it has been possible to carry out this plan in detail with a "human mother" and a young male dolphin by the name of Peter. Techniques used may be of interest to others planning similar research; the major barriers to close contact for the full twenty-four hours per day six days per week have been found and more or less satisfactory solutions worked out. The design and construction of the facility was aided by previous planning and construction of a building which was eventually adaptable to this type of work (Plate 5).

The special modifications of the already existing laboratory on the island of St. Thomas for the "mother-child" type of environment was designed after an initial experiment consisting of seven days and nights of continuous contact of a human with a dolphin in a shallow pool. The results of this experiment were sufficiently encouraging to plan a longer, two-and-a-half-month experiment. Between the two experimental periods the changes in the facility necessary to carry out the longer program were completed.

The longer experimental period was done in the summer

of 1965, started in June and completed the beginning of September.

In the past this research has been approached with dolphins individually isolated in small tanks for short periods of time with sometimes informal, sometimes a more formal ("operant conditioning") frame of reference. In the past "food reward" was tested, found successful, and later was shown to be unnecessary with a trained animal. In the past the dolphin was put with one other dolphin between experiments to avoid the effects of isolation or was left alone in solitude in his tank. Informal spontaneous exchanges were explored. Words, phrases, sentences, tones of voice, and emotional involvement in the dyadic relationship were found to be important to carry primitive meaning between the human and the dolphin. Later the formal exchanges were developed; in these exchanges, numbers or nonsense syllables were used to test the dolphin's abilities to mimic 1. isolated human speech sounds; 2. numbers of sonic bursts; 3. durations of bursts; and 4. the sonic patterning psychophysically measured. It was quickly found that within limits a dolphin will learn quite complex exchange rules with single human operators, i.e., dolphins with humans establish a primitive action-reaction code.

The results were summarized* as follows: Durations, numbers, and patterning of human sonic bursts are mimicked by *Tursiops* with accuracies of more than 90 per cent. The patterns presented must be of a great number and a great variety to keep the dolphin's interest. The human operator can learn to select and control and hence "teach" the dolphin any selected aspect or group of aspects of the speech sounds to be mimicked. The dolphin's limits thus explored are: 1. final trained pitch is high (400 to 1000 Hz); 2. formants can be trained down to the second and third partials;

* Lilly, J. C. (1965) in General Bibliography.

3. general patterning is excellent; complex patterns are rendered at higher frequencies with excellent mimicry. The longer and the more frequent the contacts (human-dolphin) the better the performance. Longer mode intense contacts were thus shown to be needed.

These results encouraged the planning of the present study. In order to move fast, a chronic contact, 12 hours/day, 12 hours/night, was planned. The analog used in the new studies is the mother and her baby, human baby, being exposed to all of those actions, reactions, contexts, situations, and emotions which lead eventually to the baby becoming a child who speaks English (or other human language in the repertoire of the mother). We recognize that there are many unknowns in the mother-child relationship and in the acquisition of language by the child. If we choose 1. the proper mother; 2. the proper dolphin; 3. the proper environment; 4. the proper social milieu; and 5. the proper direction of all of these factors, we feel that these unknowns of this relationship will be brought into the new relationship between the dolphin and the human. In addition, the successes with the previous mimicry research and its encouraging results are brought to the new studies. One basic purpose behind this project is expressed by the "mother" involved as "no matter how long it takes, no matter how much work, *this dolphin is going to learn to speak English!*"

Assumptions

The basic meta-assumptions ("assumptions about assumptions themselves") and assumptions made by the investigators on this project are important heuristically. The assumptions are pragmatic; if one assumption works it is made and used; if another doesn't work it is dropped. Success or failure of a given assumption is measured by the results achieved by a human using the assumption sufficiently vigorously for

PLATE 23. *A View of Some of the Apparatus in Teaching Peter.* The spheres on the left are used to teach numbers, and the different-colored plaques in the center are designed to teach color. The plaques at the far right are used to teach shape.

PLATE 24. July. Margaret says the word "diamond," shows Peter the shape. Peter's blowhole is closed; he has learned not to vocalize while Margaret is speaking.

PLATE 25. Peter has made a good vocal attempt at the word "diamond" and Margaret rewards him with a butterfish.

PLATE 26. In quiet of "play period" following shape lesson, Margaret is gently squirting water from her mouth toward Peter's beak. He usually responds by opening his mouth so that water squirts against his gums, or by gently squirting back. The close "face-to-face" play — conversation-inspection, is the type of play that develops frequently during activities, and often at night.

PLATE 27. Peter interrupts Margaret's telephone conversation and she is obviously delighted. Peter often enters into a three-way telephone conversation and was encouraged to do so in his loudest voice.

PLATE 28. Margaret lifts feet out of Peter's reach and scolds him for mouthing her foot. His teeth are sharply pointed. Note bright eye of Peter.

PLATE 29. A moment later the mood changes, Margaret wriggles toes at Peter while smiling and talking to him. This type of discipline and scolding is usually brief; Peter is scolded and the incident forgotten.

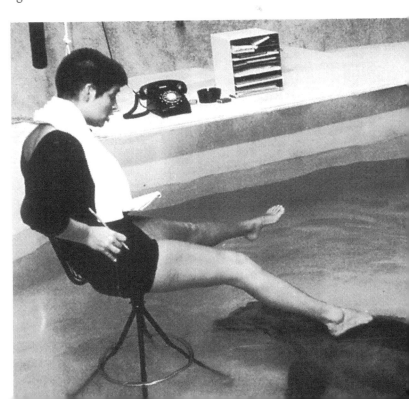

PLATE 30.   Close contacts are obviously welcomed and enjoyed by both participants.
The dolphin will spend time being completely limp, free to be pushed, pulled, carried,
towed around, etc. by Margaret or will turn the tables and demand that she go limp so
that he can push her around, inspect her knee joints, look at fingers, etc. These are very
happy "getting to know you" periods.

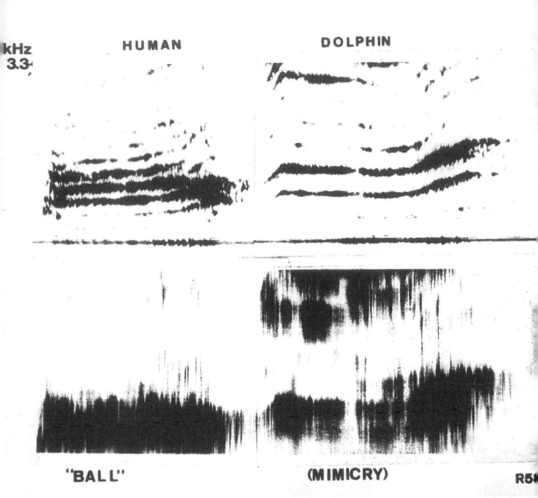

kHz
3.3

HUMAN   DOLPHIN

"BALL"   (MIMICRY)   R5

PLATE 31. *Spectrograms of Margaret saying "Ball" and Peter's Reply.* The sonic spectrogram plots here (in contrast to the ones earlier in the book) are limited to 3300 cycles per second as upper limit for the human carriers of meaning in speech. The upper traces are taken with a narrow-band (45 cycles per second) filter, the lower traces are taken with a wide-band filter (300 cycles). It is to be noted that Margaret's pitch is not exactly matched by Peter, his is somewhat higher (as is shown by the wider spacing of his lines in the record with the narrow-band filter). In addition he starts his answer in an abrupt fashion, copying Margaret's start with her word "Ball." She tends to lower her pitch at the end; he tends to raise his at the end. (Thousands of such spectrograms are needed for a complete analysis of the Margaret and Peter exchanges.) (From manuscript cited by Lilly, Truby, Miller, and Grissman.)

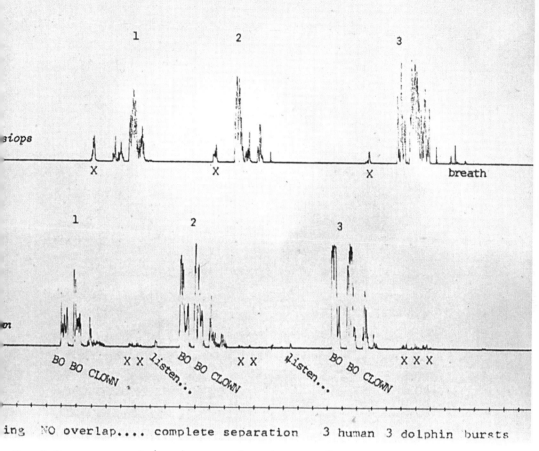

siops

1 2 3

X X X breath

1 2 3

BO BO CLOWN X X *listen...* *BO BO CLOWN* X X *listen...* *BO BO CLOWN* X X X

ing NO overlap.... complete separation 3 human 3 dolphin bursts

Peter's Learning Period. The upper trace shows the amplitude of the sound emitted by Peter and the lower trace of the sound emitted by Margaret. First Margaret says the words "bo bo clown" and Peter replies with three bursts of sound. The part of his curve showing an "X" is where some of Margaret's voice shows in Peter's channel; "X's" on her trace show where Peter's voice shows in her channel. This example illustrates that Peter will work many times to perfect the same words. He does not copy Margaret when she says "listen." He copies only when she says the words "bo bo clown." Each of his copies are quite different as can be seen by the top trace. He varies them as she varies the use of the same words. This figure illustrates some of the complexities of evaluating the vocal performance of a dolphin with his great degree of flexibility, plasticity, and quick learning (from manuscript cited).

a sufficient period of time. The human involved is only one judge of the results: independent judges not working directly with the dolphin make their judgment on the recorded material on tapes.

The basic beliefs of the human participant operator are important and determine how he or she handles the dolphin in the interactions with the dolphin. For example, if one believes that all dolphins are dangerous (though bright) animals he does not approach a dolphin closely, whereas a person who believes that the danger comes only with improper approaches to dolphins at least tries. In the first case the trial approaches are not made to test the assumption; in the second case tests for the correct pathways to the dolphin are made.

One's assumptions about the possible levels of understanding on the part of a dolphin are important. If he believes that dolphins are "bright animals easily trained" then he does only "training" and ignores clues to other paths to the dolphin. If he believes that dolphins can become quite as understanding of his actions and words, given the opportunity, as another person, then he arranges to give the dolphin a long-term opportunity to learn the meanings of his actions in close quarters. With this belief he not only interacts with the body of the dolphin and his own body, but uses the voice and its actions as well to express himself completely and forcibly. If he believes that dolphins cannot ever learn English he never tries to teach it to them. If he believes that they not only have the brain to learn it but the ears to hear it and the vocal equipment trainable to speak it, he then tries to induce the dolphin to speak English.

A belief does not make a true fact. To obtain the (future) fact "dolphins speaking English" one must invest the requisite time, interest, energy, money, and self-dedication to make the attempt over a long enough period of time to see if the fact can be created through one's own efforts.

The human participant's basic assumptions and the progressive changes can be seen by reading the notes written by this person before, during, and after the period of exposure to the interactions with the dolphins. These are part of this report. This method of seeing the assumptions gives the detailed picture; except by connotation, it does not give the general assumptions under which she operates. Many different ways of expressing these generalities are possible. One of the investigators' view of them (John C. Lilly) as expressed before the beginning of this project, was given in the book *Man and Dolphin* (the mother-child view). Another way rephrased by him after exposure to the experiments, to the human participant, and to the results and to the recordings is as follows:

1. In an environment suitably arranged for meeting one another on as equal terms as possible, a human and a dolphin can develop mutual trust, mutual understanding, and shared communication methods.

2. The human can communicate her emotional reactions to the dolphin, and he can respond appropriately to these reactions.

3. The dolphin can communicate his emotional states to the human and she can respond appropriately.

4. The dolphin has strategies he can use and others he can develop in the interactions; like the human he plans ahead.

5. Not only can techniques of transmitting information be worked out, but the dolphin understands "meta-language" directions given to him. These instructions are about how to mimic, how to pronounce, how to raise volume, how to lower pitch, and so forth. (The astonishing result is that he mimics only what he is told to mimic. He does not mimic the directions [meta-language] given with the words [language] to be mimicked.)

6. The dolphin tests the human: he knows what is wanted

in a given instance, can purposely do it "wrong" to provoke a reaction from the human; he can do it right but won't for purposes of his own. One of these purposes is to keep the human reacting and interacting with him.

The human participant's assumptions, i.e., those of Margaret C. Howe, in her own words are as follows:

1. Dolphins are capable of communication with man on the level of high intelligence.

2. Dolphins are not only capable of this communication but are eager for it and are willing to cooperate with man to achieve it.

3. Possibly the best way to go about establishing this communication is to set up a situation where the man (woman) and a dolphin live together as closely as possible for an extended period of time.

4. This is a long process and involves many steps, each of which must be recognized and encouraged. The attempt to communicate with a dolphin in English involves two main parts: (1) the dolphin must learn how to physically say the words, and (2) he must learn the meaning of what he is saying. These two parts may be worked out individually or simultaneously.

5. One first step is the creation and the maintenance of mutual trust and reciprocal rewards one for the other.

Her assumptions fundamentally agree with those of John C. Lilly.

Design Needs of Man-Dolphin Facility

The first basic needs are air and sea water at the proper temperatures. The water temperature is 80°F to 84°F. A satisfactory air temperature is 80°F to 90°F. Both air and water must be continuously flowing through the facility. New clean tropical sea water must wash through the facility rapidly enough to dispose of wastes and maintain the temperature. A natural flow as the result of wind and wave action and tidal action is better than electrical (or other power) pumps (Plate 6).

There are several distinctively separate necessary areas in the facility. These areas must be immediately adjacent and have non-dangerous boundaries between them. The areas themselves are as follows: a deep-water area, a shallow-water area, and a "no-water" or dry area.

The deep-water area is for the dolphin to relax as dolphins relax, i.e., if he wishes to swim at high speed or do fast three-dimensional maneuvers, he is free to do so. If he wishes to leap out of the water it is deep enough for the takeoff and for the landing. This area has water that is too deep for the human to be comfortable with the dolphin for long periods of time.

The shallow water is the area in which the results of interest are obtained. This area is shallow enough for the human to walk comfortably and yet deep enough for the dolphin to swim comfortably. This is the zone of encounter of man and dolphin: the mutually adapting area. Each of the dyad compromise something of their comfort in their cooperation with one another in this area. At any time the dolphin can leave this area. He can safely and comfortably scoot into the deeper water area. And at any time the human participant can safely and easily move into the "no-water" area.

The no-water area has two sub-areas within it. The one immediately adjacent to the shallow water may be called the damp area. It is inevitable that splashes from the dolphin's actions put water into the damp area. It is also inevitable that the human in shedding the water acquired in the shallow water will shed it in the first part of dry area available. In the other part of the human area there must be a definitely dry area, i.e., with no sea water allowed anywhere in this area. This is the zone of human relaxation as a human. It is comfortable, is so designed for human beings. It is an area which is totally uncomfortable, anxiety-provoking and sometimes even dangerous for a dolphin.

It is convenient to think of two additional areas adjacent to these. At the deep-water end of the facility should be the sea itself. This is where dolphins come from in the first place. At the other end of the dry area is all of civilization on dry land. This is where the human participants come from and return to for refreshment from the isolation from humans.

If we could only arrange for the dolphin to return to the sea for his refreshment in a similar manner, we would consider the facility ideal. Some of each of the above areas should be inside, out of the tropical sunshine, and some should be outside, in the trade winds and in the tropical sunshine, subject to all the vagaries of the weather of the tropics.

It is to be noted that in any practical facility made with a limited budget the areas of deep water, shallow water, dampness, and dryness are of necessity relatively small. In fact, they are unsatisfactorily small from the standpoint of evenness and monotony for this study in dyadic isolation. Ideally the facility should have all of the complexities built into it that the dolphin values in the sea and that the human values in an ordinary everyday civilized life in a home.

The food problems have practical and ideal aspects. Ideally the dolphin should be free to hunt in the sea for his own diet and return to the facility for his education with the human participant. Until the day that is possible, the humans must supply fifteen to twenty pounds of fish per day per dolphin. Butterfish is, in our experience, the best and most complete diet for the dolphin. At certain times of the year it can be obtained in large quantities frozen and shipped in from the United States mainland. With deep-freeze freezers and a supply of electricity, satisfactory maintenance of the fish supply can be successfully achieved.

The food for the human participant is the participant's usual purchase-stored-cooked diet in the completely dry area. In the special circumstances of the wet live-in, most of the usual foods can be used. However, pragmatic experience shows that special, easy-to-prepare-and-to-cook foods are best. One special food for the human is the food of the dolphin. It has been found that fried butterfish is a good compromise food at times.

The questions of power and light sources inevitably come up. We have used electricity as our major power source and propane gas as the heat source for cooking. Electricity (115 volts A.C.) is dangerous around thoroughly grounded salt-water in large quantities. Either the dolphin or the human could be strongly stimulated or badly burned or even electrocuted if mistakes are made involving switches, power outlets, and appliances. We have found that no wall switches, outlets, or electrical appliances can be anywhere near the walls or area enclosing the sea water. We have found that if we put in waterproof lights, run the cables out of the room and plug them in a dry isolated room which includes the switch, we avoid fires and shocks. In the current cooking experience a two-burner propane gas stove has been used with the gas supply outside of the building. The stove is raised far enough above the water to prevent sea water splash corroding the stove or spoiling the food. One suggested addition for a long-term living-in is some form of oven. For purposes of keeping food that needs refrigeration a gas refrigerator would be a welcome addition. Possibly low-voltage A.C. lights would be preferable to the present 115-volt lights.

The actual facility used departs from the above ideal in

some respects. The deep-water area is sixteen feet below the shallow-water and dry areas. It is necessary for the dolphins to take a trip on an electric hoist elevator in order to move from the shallow water to the deep water and vice versa (Plate 11). The deep water is a sealevel pool approximately sixty-five feet long, twenty feet wide, and 4½ feet deep, with its supply of fresh sea water furnished by the trade wind waves (Plates 9, 10). This is our emergency facility in case of power failure cutting off the pumping facilities at the higher levels in the building.

The shallow-water zone, the "encounter space," consists of two areas. The inside one is forty feet by twenty feet and the outside one is twenty feet by twenty feet (see photographs).

In the inside shallow-water space are the sleeping, cooking, and office facilities for the human. Analogous functions for the dolphin are carried out anywhere in the two areas.

The dry area is the rest of the building and contains fish storage, human food storage (including a refrigerator), human toilet facilities, and human dry sleeping facilities when needed.

Special aspects of the shallow-water facility are as follows: the inside room has a "recording studio" hung with carpets on walls and ceiling in an area twenty by fifteen feet to facilitate sound recording in air with minimal echoes. The recording itself is done on tape machines in an adjacent dry room. The microphones are protected by proper plastic bags and are hung from the ceiling in the recording area. Insofar as it is possible, vocal exchange lessons take place in this area. However, some interactions take place outside on the balcony and hence cannot be recorded.

The details of the construction of the facility can be adequately seen by careful inspection of the photographs and the captions. A floor plan of the facility is included in this report (Figure 14).

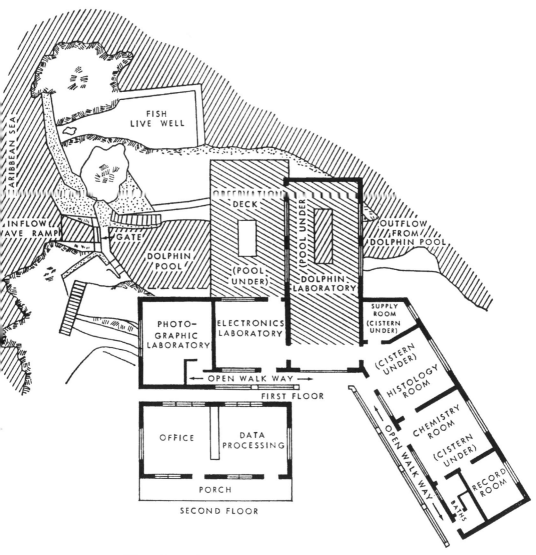

FIGURE 14. *The Floor Plan of the St. Thomas Laboratory Showing the Location of the Flooded Areas for the Living-in Experiment.*

The balcony is to the left and the inside room is to the right (marked with 45-degree lines). The sea pool is immediately below these two rooms, 16 feet below the floor level. The seawater in this space was kept at 18 inches for the period of the experiment.

History

It is considered desirable at this point to present what we can in the limited space of the history of the human participant in her relations with dolphins.

On February 7, 1964 Miss Margaret C. Howe joined the Communication Research Institute staff in St. Thomas. Up to that time she had seen dolphins once briefly in a Florida dolphin circus. From February 7, 1964 through April 5, 1964 she worked with dolphins, mainly with Peter, a male dolphin, in the Fiberglas tank (at that time in the upstairs room which was later flooded). The other two animals were in the sea pool. During this time there was a four-day period (April 10–13) in which she did her first vocal work with Peter. In this work she demanded that he make a sound before he was given a fish. This was Peter's first exposure to vocal work in the operant conditioning kind of situation.

On April 15, 1964 Pamela (a female dolphin) was brought upstairs and put into the tank with Peter. From this date until the seventeenth of May Margaret Howe worked with both Pam and Peter in the Fiberglas tank.

On the eighteenth of May 1964 Sissy was moved upstairs and put into the tank with the other two dolphins. Margaret continued to observe and work with all three. No vocal work was being done nor had there been any done since the four days in April with any of the dolphins.

On the twenty-second of May 1964 all three dolphins were moved into the sea pool and Margaret had her first look at all three together underwater through the observation bubble (see photograph). On this date several of the personnel at the laboratory began serially observing through the bubble and recording animal behavior in protocol book form. This type of work continued through the twenty-fifth of August 1964 (Plate 7).

From the twenty-fifth of August to the first of October Margaret continued to observe the dolphins underwater. Her main effort was spent in working with data of the past several months. Tapes and motion pictures of animal behavior were being worked on and developed. All three dolphins remained in the sea pool during this period.

From the second to the fifteenth of October 1964 there was a general transition period in the laboratory. The personnel were being changed and plans for a complete change in the research orientation and program were taking place. The three dolphins remained in the sea pool.

From the fifteenth to the thirty-first of October 1964 Margaret Howe was for the first time on her own at the laboratory. She was placed in complete charge. She learned to set up the electronic apparatus for recording vocal and underwater sounds. She made her first attempts at independent vocal work with each of the three animals in the sea pool. Some tapes of importance were obtained after this period.

On the second of November 1964 Peter was brought upstairs and put into the Fiberglas tank alone. Margaret concentrated on vocal work with him at this time. This is the beginning of the currently important data. Here Peter went through the transition phases of first responding to Margaret with no airborne sound at all and learning the rules of this game. When he gets the idea of responding to air sound with air sound he begins to click in air, to whistle in air, and to make humanoid sounds. This attempt is encouraged with special emphasis given to his "humanoid" emissions (these are the dolphins' sonic emissions which resemble somewhat some of the basic elements of human speech). Once Peter does learn that it is a humanoid sound that Margaret wants, he consistently interrupts her and has to learn to listen. Teaching him to listen is the next part of the program. Progress was made during this time up through the ninth of January 1965.

On that date Peter was put downstairs into the sea pool (Plate 8). Pam was moved upstairs into the Fiberglas tank. From the ninth of January through the nineteenth of March 1965 Margaret worked with Pam on vocalizations and on close human contact. In the period March 20 to 27 the seven-day experiment was accomplished. Margaret lived in the tank with Pam (see photographs). From the twenty-eighth of March through April 19 Pam remained upstairs, Margaret continued her vocal work with her, Peter and Sissy were in the sea pool. On the twentieth of April 1965 Peter was brought upstairs and put into the Fiberglas tank. Pam was brought downstairs and put into the sea pool.

Until the twelfth of May 1965 Margaret and Peter worked together on vocal responses. On the thirteenth of May Peter was put back into the sea pool with Sissy and Pam. He stayed here while Miss Howe made changes in the facility in preparation for the 2½-month experiment (see photographs).

On the fourteenth of June Peter was again brought upstairs, and put into the new flooded room area (see photographs). On the fifteenth of June Margaret Howe moved into the room with him to begin the "wet live-in" program for 2½ months.

On September 1, 1965 Margaret Howe moved out of the wet room. Between the fourteenth of September and the fourth of October Margaret was away from the laboratory. Peter was moved to the sea pool on the thirteenth of September and he was put back upstairs on the nineteenth of September 1965.

The above history does not give a description of possibly important factors in the development of Margaret Howe's training and experiences. The results of her experience are best given by Margaret herself. From this point on when it is germane Margaret's words will be given verbatim.

In summary Margaret Howe's experience at the Communication Research Institute, Dolphin Point Laboratory in St. Thomas, is as follows:

From the seventh of February 1964 to the latter part of October 1964 Margaret was a member of a group of nine humans. Eight and one-half months were spent with a group working on animal behavior with the three dolphins. From approximately the twentieth of October 1964 to the present, Margaret has been running the laboratory herself on this particular project with the aid and encouragement of Dr. Lilly, who has been able to spend approximately five days every month at the laboratory. Margaret's staff during this latter twelve months consists of herself and two or three workmen. Two workmen, Richard Turnbull and Aubrey Pickering, had experience previously in particular ways of handling, feeding, and caring for dolphins.

During the period that Margaret spent in the laboratory with eight other humans plus the three dolphins, she spent three months observing and writing her observations on the dolphins' behavior. This experience is very germane and useful for her in the context of the current experience. The perspective of the preliminary period leading up to these experiments in Margaret Howe's life is best given by a sample from her notes:

Date is Thursday August 13, 1964. Time is 1104 hours. Visibility is good. Pam is now swimming full length of pond. She is in her "spot only" routine. (What is the spot routine? I don't recall but I explain somewhere.) Pam and Peter rest by the inflow. Sissy is circling, sonaring by the hydrophone. Peter circles slowly. Now Sissy chases Peter. He bites along her. He does three half-leaps, they swirl, Sissy opens mouth wide and slides her teeth down his back. Peter turns over, he is now underneath her. Peter bites her throat. Lots of creaking door sonaring going on. Sissy swims to Pam, Peter follows her, biting at her tail. They hassle. Peter upside down again. They come mouth to mouth.

1110 hours. Peter bites hard on Sissy's eye. He puts his head under her genital region and bumps upward hard, squealing starts now. Whoooooo, whoooooo, by Sissy. She circles away from Peter, now back to him. He is after her tail in tight circles, lots of loud whooooo, whooooo. Sissy makes it and lets out a steady stream of bubbles from her blowhole as she does so. In center of pool the two line up face to face, not touching. Noses about four feet apart. Peter suddenly lurches forward after Sissy with mouth open. Sissy goes to Pam and they cruise together. Peter cuts in, haggles with Sissy, making whah, whah complaints. (Time for writing.) Pam's right eye closed now cruises with Sissy. Peter is alone, swimming around outside pool with his belly facing in towards the wall. Peter flips upside down and goes into chasing Pam. Pam leaps clear of water three times, turning to face opposite her way as she does. Pam slows down, Peter is immediately less intense in this chase, Pam noses along Peter's genital area, Sissy joins them and the three circle together.

1115 hours. Peter upside down nibbles Sissy. Sissy also turns upside down and continues whooo whoooo while upside down. I can see the stream of bubbles . . . the three cruise silently, aimlessly, Peter ahead by a length, Sissy outside and even with Pam who is inside. They come to a pause and rest at the surface (time gap for writing).

1120 hours. Peter and Pam both have their right eye closed. Sissy circles pool slowly. Fiddles with piece of grass. Pam undulates in place, Peter starts to circle her excitedly, always facing her with belly turned towards her. Sissy hovers nearby—Peter moves in and sonars Pam's genital region. Pam moves slowly in circle, Peter follows. Peter leads Pam sonars fish under grate, Sissy is resting near Pam. There is no intensity here, all three seem to be resting and doing not really much of anything. Nosing each other, sonaring genitals, fish hovering, grass playing, all seem to be just passing the time of day. Sissy is alone. Now she half leaps whapping the water with her side, again and again, fonp,

231

fonp, she smashes down. This must feel sensational. No one pays any attention to her for a while. She continues. Suddenly Peter from the opposite end of the pool faces her and I can hear him sonaring like mad. He slowly advances towards her, speed increases and he ends up flying at her with mouth open. They hassle. Pam comes over for a look. Peter squeals, races, trying to press genital regions to Pam, no erection, they have a big hassle, lots of bubbles, Sissy starts leaping and Peter follows suit. Pam dashes around, Peter noses into Sissy's neck, Sissy's flukes flick across Peter's genital, suddenly it is quiet. Rest period. Just as suddenly Sissy is whining and chasing after Peter's tail (gap for writing notes). Peter and Sissy swirl, Peter seems to be directing, pushing her around, nipping her here and there, and it seems that quite often their genital areas come in contact. This is very vigorous. Pam mildly observes an attempt.

1135 hours. Pam stays close to Sissy. Peter and Sissy seem angry at each other, are bopping and nipping and whah, whah, scolding each other. Sissy passes by Peter and wham. She slams him with her whole tail. I can feel the swell in the water as it hits the bubble. Pam is out of it but stays close to Sissy.

1145 hours. Suddenly the fight is over, and the three rest quietly together by the inflow.

I am confused by the way a vigorous looking and deathly sounding squabble can end with a big "nothing." Just suddenly turned off, then resting side by side, seemingly no interest in continuing the squabble????

M. Howe

The accumulated notes, observations, and to a certain extent, tapes, of this period of Margaret Howe's investigation of the dolphins is conserved and used by her in writing a report on this research.

I asked Margaret early in March 1965 to 1. give an account of her feelings of dolphins and their possible "code of living" with the directions "begin from the heart and work out," and 2. read and comment on the book *Planet of the Apes* by Pierre Boulle. These two papers contain information about Margaret's basic ideas and for that reason are included here.

Begin from the Heart and Work Out

I have worked with dolphins in two different ways: first, I spent time observing three animals (Peter, Pam and Sissy) together in a large sea pool with underwater vision available. Second, I have worked intensely with one animal at a time, both in lessons in English and in number systems and in close physical contact. I have been swimming with the animals involved. For half a year I have lived in a laboratory the only other occupants of which were the three dolphins. This is the longest period of time since I left home to go to school that I have shared living quarters with any other living being.

Living in a different environment from your roommate does eliminate certain obvious communal factors (clothes, social life conflicts, food sharing, and so forth): it does not eliminate communication and awareness of each other. I can hear or speak to any dolphin from any part of the building. This does not include their very high frequencies or their underwater sounds of course. It does include any air emissions or loud underwater sounds. I am usually a fairly light sleeper and at least one dolphin (the one who happens to be in the tank nearest my bedroom) can awaken me during the night. Let me say here I would like to work out and materialize an even closer living situation for man and dolphin.

From my work days with the dolphins and from my close living with them I have learned many things about their specific intelligence and learning ability and about their personalities. I have learned something of the dolphins' society as it exists among the three of them and man and dolphin society as it exists among the four of us. I have learned something of their ethics or civilization. This account will not deal with the intelligence and learning factors directly; it is more a general approach to the dolphins' code of living.

In observing animals together there is so much to see that it takes a good while to be able "to see" anything. And there is such a constant interaction and so few immediate repetitions of any one act between any two of them that it is hard to be conscious of what one is seeing. In fact for a while at least you are seeing simply a beak and an eye or two staring back at you! After a time it is possible to note not only the type of action, i.e., sex play, sleep, idle play alone, and so forth, but also to get a feeling of the mood in the pool in general or of that of any particular dolphin, i.e., extreme excitement, annoyance, or dissatisfaction, pleasure, boredom, and so forth. I do not deal here with the specific actions but rather I generalize about the mood.

The three animals consist of a young adolescent male and two more or less adult females: a dubious triangle. Sex play can occur between a male and a female, between two females or between all three animals at once. I did not witness jealousy between two animals strong enough to cause any real battle. Indeed never did I witness a situation that caused a real battle between any two of the dolphins. And yet, because this seemed an obvious outcome, we tried inducing outside factors to enable us to witness just such a show of strength or of dominance.

We tried tossing one ball into what seemed neutral territory of the pool occupied by the three dolphins. In most cases the dolphin to first reach the ball became its "owner." This dolphin would then "possess" the ball as it were, and play with it in front of the other animals. Only a few times did the ball "change hands" during such a period. More likely, even if "the owner" became distracted and left the ball for a moment, the ball would remain free and not be picked up by another dolphin. The owner was somehow secure and could return at his leisure. Several times the ball would be held onto the body of one dolphin by another dolphin but this could well be some sort of game brought about by invitation from the owner of the ball. We tried setting up the feeding situation where a neutral fish (this was later questioned—the fish had come from one bucket "belonging" to one of the dolphins) would be tossed out into neutral water in the center of the pool. The feeder avoided eye movement or any other indication of where the fish was going. Again the first dolphin to it, and there was no great hustle to get to it, was the owner or in this case the eater and that was that. This experiment was not repeated often enough to discover any patterns of who got the fish the most times, and so forth. But in all, a very mild, unemotional, organized and somewhat surprising and disappointing display to the human observers.

Does this "what's mine is mine and what's yours is not mine" attitude continue from dolphin-dolphin behavior to dolphin-human behavior? It would seem so.

We set up an experiment to get some sort of possessive or dominant reaction from a dolphin by attaching a ball to a long piece of stretch cord. We lowered the ball into the pool from the observation deck above, the ball touched the water, was sonared by the dolphin but was not touched by the dolphin. The game of "tug-of-war" on the ball did not materialize at all! Again this surprised and was somewhat a disappointment to the human observers.

(*Note:* in other experiments of this sort the animals have been known to not play tug-of-war with the ball but to bop it out of the water into the air and have it sink back into the water again.)

It must be emphasized that any of these experiments are subject to such uncontrollable factors as the mood of the dolphin, preference at the moment for a certain ball, interest in other activities, and so forth. But not once was there the slightest suggestion of taking the ball and "pulling" or trying to "take it away from" its original source, i.e., another dolphin.

What does not happen is quite as important as what does happen. Again it was observed that during feeding (and all animals at CRI are hand fed) animals preferred a slight toss of the fish. This could be a very slight passage of the fish into the air (even one-fourth of an inch), between human hand and dolphin mouth. One of our animals when hungry (I have tested this many times myself) is very reluctant to "take" a fish out of a human grasp. A dolphin will come and take an end of the fish in his mouth, feel even a slight resistance and let go or continue holding—but seldom will he pull it away. The dolphin must know that eventually that fish will "belong" to him but it would seem that they are reluctant to "take fish away from" a human hand: rather be given the fish with some neutral territory in between.

Along these same lines another incident occurred between Sissy and myself.

A camera crew was filming beside the pool, I was in the water swimming with Sissy. We had played a bit and I was without a mask. My mask was lying on a wall just above sea level. Apparently wave action knocked it into the water and it sank to the bottom about two feet down. For a moment I could not find it and then discovered that Sissy was hovering above it. I approached to pick it up, Sissy sank a bit and "sat" on it. This indicated to me that it was, for the moment at least, "her" mask. I tried for several minutes (with an amused camera crew looking on) to get the mask from Sissy. Sissy bopped at me with her beak and I withdrew. We had to get on with the filming and that was the one mask I was most comfortable in. I obtained another mask and tossed it five or six feet away, it sank. Sissy was distracted and went to investigate. I bent to pick up "my" mask and Sissy came streaking across the pool, barking and opening and closing her mouth at me. I was threatened and withdrew. Looking back I am annoyed at myself for breaking the "dolphin law." I knew perfectly well that I was not to "take" that mask but human trickery had taught me how to get it. Another dolphin, I believe, would not have "taken" the mask from Sissy nor used trickery.

Another interesting point: I went back into the water with Sissy several minutes later and finished the filming. I was a bit cautious expecting Sissy to be annoyed or resentful. Not so. Sissy had forgotten the incident or considered it closed. It was "my mask" again.

With single dolphins alone I started a new series of encounters. In a smaller tank on an upper level I worked intensely with one dolphin at a time, teaching English and a number system. I have worked this way with Peter, a young male and with one of the females, Pamela.

Peter is young, boyish and tends to be the "naughty" one of

the three dolphins. He delights in such mischief as plugging up the outflow of his tank with a toy so that the tank eventually fills to the brim and spills over. I came in to find Peter joyously leaping about in this great sloshing tank. I scold him in English. (I had not tried the dolphin discipline actions, such as a firm whack over the head.) Peter responds with a slight sulk but is very inclined to be "naughty" again when he has the opportunity.

When I first met Peter he was very used to a game with other persons that involved a human arm or hand inside his mouth rubbing his gums. Being a "green novice" I was having no part of this game and refused to play it. Peter soon learned that he was not to scare me with his open jaws and now is very gentle with me and seldom opens his mouth. I say seldom because this involves another point.

Without exception I have found that when displeased or angered by human actions that any of these three dolphins will "threaten" or "warn" the human before going into further discipline. This threat is in the form of 1. opening and closing of the mouth in a warning manner: 2. a rapid bobbing up and down or sidewise movements of the head in a "go away" gesture; or 3. a vocal "whah, whah" indicating annoyance. I have seen all three methods of warning used by an animal to humans and also to other dolphins, and one soon learns to respect such a warning. One is expected to.

All of this builds into such a nice way of life. Possessions are "owned and not fought over." People or animals are "warned" that they are doing something wrong. Discipline is brief, quite clear and then over. Can these animals not be incited to some very aggressive, hostile, in a word, "human" act?

On one occasion I observed Peter in a situation that certainly seemed to call for such a reaction. For several months I had been carrying on a personal battle with a rat in the laboratory. A sly character who occasionally gave me glimpses of his disappearing tail and left lovely traces of his presence during the night. He was also seen on the wires to the lights above Peter's tank. One night I turned on the lights apparently startling the rat and he fell smack dab into the middle of the tank with Peter. Three human friends visiting me and I rushed to witness the action. The sides of the tank are smooth and slightly slanted, the rat could not climb out. All of the humans around that tank including myself were anxious to see Peter snap at, bop around, drown, flip into the air, *something* that rat. Peter looked at the rat, sonared it briefly, nudged it a bit and then ignored it. Peter was much more interested in the people around him who were obviously very excited about something. I tried putting the rat afloat on a piece of board in the tank (see photographs). Again Peter took a look at this setup and nudged it briefly and then *nothing!* We stayed with it for a half an hour, simply not able to believe that Peter was not going to open his jaws and devour or at least mutilate that rat. Indeed not, the incident ended and the anticlimax was my putting the rat into the outflow and sending him to his burial at sea. Again Peter had displayed to me the possibility of a non-hostile code of living. How delightful!

And along with this lack of hostility in the dolphin must be explained a certain caution, possibly stemming from their life at sea and the needs for caution. Any new object that is introduced into a pool with the dolphin is first sonared and observed visually before being touched. This extends from a small piece of paper to a human being. Even a small living fish tossed into the pool is carefully sonared before it is snapped at, if indeed it is snapped at at all. Our animals are fed dead fish and are fed so well that it is difficult to get a normal reaction to a living fish.

By citing these various instances I do not mean to give the impression that dolphins are totally devoid of moments of violence. These are very powerful, fast animals capable under moments of stress of a very impressive show of strength.

But I am implying the possibility of a lack of wheeling and dealing, of cheating and stealing and lying and other seemingly small but nevertheless devious ways of life stemming from human foible. From what I have observed and felt I do not feel that a dolphin newspaper, if one could exist, would contain articles on robbery, murder, dishonesty, delinquency, riots.

This business of communicatively joining the two species, man and dolphin, is very new but is progressing rapidly in proportion to the obstacles to be overcome. The biggest factor in this rapid progress is not only the widening human interest and anxious anticipation of the wide possibilities, but also of the dolphin's own interest and cooperation in seemingly just as strong anxiety to "get on with it." We must remember that as they live and work with us they are learning not only the lessons in English and number systems, etc., they also are learning, just as are we, about another way of life. A new set of ethics and morals. Let us determine at the outset to be cautious of what we let the dolphins observe, learn and instinctively "feel" about all this. Let us be open to the possibility of learning and practicing what we learn from the examples set by the peaceful, gentle, and not to be overlooked in a time when ulcers and nail-biting are part of our every day life, *happy* dolphin!! [End of Margaret Howe's account.]

Planet of the Apes by Pierre Boulle

I found this exchange of man and apes on the evolutionary scale delightful and witty, and substituting dolphin intelligence for that of the apes, entirely believable.

But there is one point raised by the overall pattern of the book that bothers me deeply:

The pattern runs . . .

(1) Earth: Man dominate, ape subordinate,

(2) Betelgeuse: Ape dominate, man subordinate,

(3) Earth: Ape dominate, man subordinate, and we have every indication that had our travelers returned to the planet of apes, the time lapse would have allowed for

(4) Betelgeuse: Man dominate, ape subordinate.

Why why why must there be a dominance and a subordination??? Why must man *take over* or why must the apes *take over*?

I have occasion every day to look an animal (dolphin) straight in the eye and to speak and listen and smile and scold and somehow try to bridge the verbal gap that does exist between myself and this other intelligence whose existence I accepted as fact long ago.

But never never have I imagined that when the dolphin one day learns the form of our intelligence would he then proceed to "take over" this planet. No more than I have imagined that man must strive to keep the dolphin subordinate and "under control."

Can it be, as Boulle suggests, that within one environment, land, only one species will be allowed to hold superior intelligence? This may well be so. In this case man and dolphin could exist on an equal level . . . man on land and dolphin in the water.

But this simplicity is poppycock. Land, sea, and air melt into one to intelligent beings. So we cannot accept that man is most intelligent on land and Cetacea (dolphin) in the water. We must face the thought of the two equal intelligences on equal footing on this planet. This may well already exist, with the only missing link being communication. When that link is no longer missing and dolphin and man can communicate thoughts to each other (and that day will come!) will we be faced with a war situation? With a conquer-or-be-conquered atmosphere? I sincerely hope not.

Looking back it could have been that instead of the happy bisexual society that we live in, fate might have swung us to a monosexual society simply through this boring "one must be superior" routine.

Looking ahead it may well be that one day we will find it hard to imagine a monospecies society . . . as we live happily in our quite normal bispecies culture . . . that of Man and Dolphin.

Margaret Howe

My comments:

This account clearly shows the basic feelings and enthusiasm of Miss Howe taking hold with the dolphins. She sees clearly, writes clearly, thinks and feels clearly. She thinks well on her feet; her actions are appropriate. These are the talents she brings to this project. We avoided choosing a psychologist, a psychoanalyst, a comparative zoologist or any other person in a specialty within science itself. A more pragmatic, general yet direct approach than any one of the present sciences offers is sought. I felt that to carry out this project a rather rare human being uniquely herself is needed. She is dedicated to getting the project finished. Keeping her eyes as open as she possibly can, as open to all lines of evidence and truth testing as she herself is capable of, she operates without reference to artificial criteria generated by scientists.

In the preliminary experiment of seven days and nights with Pamela Dolphin, Miss Howe found much information useful for planning the 2½ months' experimental period. She found data on herself, the dolphin, their interactions, she found by experience the problems and some solutions regarding the clothing, the wetness, the walking, the cooking, and the rest of the real living-in situation. She wrote an account of this full week.

The full progression from the past into the future includes a long-term plan of setting up a house which dolphins can share with humans. Among other things, Miss Howe is planning such a house in the following write up. As a result of the seven days' experiment, she has many suggestions in the way this house should be constructed. These suggestions insofar as can be done are then followed for the 2½ months' experiment which follows the seven days' experiment. The 2½ months' experiment is the second phase of the long-term plan to develop a living-in program between Margaret and a dolphin. The house is an essential facility for this future development and these preliminary experiments are necessary for the proper design of this house.

CHAPTER 11

Living with a Dolphin:
Seven Days and Nights with Pam

A PRELIMINARY seven days and seven nights with a dolphin was arranged with Margaret Howe. The aims of this experiment were to test human and dolphin tolerance to a set depth (sixteen inches) of sea water, to find particulars of human needs such as clothing, food, fresh water, dry items (pens, paper, books), to find the limits of human tolerance of sleeping on wet bed in wet clothing, to see progress in human-dolphin relationship during such close living, to continue vocal lessons with dolphin and record same, and show vocal progress under such conditions.

The following is Miss Howe's account of this period:

In sixteen inches of water a human can maneuver, walk, work at a desk, sit in a chair, eat.

It was shown in this experiment, however, that at least with this particular dolphin, sixteen inches is not enough to allow her back, over a period of time, to remain wet enough for a normal, healthy skin. Pamela could have kept wet by constantly bobbing and causing waves to wash over her back. A tiresome task and Pam chose not to. Her back at the end of the week was not seriously dried and cracked, but it was bad enough to show that longer exposure to this environment would lead to trouble.

In this depth there is a limit to the maneuvering a dolphin can do (Plates, 12, 13, 14, 15). Jumping, swishing around, high-speed swimming are limited if not eliminated. It must be remembered that Pamela, at the time of the experiment, had an injured flipper and was going through a very inactive period. I believe that a healthy animal with no injuries would, after not very long, go "stir crazy" and long for deep enough water to leap and dive in. I feel that this should be available to her or him.

This depth (sixteen inches) seems rather ideal for the human: it is shallow enough to walk in without any great hindrance. (Knee-deep water is very difficult to walk in. Sixteen inches is midway up my calf, 19½ inches is at my knee joint.) It is shallow enough to allow a chair to sit in it with the seat above the waterline. It is shallow enough so that normal splashes made by the dolphin rolling or turning over are not high enough to reach human things—desk, papers, TV, etc. It is deep enough to allow humans to sit and float with ease and therefore get "down next to" the dolphin. And a small point but important in this experiment: it is deep enough so that when sitting in the chair I could drop my hand loosely over the side and have it in the water, thus affording Pam an opportunity to rub my hand.

I would recommend that in the final experiment, sixteen inches of water flood the entire house. There must also be, however, a deeper (thirty inch) passageway through the house in which the dolphin can travel and maneuver; thus he could lie in "his" space in the kitchen, watching you, decide to come to you, and simply go from thirty inches to sixteen inches of water to do so.

I also recommend somewhere in the house a deep pool, at least six feet deep for the dolphin "to be a dolphin in." This should be connected to the other waters. While thinking of all this I have also thought about walls and doors.

A special "dolphin door" is used by both humans and dolphins. The open space under the door has double purposes: 1. humans walking through the doorway will not have to pull the door against the weight of the water; all of the swinging part of the door will be in air; 2. the bottom of the door is higher than sixteen inches above the water level to afford the dolphin dorsal fin space to go through with the door closed.

Living for a week is very different from living for a year or more. However, from my experience I have found that clothing —wet suits, top and bottom and two-piece so that one can be removed—is vitally important in a room where air temperature is between 79°F and 83°F. I found leotards good for drying speed and protection (warmth), but the top piece fits too closely through the crotch. It was from this garment that I got so chapped. I am not sure, however, that a looser garment would solve this problem. Loose garments can chap too . . . they even rub the skin more. One note on bras: hooks on the back can tend to "wilt" and I found that one was at a bad angle and was digging into my back. I had to bend it back into place several times. A bra without hooks would be good . . . but elastic would not hold up either. A problem.

It is very important, even during one week, to have dry clothes available. Shorts, shirts, anything. The human is used to changing clothes and feeling "fresh," and just because the clothes will end up wet 95 per cent of the time is no reason to assume that there is no reason for change. Wet clothes get a soggy feel to them after a while, and it is desirable to get into dry clothes and then get *them* wet. They will not have the same soggy, rundown feel. Example: it is desirable to change daytime clothes to sleep clothes, and in the morning to change from sleep clothes to daytime clothes. The outfit is unimportant, the wetness of the clothes is unimportant . . . the change is very important. I recommend more experiments on what clothes are comfortable when wet. That a supply of clothes be available. At the house or an outside source there should be a setup to handle the laundry problem. Include sheets (not necessary), towels, blankets, quilts, etc. (see discussion on sleeping), all of which must be attended to.

I found that during this week I did not covet fresh water as much as I thought I would. I was seldom thirsty, not that I was seldom overheated. I did need fresh water for washing my face in the morning, and for my teeth; (saltwater toothpaste is so-so and promises to get boring after a period of time). I did not rinse my hands with fresh water before reading, writing, and so forth. Perhaps this should be done as I did have slight discomfort with my fingers, probably from constant salt contact.

I recommend fresh-water taps in each room. Bathroom with fresh-water shower. Clean hair, and body become important even after one week although not desperate. But long range . . . shower would become very important. None of these fresh-water outlets would need a drain. They could run right onto the "floor" of the sixteen inches of salt water.

If there are (a) water and (b) a dolphin in the same room, things are going to get wet. In sixteen inches of water, Pamela could soak the TV which was a good six feet off the floor. Obviously, the human things need to be dry. Pen, paper, TV, electrical items, etc. I had relatively few items during my week's experiment and Pam was relatively quiet and still. [This quietness may have been because of her injury.]

I recommend that more experiments be done in setting up and care of objects for humans. That the house have high shelves, high electrical outlets (if any), high electrical equipment (if any), and a design of covering to "dry store" things. Perhaps "dry" areas of work, a raised platform with a desk on it. Cupboards at top of walls with access only to humans. This is purely a designer's problem.

During this week, all my food was cooked outside the room and brought to me. The problem in the flooded house would, of course, be different, as the person would have a kitchen. I do not think that any rigid diet need be set up for the human. I do recommend that canned foods be kept in dry store and that the cooking facilities be as simple as possible. Two burners are quite adequate. Butterfish is excellent fried and this could be a simple source of food [but possibly monotonous]. Electric or gas facilities in the design of the kitchen must be thoroughly investigated; I will not do that here.

During my week I slept usually in daytime clothes, wet, in a bed that was wet, with a dry quilt that got wet, with a dry pillow that got wet, except for a corner I would protect with my cheek. Several times I went to bed in dry clothing, but the bed was still wet. This meant that the clothes became damp through the night. Several times I became uncomfortable when sleeping, because my skin itched. I suspect that this was due to the amount of time I spent in the same clothes, rather than to the fact that I was damp or wet. Usually I slept well and several times was surprised by a very sound sleep.

Sleep patterns are broken with a dolphin. Many times I was awakened in the night by a restless-hungry Pam. This is O.K. but must be accounted for. I solved it by taking daily naps, as closely as I could matching my sleeping patterns with the dolphin's sleeping or resting patterns.

I recommend that more experiments be done to determine results of "wet" sleeping.

NOTE: I had a stiff neck on my last day in the tank and on the day following my getting out. Did wet sleeping cause this? I would like to see experiments done to determine if dry sleeping, still in close proximity to the dolphins, is possible. Sleep for a week is unlike sleep for a year or more. Is "wet" sleeping the answer?? Is sleeping in heated water the answer?? Is dry sleeping the answer?? I do not know. I do recommend being flexible enough to match the dolphins' sleeping pattern. A man and a dolphin will have a year of wake hours and of sleeping hours, and there is no necessity for eight hours awake, eight hours asleep, and so forth. What *is* important is enough sleep/rest for both, *not* when it is obtained.

A note on cleaning; during even one week in this small tank, dirt collected and sat on the bottom. In a house, where the dolphin is not constantly stirring up the bottom of each room, this would surely happen. There must be a system for draining that would allow scrubbing. Also a "vacuum" of a siphon hose should be available. This seems to be the best way to clean dirt out of water . . . without draining.

A week is a very short time and every animal is different. I decided only one thing at the outset of my experiments: to be in no rush "to make anything happen between us" and to let Pam take the initiative as much as possible. I was glad I made that decision; I stick by it, whether for a week or for a year. I found, during this week, a nice slow, steady, sweet binding of the relationship between us. Our mutual relationship was, for a day and a half, zero; we had no contact—slowly I approached Pam . . . and she allowed stroking.*

Then she invited this . . . turning on side, etc. Long rub sessions slowly turned the tide so that soon she was coming to me . . . rubbing my legs, hands. Until almost the end of the week Pam would not eat from me in the tank. She would not even take food from an outside source with me in the tank. Slowly all this resolves itself until Pam, at the end of the week, is taking fish from me while I am in the tank . . . sitting or standing.

Progression in familiarity and boldness can be seen throughout the week. In the beginning there is a very polite, gentle, "tippy-toe" business of getting to know you.

Toward the end of the week, we were both loosened up to the point of Pam demanding attention from me, interrupting conversations, flapping tails to get my attention, etc. And I am feeling freer with her . . . at one point I let loose and yell at her to stop something that is annoying me.

I think that this change of mood in the tank is interesting and important. I am not saying that any politeness or gentleness stops; I am saying that both parties become freer to make their wishes known to the other.

I recommend that in any other preliminary experiment or in the flooded house itself . . . nothing should be rushed. That the dolphin be allowed to go at its own pace . . . and each animal may be different in this. Over a longer period of time, lessons are scheduled throughout the day . . . and that the time in-between living be as easy and free for both parties as possible.

During this week, I recorded only one lesson with Pam. It was not until the end of the week that I was able to feed her from within the tank anyway, and then very often she would eat only a few fish. Over a longer period of time, I feel sure that the dolphin vocalization would increase . . . encouraged by the human

---

* [A clinical note on Pam. This dolphin had been badly traumatized. Her behavior is in general "distant," "remote." She is shy and retiring. She is wary and cautious. She gives one the feeling, however, that she is also gentle and wants to make contact but something is keeping her from that contact. We know that before she joined us she had been through two traumatic episodes which we do not describe here.]

247

. . . and would become part of the in-between living as well as part of the lesson.

Pam did, immediately upon my entering the tank . . . show a willingness to respond vocally to me. It was in delphinese, however. And only after a period of time did she begin to vocalize in any humanoids. I believe that the closer you are physically to the dolphin the closer you can get vocally. And during a week's time the progress here can be very slow, but over a year(s) . . . such a situation should have spectacular results.

I would like to see a house built so that a man and a dolphin could actually live together for one, two, or three years. If dolphins are truly going to learn to speak to us in English, I think they must have a much greater exposure to us and our language than the two hours or so per day they get in the present lessons at the laboratory. Eventually the whole living situation could be a lesson with us. With the animal learning more and more and the human demanding more and more English words before he will respond to the dolphin's wishes.

No one will ever know the outcome of such a living experiment until it is done. We owe it to the dolphin and to our curiosity to try it.

This is Margaret Howe's seven days and nights with Pam as she reported it. In this report the planning ahead for a much longer experiment of living in the wet environment, Margaret with a dolphin, is given. At this point she was willing to commit 2½ months or approximately one thousand hours to the project. This is in spite of interferences with her private life and the satisfaction of her social needs. In a sense Margaret is insisting that the world come to her and her dolphin. She cannot go out to the world during this experiment. Let us now enter into the experiment through the program that she set up for herself to carry out. After this we will give the detailed reporting during the 2½ months, as written by her at the time.

It is to be emphasized that the experiments are considered by Margaret to be still preliminary. The flooded house program for "permanent" dolphin-human living is uppermost in her mind. Therefore she calls this a "program for a 2½ months' preliminary experiment."

Margaret and I had many conferences before, during and after the seven-day experiment: planning strategies, compromises, costs, materials, personnel, were all discussed. After such conferences, Margaret then took the initiative within the limits of the possible and carried out the actual details. Since what she *did* is the important data and since this is based on *her final plans,* the content of our conferences is not recorded. Though possibly important, only the reflections of this content through the mirror of Margaret's writing is left in this account.

CHAPTER 12

Program for a 2½ Months' Preliminary Experiment: Living with Peter Dolphin in a Special Facility

Before the live-in began a program was laid out as follows: The experiment is to be carried out at St. Thomas, U. S. Virgin Islands, in the Dolphin Point Laboratory of the Communication Research Institute during the months of June, July, and August of 1965. One human and one dolphin are to live together day and night, for the period. They will eat, sleep, play, and work together within the boundaries set up by the experiment. Details of these boundaries will be included in this report (Plates 17–21).

The purposes of the human are 1. to gain information about the learning ability of a dolphin exposed to such an intense and prolonged interspecies isolation with the human; 2. to attempt to teach the dolphin to "speak" English and to "understand" English; 3. to gain additional information in order to properly design the flooded house. (The only previous experiment known to us along this line is a one-week period, March 20 to 27, 1965, during which Margaret Howe and Pamela Dolphin lived together in the Fiberglas tank at the St. Thomas laboratory. The results and recommendation for that week's experiment have resulted in the extended experiments started in June.)

Daily notes and recordings are kept in the St. Thomas

laboratory by Margaret Howe. Included is a general weekly summary report by Miss Howe. No visitors are accepted in these two rooms or to the electronics room without an appointment set up by Miss Howe. All visitors are to be recorded in the notes.

Any changes in schedule are to be made only if initiated or approved of by Miss Howe. She accepts responsibilities to make changes as she sees fit. She will be out of the tank all day Saturday. In part the time on Saturday is spent organizing tapes of the previous week and setting up tapes for the following week. Weekly reports are to be done.

At any time during the 2½ months, should Miss Howe become ill or in any way physically discomforted, she may withdraw temporarily any time she finds necessary. Any withdrawal must be noted.

Following is an outline of the daily schedule to be followed, subject to later changes by Miss Howe.

7:30 Miss Howe gets up, washes, eats.

8:00 to 8:30 Recorded lesson with Peter, five pounds of fish.

9:00 Miss Howe daily cleaning, vacuum, etc.

9:30 Miss Howe does feeding, notes, protocol, check workmen.

10:00 to 10:30 Miss Howe and Peter play . . . involves some lessons.

11:00 Miss Howe and Peter outside . . . together but relaxed.

11:30 Miss Howe gets lunch.

12:00 to 12:30 Recorded lesson with Peter, five pounds of fish.

1:00 to 2:30 Miss Howe sleeps, fun, write, read, relax.

3:00 to 3:30 Recorded lesson with Peter, five pounds of fish.

4:00 to 4:30 Time spent working with Peter.

5:00 to 5:30 Miss Howe works on notes, bills, tomorrow's schedule.

6:00 Miss Howe has dinner.

6:30 Games with Peter, visitors, reading . . . always with awareness of living with Peter.

End of day and work is over, the two are still together.

10:00 Bed.

Above schedule to be followed Sunday through Friday. Saturday is a free day for Miss Howe; Saturday night sleep with Peter.

The language lessons will use a basic vocabulary in various categories as follows:

Basic vocabulary for both pronunciation and comprehension: numbers (1–5); personal names (Peter, Margaret, me, you); greetings (hello, bye-bye); objects (ball, toy fish, bucket, bobo clown, kinipopo, baby block); actions (speak, listen, come, go, give me, etc.).

To teach number, it is planned to use a series of balls with hooks in each end. The balls can be easily put together by the operator in any combination or taken apart. Many ways can be used to teach numbers. The human can hold a string of balls and point at the balls as she says them . . . "one, two, three," etc. The human can hold a string of two in one hand and a string of three in the other, and correspondingly show that one is two, one is three. Addition and subtraction are endless.

One problem is to teach the dolphin to say the name of the number, rather than to teach him to make the appropriate number of sounds for numbers. First, have the dolphin repeat after you. Second, demand that the dolphin name, number, or count the series of balls you hold up without you speaking.

So little is known as to what dolphins do and do not know about color. I suggest this not be among the first lessons, as the response of the dolphin may be nil anyway. Use wooden plaques all the same size and shape, the only difference being their color. First, have dolphin repeat after you; second, demand that the dolphin name the color as you hold up the plaque.

Shape can get involved with various named angles and so on, but I suggest one begin with basic shapes. Use wooden plaques of the same approximate size and color, with the only difference being shape. As above, dolphin comprehension can be kept track of by first having the animal repeat after you and, second, demanding that the animal name the shape of the plaque that you hold up.

If we are going to get into small sentences with these dolphins, it seems essential that names be used, both proper, "Peter," "Margaret," etc.; also, such as "you" and "me" should be taught.

Greetings explain themselves. The only reason I used them at all is 1. as a signal ("bye-bye . . . lesson is over," etc.), and 2. "hello" is such a natural thing to say when entering a tank or a room. These are getting into the area where it is hard to know if the dolphin understands.

The list of objects can be changed according to the animal and the surroundings. It should be flexible . . . if the dolphin should get an ashtray into the water and play with it, it should have a name.

I suggest, as with all of these words on the vocabulary lists, that once a word is learned and the meaning understood, it should not be allowed to lapse from the list. If Peter learns what an ashtray is, it should not then be put into another room and forgotten. It should become part of Peter's things and should be used.

Anatomy is a difficult area in that it is hard to get the dolphin to identify the object with the word. I suggest, when patting Peter's tail, to name it over and over. Then change to saying "tail" to him and coaxing him to offer you his tail.

Getting the animal into some sort of game is a good way to bring action. I "throw" ball. Peter, "GO GET IT" or "PICK IT UP." "BRING IT HERE" . . . "GIVE IT TO ME" . . . , etc. This list should be added as new actions are taught and played with. This is more readily done with human speaking and animal acting. Not until much later will we probably have such a thing as Peter telling me to "go and get" something (at that point I will become his most humble slave!).

In all of the above I suggest the gradual getting away from fish as a reward, and using instead as a reward the human's obvious pleasure with results, petting, vocal rewards, etc. To do this I will try:

1. Fish as a reward after each response.
2. Fish as a reward after every other correct response.
3. Gradually move to having lessons just before feeding.
4. Gradually move lesson farther away from feeding.
5. Make feeding at this point as dull and unrewarding as possible. The feeder not to speak to the dolphin and to feed at a rate so that the dolphin has no chance to speak.

Usual human participant will not feed the dolphin.

This is all a long-range program. It is essential first to get the animal volunteering humanoids and to obtain a sense of listening, then speaking.

WEEKLY REPORTS—M. Howe. Written during the 2½ months' experience:

June 15 to 19, 1965. First Week

I must say that this week for the main part, is a week on preparation and adjustment. Peter was brought upstairs on Monday. He seemed happy and contented with his new home, but as yet he has not ventured outside. I tried coaxing him during one meal but no go. I may force him out next week just to get going.

I have been so busy getting ready for this experiment at the beginning and had two very disappointing times of filling the completed tank rooms only to find leaks. Once I was ready and the rooms were flooded to twenty-two inches I found that there were a lot of last-minute things to get and hence a day of in and out of the flooded room. On Tuesday night I was fairly settled.

The first few nights in the flooded room were awful. I was uncomfortable and hardly slept. Later I seemed to adjust to that and by Thursday I was fine. I found that it was very tiring just to walk across the flooded room. Everything I do takes more energy than it normally would; but I take a nap in the afternoon and that seems fine.

Peter is his energetic self and a bit nippy on the toes. I carry a long-handled broom with me for that and ward him off. This is not always the case, of course: we have had several long "loving" sessions. The water is deep enough for him to roll over and this he does for tummy rubs. He sleeps just next to my bed . . . some nights he has been quiet and others he just has to yell and splash around. He is always hungry . . . and usually wakes me early in the morning to tell me to feed him.

Lessons have gone fairly well . . . I start with counting and shapes. I am stopping, however, for the moment . . . go back and get Peter into the habit of listening. Speaking. He seems to have lost his sense of conversation. He often overrides me. One thing at a time. I cannot teach him if he is going to yell every time I open my mouth. He has said, for the tape . . . one clear word, "BALL." This came in the middle of one of his ramblings by himself and it could contain no meaning. But it is good pronunciation . . . in a nice comparison with Pam's "BALL."

We have several games—the most promising of which seems to be a retrieving game with the dishcloth or the ball. I throw the cloth, squeal "Go get it" to Peter . . . he dashes away . . . brings it to me . . . and willingly flings it in my direction. This seems endless. I would like to work it into a business of "Bring ball" or "Bring cloth" and get him to tell the difference. A step in the right direction.

He had picked up a nice business of following the inflection in my voice . . . "one, two, three, four" . . . with an upturn on the "four."

We have played several times with his brush . . . he loves to be brushed gently with it. I usually do this in front of his mirror where Peter spends a good deal of his time. I name the brush as I use it. So far Peter has not copied this.

Several personal notes that I will put in here and be done with. I find that clothes are no problem. I spend the day in a bathing suit . . . shower before dinner and put on the top of a leotard. I have not been cold yet, at night I do not use the wet suit. The room is warm, the nights are not . . . I have not had the problem of cold that I had with Pam.

The bed is usually damp by night, but it wipes off and half the time I don't use the quilt. I have sprayed several times for bugs, but they have not bothered me.

Cooking is fine.

Cleaning is interesting. I find that I must do it several times a day, the waterflow is in my favor. Each morning most of the dirt is neatly deposited at the foot of the elevator shaft. All I have to do is suck it up. This I tried with the vacuum from Miami . . . found it did not pull enough; I put a hose through the elevator down to the sea pool, fill it with water to start a siphon, and find it has a good pull. Only problem is a small mouth. Perhaps a funnel at my end of the hose will fix that. Also, the dirt collects several times a day . . . so I have to do this several times a day. Outside is another problem: algae grow on the walls . . . I clean it daily . . . cleaning the floor is not so easy. There is a stronger flow there and the dirt scattered. It will not collect in a pile. But in general the place stays cleaner than I thought it would . . . and the seawater is always clear . . . not milky.

In the shower I have been using a children's shampoo; it does not sting the eyes. Peter stays under the shower with me and does not seem the least affected by the soap so I will assume that in a large quantity of water its effects are negligible.

When the phone rings . . . it usually takes me a while to get to it . . . and on the way I explain . . . "telephone" to Peter. He often hears me talking and starts in vocalizing . . . very loudly and in a competitive way some time . . . it is amusing. I encourage this. (See photograph.) Peter uses the mirror . . . talks to himself . . . scolds . . . shoots water at his image. I plan to get a microphone over him to get some of these private conversations. A good deal of the talk that Peter does when he is "alone" is now in humanoid. Interesting and encouraging.

The one thing I really don't like is Peter's loss of ability to listen. He must learn this soon or I will be tempted to get Pam up here. Peter is good and loud and humanoid but he is slow to really pronounce . . . and he is forever interrupting. But I will give him at least another week.*

Another interesting point . . . I found that when I listened back to the tapes I had made during the week . . . I was much more encouraged than I was at the actual lesson. I do not get to listen to the tapes during the week. I have just spent all day Saturday checking up on records, bills, and tape listening. I may change my schedule to Saturday out of the tank but working in the electronics room on work done previous week . . . and take Sunday out of tank and use it as a free day.

Outside work is being done . . . I looked at the wall around Pam's future tank. It is about four feet high all the way around, it may be finished this week . . . in which case we can get the water systems in and make it ready to get Pam up the following week. Pam and Sissy are both downstairs in the algaefied sea pool. But that will have to go for the moment. New concrete should be in soon to fix that situation.

To sum up . . . a good few days' beginning . . . and several nice games, lessons, habits started. I am pleased . . . and look forward to the next week.

June 19 to 25, 1965. Second Week

Several new things developed this week.

First, Peter and I got on a more sociable, physical level. Peter began to be gentle with me, and allow me to go to him without

---

* Before these experiments began, it was questioned as to whether to work with Peter or with Pamela. Pamela (from the previous work with her) had good pronunciation. Peter was more vigorous but had poorer pronunciation.

the broom. He did not nip at me as he used to . . . rather he was making a thorough study of my feet, legs, ankles, knees. Doing this he is very gentle . . . the rough part being when he tries to push me around. He gets between my legs and pushes me apart. When he starts to nip . . . I make a big fuss . . . shout at him and retreat. But we are getting much friendlier . . . and I feel more comfortable with him.

Second, my earlier thoughts on Peter are coming true; Peter is more and more inclined to "play games" and speaking is going rather slowly.

I will take advantage of this . . . and use the games all I can for speaking. We will continue to play the "towel fetch" game and the "cloth fetch" game. We have gotten so far as to have three balls thrown and collected and brought back to me. From this I can start to name the number of balls, and try to get him to fetch only one, or only two. He is very enthusiastic about this game . . .

Listening to the tapes . . . I find the most encouraging thing is that Peter does seem to be working. He is taking his sweet time in really beginning to listen to me again . . . I have had several sessions where I have really had to yell at him to bring order to the lesson. One time I let him ramble on and on, but I tried to copy all of *his* sounds. The tape was interesting. I was surprised at how well I was able to copy at least his pitch . . . and how he seemed to test me with new combinations of sounds.

I have concentrated mainly on counting and shape lessons.

I recorded one spontaneous game developed when we were watching TV. The TV is on in the background, and Peter and I are playing with the towel. Peter speaks for it, I throw it, he gets it, brings it to me, and on and on.

I do not know how long Peter will stick at this game . . . I always get tired before he does. It would be interesting to just keep going until he tires of it.

Peter eats well. Only once has he refused a meal, and then he ate it about an hour later. Occasionally when I am eating something he sets up a row . . . open mouth "feed me" kind of thing . . . and I toss him a piece of whatever I am having. A sardine was the most interesting . . . he mashed it up a bit before dropping it.

I am well pleased with all of Peter's activities except his apparent vocal ability. He is more than eager . . . works hard . . . but he just does not seem to hear or be able to copy the pronunciation aspects of speech. Perhaps this will come . . . perhaps not. He has said a clear "ball"; he has worked well on the beginning of the word "one" . . . the "wa" . . . and best of all he does seem to have a nice sense of pitch.

By this I mean that when I count, "one, two, three," my voice will often rise on the "three" . . . and often Peter will copy this rise in the last of the three sounds. This is true of words like "triangle" also. And "hello." I try to say one word the same way each time . . . sometimes I fail but for the most part I am consistent in my inflections and Peter is beginning to pick this up.

He has been practicing with the pronunciation of the letter "M" from "Margaret," no doubt . . . and is discovering that rolling slightly so that his blowhole is just under the water gives a satisfactory "M" effect. (Pam has done exactly the same thing.)

Peter is certainly many times more humanoid vocally than he was two weeks ago . . . and some of this is beginning to creep in to non-lesson time such as when he wants my attention, he is annoyed, etc. I always reply in some form to an uncalled-for humanoid and encourage him. Peter continues to "chat" whenever I am on the phone . . . and this is mostly in humanoid. I don't think anyone has called here recently and not heard Peter in the background. I have asked people how he sounds . . . and they say that they can hear him very well. I think incidentally that Peter is quite happy. I would not have said the same thing of Pam in that other situation . . . but here the water is deep enough so that Peter is well covered . . . moves easily, can race around . . . and I see no bad effects at all. I am also quite comfortable except for the sleeping. My bed now has about three inches of water in it . . . that will not come out . . . it is saturated. I have been on and off sleeping out of the tank . . . and I am waiting for some polyethylene sheeting to make my bed more waterproof. I will screen it in. I had a fever of 101°F for a day . . . and spent the day out of the flooded room in bed. Aubrey Pickering had been ill and I think this accounted for my fever.

We have not forced Peter outside yet . . . I am waiting for special workmen to come and look at the balcony to see about cleaning it and I don't want Peter there when they do. And for the moment he seems happy inside. Each day he moves farther down by the elevator . . . it may be that he will get outside himself (see photograph).

Monday the sea pool will be cleaned and Tuesday the concrete will come and start being poured as was planned. My boys will continue on wall . . . and by the end of next week Pam should come upstairs. Here's hoping! [The reference is to the wall around Pam's new tank outside this building referred to earlier in this report.] (See photograph.)

I am anxious to start work with Pam . . . I miss her pronunciation capability!

June 27 to July 2. Third Week

Monday and Tuesday of this week we start in the first out-and-out cleaning of the new flooded room. The inside was drained and scrubbed down. Peter was put outside . . . we were going to get him into the sling but it was not necessary. He was gently pushed and went through the door. He spent a happy day outside . . . moving freely all around the center wall. (See photograph.) We worked inside and repainted the bottom with Thoroseal. Tuesday we cleaned outside. Peter had to be brought inside in the sling and he was reluctant. When he was in the sling I saw that his belly had some red marks, probably from the rough floor inside. They did not look open or even very sore, just pink. We were able to clean outside fairly well although the drainage is not complete and it is hard to get all the mucky water out. Most of the algae growth was at least scrubbed off, if not flushed out.

Draped shower curtains around my bed . . . dried all the parts of the bed . . . looked forward to dry sleeping. Found during the week that it works very well . . . Peter will get my attention by throwing ball up against the curtain . . . "whap, whap" . . . but he cannot get me drenched any more.

Several of the lessons this week were very poor. Peter has picked up this monotonous tone, a whine . . . and it goes on and on . . . he seldom stops to listen to me. I will do anything to break this, and several times I lost my temper and really yelled at Peter. Other times he listens very well . . . and at least seems to be trying to do the right things.

I still feel very strongly that I can do what I am trying to do . . . but I have not succeeded in doing it yet. I must teach Peter that he is to learn. Just that . . . and then we will have something. I can go through five lessons with him and be so fed up . . . and then I will give a counting lesson, say, and suddenly Peter is listening . . . rolling over and looking at the balls as I point to them, looking back up at me . . . trying sounds, listening when I repeat. It may be that Peter is not sure exactly what he is supposed to be doing. I must try to make it quite clear.

I find in going over the tapes of the week that they are very helpful . . . I get a condensed version of what has gone on. It all comes back. I am picking out some things that I find interesting . . . a good beginning of a word, a good copy of inflection, pitch, etc., but I have not started rerecording any parts of it yet. I am so lousy at the mechanics involved that it will take forever . . . and I don't think I have enough good material yet to make it worth the time spent. [When I asked Miss Howe what she meant by "good material," she added "good pronunciation."]

Peter has still not gone outside on his own. He inches his way . . . I have decided it is just too shallow. This weekend I will raise the level and see if he will come out.

Toward the end of the week on Friday afternoon, I had the first really bad spell of restlessness. I just could not stay at the lab another moment. I got into the car and drove around a bit . . . and felt better. [Margaret has enlarged on this state of mind in a longer note, which will be inserted later in the summary of problems encountered.]

I am physically so pooped I can hardly stand . . . my legs from the knees down are numb. Note that I got my period on Wednesday . . . that may affect me. I sleep in my own bed Friday night . . . and feel better on Saturday. All of this fatigue was also combined with a depression . . . wanting to get away and see some people. I think I reached a point where my mind is not all on the job and I do not function well at all. At any rate . . . I went out and around on Sunday . . . and felt much better facing Monday.

To sum up . . . it has been a sort of neuter week. Not much visible progress, but no backslip. This is fine with me. The fact is still there that Peter and I have spent another week together . . . have yelled at each other . . . have had long, loving sessions, have scolded . . . had lessons . . . etc., and that we are a week closer in awareness of each other than we ever were before.

And for the moment that is all I expect. It has taken this long to really iron out the physical problems in the system, and with the exception of food, I think we have now done that. The cleaning people will be here on Tuesday to see about cleaning. About time!

The concrete was poured into the sea pool this week . . . that was a large distraction. Noise most of the day . . . I had to get out several times to see the work. Pumps would not work, the crew was there to pour, the pool was still full of water . . . I had a lot of outside problems on my mind. Saturday morning the crew was due here at seven-thirty to finish pouring concrete. I got up at 5:00 A.M. and put on the pumps to have the pool empty for them, and the power was off.

Most of these are small problems, but somehow this week they added and loomed very big for me. Pam stopped eating for several days. I was worried about her. She is fine now . . . back on her norm.

Peter continues to be very interested in games. He loves to go and fetch things. I must find a way to make this more worthwhile. The more of this kind of thing the better. I look for any kind of action or performance that has an order to it and some control on Peter's part. This "go and fetch" is ideal. Once again, I am eagerly looking forward to next week.

July 3 to 10, 1965. Fourth Week

During the early part of the week, work was still going on in the sea pool to get the sump properly concreted. Saturday morning the electricity was off and somehow the small tank by the sea pool was half drained. Having no power made it impossible to fill. I have purchased a fifty-foot flexible coil hose for a vacuum upstairs and it works as a siphon. I dropped it over into the tank, and filled the tank from the water upstairs. It is a very good emergency measure. I find that the vacuum takes out more water than the regular outflow upstairs.

I have also discovered that Peter's reluctance to go outside is not due to too narrow a space, or the doorway . . . rather it is due to the water being too shallow next to the elevator. (On the south side of the elevator the passageway floor is slightly elevated so that Peter would have to pass over a hump in the floor). I raised the water to about twenty-four inches . . . and he goes outside on his own. Peter was outside one day . . . and I closed the top part of the Dutch door arrangement, assuming that he would not go under the door . . . as I wanted him to stay outside so I could clean inside uninterrupted by his presence. Not so! Peter very willingly came in under the door . . . went back out again. As long as he has enough water . . . he moves freely.

We spent a lot of time outdoors, I gave him several non-recorded lessons on the balcony and played with him while floating on the raft. (See photographs.)

I have begun working with Peter more and more at times other than feeding. When I am not going to give him a lesson at feeding time, I make feeding as dull as possible. I simply dump the bucket of fish into the water and leave him alone. He eats all the fish, but I do not speak to him, stroke him, etc. I find that more and more Peter is humanoiding to or at me to get attention. I respond as often as possible. I will be in bed, or cooking, and if Peter speaks to me in humanoid, I drop what I am doing and go to him, or else try to engage him in conversation. I do not respond to his attention-getting clicks and whistles. They mean nothing to me and I make that clear.

Peter is more and more interested in games, and often starts them himself. He can toss the ball, bunt with some accuracy to me or at me, and I find that I am suddenly necessary to his game . . . he seldom plays with these objects by himself. We play two games. One is "fetch" . . . Peter brings me the ball, cloth, or bunny, I throw it out, he dashes to it and brings it back to me. The other is catch . . . he hits the ball into the air to me, I can often catch it, and I toss it back to him. He is very willing to toss it back to me. There is no hoarding, or "keep away" instinct. [It is well to note that this is Margaret's special use of the word "instinct."]

I can come into the room, find Peter sitting at the mirror and the ball floating at the other end of the room. I can say "ball" to Peter several times and if he wants to play, he can go and get it . . . and does. It is hard to tell if he can make the distinction say, between the ball and the cloth. They are both lying around and I ask him to get the cloth, he will often get the ball. He seems to prefer the ball and I am not sure he isn't simply ignoring what I say in doing what he wants to. When this happens I ignore the ball, continue asking for the cloth, and if he will not get it I drop the whole thing.

John Lovett came during the week and took black-and-white photos. I have some on file, with the contact sheets but had sent the rest to Dr. Lilly. They are good shots and are an excellent record of the progress here. (See photos in this report.)

Recording sessions with Peter have improved. He is finally able to listen again! I have a nice system with him of hushing him. When he is wrong I simply put my fingers gently on his beak or over his blowhole and he is still. I repeat . . . and he follows. He seems to have lost the impatient squealing that was so annoying and we are working much better together. I have not yet gone over the tapes of this week so I cannot report.

I am not capable of using these tapes as I would like to. But I know what should be done and what I would like to do. I think that I will simply continue making the tapes and going over them as best I can . . . and at a later date I will have to take several days and perhaps get someone in who can properly re-record. Listening to all the tapes is endless and I will make re-

recordings of those parts that show progress. This must be done but it can wait.

Peter has become sexually aroused several times during the week, and I have thoughts and questions on this that follow in a separate paper.

[The paper in question is dated July 11, 1965.]

CHAPTER 13

Observations and Thoughts on Four Weeks' Experiences

Margaret made a special report at the fifth week of living with Peter twenty-four hours a day.

Over the past several weeks I have had thoughts and made observations that have not gone into the weekly report. This will be sort of an intermediate report including these thoughts and observations.

To actually live with a dolphin twenty-four hours a day is a very taxing situation. Much more so than I had anticipated. Unlike a dog, unlike a cat, unlike a human, a dolphin is more like a shadow than a roommate. If given the opportunity, *he will never leave your physical being*. To try and sweep a floor *with* Peter, means that Peter is continually at your feet . . . touching you . . . pushing you . . . nibbling you . . . perhaps speaking (humanoid or delphinese) to you. *He does not go away*. To cross a room to answer a phone means that Peter meets you when you come into his immediate range and he walks with you, pushing, nibbling, slapping, *the whole way*. And if you are on the phone for half an hour, Peter does not get distracted or bored, *he stays right with you* . . . again touching you, pushing you, nibbling you, speaking, squirting.

At the moment, I am in a situation where Peter is still reluctant to move down by the elevator and outside. I can "escape" from him. But he has gone outside by himself . . . he can move all around the room, and it is just a matter of time before I will not have a place to "escape" to. This is, of course, what I want to happen, but I had not realized the intensity of the situation. If not actively involved in a game, Peter will be touching me in some way and demanding attention. This may sound mild, but I literally cannot take a step without Peter getting all tangled up in my feet. And if I should continue to ignore him, I am likely to get a slap with his tail that can take my feet out from under me. My shins are bruised, up and down, from the constant butting with his nose and the front of his flippers. *And all of this suits me just fine.* We will never be comfortable with the dolphin until this business is solved. Peter *must learn that I can get hurt* . . . and he must learn that no matter how annoyed he may be, he is not to hurt me. Until that is clear, there will be an element of danger with dolphins, that is, for me anyway, too much to live with. I cannot feel that, if suddenly in the middle of a game or a lesson Peter should become annoyed, he would be likely to physically damage me. In this respect we are dealing with a "wild animal" and we must domesticate or civilize them. [I questioned her on the term "wild animal" and was wondering if maybe a "wild man" might not be better. She said no, she meant "wild animal" and that is the sense in which she means it.]

This, of course, makes no sense to the person who has had a "nice swim" with a dolphin or with one who has "played for a while" with a dolphin. When you expose yourself to a dolphin twenty-four hours a day, you are becoming the "other dolphin" in their life. You become vulnerable to their whims and moods throughout the day. You lack the introduction of a "human coming to play for a while." You are exposed to their sexual needs and play, their hunger, their playful antics, their needs for heavy exercise, and for rest. You are no longer a nice interlude in the day. You are a constant companion, and must make your peace with the dolphin as such.

Making this "peace" with Peter has occupied a good deal of our time together and we are doing nicely. I have my own physical fears, etc., I am not a "big brave man." Perhaps a braver, stronger person could solve this problem in less time . . . but this is what I have been able to do so far. To begin with, I went into the flooded room with rubber bootees. I have had Peter nibble at my feet before and wanted to avoid it. He did indeed nibble . . . and I took to carrying a broom with me when I walked. This thwarted him off, he came with me but I could protect my feet from his constant attention. After several days the bootees became a nuisance, and I shed them for good. I continued carrying the broom, but this soon became a nuisance too. I decided to tackle the thing.

Peter, on his own, seemed to sense a problem and became willing to tackle it too. He would become very gentle, and we began to have our first "loving session." This gave me confidence and was a reward to Peter for being "gentle." We became more and more confident with each other. I began walking freely without a broom. Peter continues to follow me and push at me with his beak, but for the most part he keeps his mouth closed and does not nibble. When he does take my foot or leg in his teeth, I make a big fuss, yell at him, kick water, even slap him if it hurts, and immediately remove myself from "his" area. I wait, and Peter usually responds by turning over, wagging a flipper at me, mouth closed and lies still. I approach him again, using a soothing tone now, and if he remains gentle we go on playing and the incident is closed. If he continues to snap at me . . . he has indeed tricked me into coming back . . . I blow my top and leave him alone for a good while. This seems very effective . . . every day Peter and I can be quite happy and comfortable with each other for longer and longer periods of time.

All of this business is hard to describe in detail daily . . . some of it is very subtle . . . but the changes in our relationship can be seen after several weeks. It is a big part of our work together . . . and no matter how long it takes to solve, it will be well worth it. I look forward to the day when Peter will yell at me rather than nip at me, to show his displeasure. This is a big anti-instinct step for him and I appreciate every effort on his part. My bruises and scrapes are well worth it (Plate 22). [Previous studies in the three months observation period by Margaret on the behavior of the dolphins show the patterns of a dolphin using his teeth on other dolphins.]

So much for my "taming" Peter. Now to my progress in and plans for teaching.

In his normal existence, Peter has no need to speak English. Before I can expect him to really start speaking, I must give him such a need. This I can do, so far, in two ways.

The first is to demand, through food reward, later hopefully to be vocal or physical reward, to repeat what I am saying.

The second is to introduce various objects, and uses for various objects, into his life and to make them so necessary or so much fun that I can then demand that he use speech to indicate, or get, or control, these objects.

The food reward, recorded or "formal" lessons with Peter have been slow. The program I have set up has been held back because somewhere along the line Peter had forgotten how to listen. Much time has been spent just trying to get him to give and take, listen, and respond. He is now back on the track, somewhat, and lessons are becoming more fun for both of us. I can stop screaming and touch Peter on the beak or blowhole to indicate that he must listen again. I think a big part of this is to make sure that feeding times are not too delayed. When Peter is really hungry he simply yells until I feed him. Feeding three times a day helps to take away the "tension" of feeding time . . . and makes a more relaxed, easygoing lesson. Peter has a good appetite and always eats everything I offer him. When I feel that he is too hungry to pay attention I just feed him straight, and get more fish for him. It is not fair to really hold back food from a hungry dolphin. It should be more of a snack or a tidbit.

Anyway, Peter is settling back into the groove and listening, and I can begin in earnest our lessons of counting, shape, and color. These are the three I will begin with and then we will see. It has been slow, but at least we have accomplished something. Peter is the pacesetter here; all I can do is to push him to his limit and then match his pace.

At the moment Peter is at this point: he can listen, he can hush up. He responds with a good 95 per cent humanoid, only occasional delphinese comments on the side. He can somewhat imitate the word "ball" and "hello." These are not too clear . . .

but are there. He is obviously working on "L" and "M" . . . probably from "hello," "ball," and "Margaret."

My first goal will be to get him to pronounce any word clearly and know the meaning. This will probably be a time coming, and is the hardest step. Once he learns that he can say something and have it mean something to me . . . then the other words and meanings will come easier. So I repeat over and over the few words he seems most able to repeat . . . and I don't think he will be bored with this repetition until he has mastered the word, at which point I will move on. It all makes for very boring tapes, of my repeating one word over and over, and Peter giving various replies. But I can hear changes; I can see changes as he tries for new sounds . . . and I will not stop this tedious chore until I feel that Peter is ready. The public, etc., will just have to wait for fancy, snappy tapes. There is nothing clever or cute about a deaf mute trying to learn to speak. It is a slow, dull, drooling-at-the-mouth, agonizing, and frustrating business, and that is about the size of what Peter and I are engaged in.

The list of objects in Peter's life is always subject to change . . . and frequently does. I think it is very important to choose objects that can both be played with . . . and talked about . . . and this is a much harder choice than it would seem (Plates 25, 26). I have gone into it blindfolded. Peter has taught me as I go. I began rather naturally, with a ball. This is appropriate . . . Peter can occasionally say ball, and I demand that he attempt it before giving him the ball. Now comes the question—what to do with the ball? In the beginning, we did nothing. Peter spoke for the ball, I gave it to him, and he happily took it off in his mouth. Period. This changed as Peter began bopping it gently . . . bouncing it on the bottom. All of this seems to come quite naturally to all dolphins . . . they *like to play with the ball. Fine!* But do they like to play with the ball with people? It seems natural to toss the ball and see if Peter will go get it. Dogs have trained us in this game. Peter knows it too! I don't know how I taught Peter this, or even if I did teach him this . . . but he very happily chases a ball, picks it up . . . brings it to me and lets me have it. *Fine!* Can he do this with more than one ball? *Yes!* Peter can hold three balls in his mouth at one time . . . and will go and fetch three balls at the same time and bring them all back. This I will tuck away for later when his counting is more developed . . . to try and see if he can bring just one, or just two.

So one of Peter's objects is a ball, small, red, and buoyant.

If Peter will go and fetch a ball, will he fetch other things as well? *Yes!* I have tried the game with a cloth . . . he likes to vary this, bringing it back in his teeth, or on a flipper.

The variation of this game is as follows . . . after Peter handed me the cloth, I started rubbing him gently with it . . . saying "rub." Peter did not respond vocally to this but several times later when he returned with the cloth in his mouth he would not immediately give it to me. Instead he held the cloth, sunk to the bottom, and ran his beak and the cloth up and down my legs and feet. I say "rub!" "Thank you Peter!" and he gives me the cloth for another toss.

So another object is a cloth: a dishcloth or a face cloth. I found a wet towel too heavy and too clumsy.

Peter has always had, as long as I have known him, a float. This is a rope with a float at either end. He plays with it alone, it is easy to sling into the air, and I have not played with it with him.

So another object is a float.

Another game Peter and I developed with his ball is "catch" . . . we are several feet from each other. I tossed the ball to Peter, where if he gets it he does one of two things . . . he can flip it to me underwater by snapping his jaws on it . . . or he can bop it from the surface of the water into the air. The latter I have encouraged and we can go several bops with a fairly good aim on his part and I am able to catch it after he bops it. This is suddenly stopped by Peter, who lies on his side and will not play any more until I stroke him and coo. Several minutes of this and the bop game continues.

I have collected two baskets, one blue and one red, and three balls of each color. I will hang the baskets and see if I can interest Peter in a brief water basketball. I will later see if he can sort out the colors.

So another of his objects is the basketball equipment.

From the beginning of this experiment I have had a brush, kept by Peter's mirror. Stupidly humanlike, but fun. It is a dust broom, a soft thick thing. Peter seems to like it . . . but can take only so much of it. I do not use it too often, but when I do I name it "brush" and as I stroke Peter with it I say "brush, brush." Peter will lie on his side and let me brush him all over. He likes to be brushed on the beak and around the lips.

Another object for Peter . . . brush.

I found a long, tall rubber rabbit . . . it floats and when you squeeze it . . . it squeaks. I gave it to Peter and explained "bunny."

I showed him how it squeaked . . . bopped it around a bit, and left it. He soon had the bunny squeaking. I went to him and named it again. I took it away when he left it. I will keep it until I am ready to play bunny again and then I will explain what it is again to Peter. I do not think things like this should be left with him for too long. They get forgotten and used-to. They should be carefully allotted time and attention.

Peter now has a squeaking toy . . . a bunny.

I have let Peter play for a while with his shapes . . . just to let him get more acquainted with them. When I use them in a lesson, I do not let him have them . . . I hold them up or dunk them into the water for him to see. I do not think he is ready to play with these yet . . . until he understands the difference, they are meaningless and they can't really play together with them. So they will only be used for the moment in formal lessons, that he has been exposed to them.

Peter has a diamond, a square, a circle, an oblong, and a triangle. These are wood, they float, are painted white with a black border (Plates 23, 24).

For the moment these are the basic kit of Peter's objects. There are daily arrivals of screws, apple cores, cigarette butts, buckets, tea bags, brooms, books, etc., that get into the flooded room and are usually named for him, but the above are steady members of his routine now. As this kit is added to, I will make a note of it in a report.

Slowly an environment is being set up for dolphin and human

living, and slowly I am learning what is needed and what is not. I am learning that I am not completely capable of complete isolation with Peter, and happily I am learning that it is not necessary. I have been very depressed and discouraged and have found that I simply must break out at least once a week.

I have found that during the day I will find any excuse to get out of the flooded room . . . to have to go downstairs and look at a pump . . . to have to go upstairs and get something . . . to have to get out and spend a few minutes loving my cat . . . to have to get out and take a shower in my own bathroom and dry my feet completely . . . and after all these "have-to's"—it has been most important *to have to go back and see what Peter is doing.*

But for the 2½ months at least I think it is very important and valuable to stick as closely as possible to the setup routine, just for the value of being there as much as possible . . . to find out what we do when the game is over . . . when a lesson is lousy . . . or I am exhausted, etc.

In a boring interval suddenly Peter will flip the cloth at me, and we both gain the sense of being stuck with each other . . . or blessed with each other . . . and the more of this there is the more we can work out things together.

I find that this living is hard and taxing on my own private life. I do not think that I would like to live with this much restriction for too long a time. But for the moment, and certainly for the next few months, I am very happy to do it with the obvious gains that have been made and will be made.

I hope with what I am able to learn in these months, I can establish some sort of system for learning and teaching that will make a future more livable nine-to-five schedule with a dolphin more profitable. Or perhaps not a nine-to-five schedule, but a looser living-in situation that will afford the human more time on his own. [This is a dull small area for living. There are definitely isolation and solitude effects showing. A mother and human child can go out of their house together, Margaret and the dolphin cannot leave together. Eventually the "delphinomobile" may be an answer for both Margaret and Peter to vary their surroundings.] (Plates 27–30.)

273

CHAPTER 14

Who Teaches Whom What: Mutual Trust

July 11 to 17, 1965. Fifth Week

Sunday and Monday nights of this week I got very little sleep. Peter was awake and slamming tail hard on water. I tried speaking to him, playing with him . . . no good. He is restless, his tail goes "whap, whap" all night. Also during the beginning of the week I find that my play periods are changing with him. Also during the beginning of the week Peter begins having erections and has them frequently when I play with him.

Peter has been upstairs with me for just a month, and up until now he has not displayed his sexual excitement. I think we must learn a lesson from this.

I find that his desires are hindering our relationship. I can play with him for just so long now and then he gets an erection and the play/lesson is broken. I find that I cannot satisfy Peter . . . I am in the water with him and he is too rough to handle. He jams himself again and again against my legs, circles around me, is inclined to nibble . . . and is generally so excited that he cannot control his attitude toward me. I have had Peter in the same condition before, but under different circumstances. When Peter was upstairs in the Fiberglas tank he would occasionally become aroused, and I found that by taking his penis in my hand and letting him jam himself against me he would reach some sort of orgasm, mouth open, eyes closed, body shaking, then his penis would relax and withdraw.* He would repeat this maybe two

---

* The male dolphin's penis appears outside his body only while erect. It disappears inside the genital slit when not erect. (See pictures, *Man and Dolphin*.)

or three times and then his erection would stop and he seemed satisfied.

Now, however, I am completely in the water with him and because so much of my body is exposed, we cannot get into the same position as above. I am completely vulnerable to him and he pushes and shoves my legs and feet, and quite pathetically tries to satisfy himself. I can feel his mounting frustration, and he is impossible to work with following this.

I have decided that Peter must go downstairs with Pam and Sissy for at least a day. I think that it is only fair, after say a month with only me, that he join them for a day or so. This, I hope, will relieve his frustrations, so that we can go on working for another month. I know that dolphins have been worked with for much longer periods in isolation without a break to romp with other animals, but I feel that at a certain point one may be hindered by unsatisfied sexual needs. I would rather lose Peter for a day and have him happy than continue as we are.

This will be much harder to determine in the females, if in fact it does exist. When Pam comes upstairs to her tank I will give her a month and then look closely for signs of frustration or lag in her learning. *This may be a very important and as yet unrealized step in dolphin teaching.* To try and keep an animal in isolation and a learning situation beyond this point of frustration may impair learning or even set it back. Each animal may have different tolerances, or they all may be somewhat alike. With Peter, so far, it seems to be about a month. I will follow this report with a report on Peter's attitudes after he has had one or two days with Pam and Sissy.

Another thought I have had on this subject is whether or not it would be best for the human to somehow find a way to satisfy the dolphin's sexual needs without another dolphin. This may strengthen the bond between the dolphin and the human. It may also lead to more and more frequent "sexual periods" between the two. If Peter knows that I can satisfy his needs, he may feel free to turn any play period or lesson into a sex period . . . but if he knows that I will not have any part of his sexual needs and that once a month he will be put with Pam or Sissy, he may reduce his excitement periods with me. This would, of course, be preferable. I will try and see. *This is a problem,* and it must be solved . . . I cannot go on having my shins belted about by lusty little Peter. *It hurts!*

Peter continues to improve his attitude during lessons. He is most attentive, listens as well as I ever hoped, and tries hard. I am working only on a very few words, trying to ram them home with him. He listens, repeats, listens again. He has that lack of pronunciation, but improves daily on inflection and pitch. Listening to the tapes, he could be speaking English from the general sound of it. It is just not yet comprehensible. In the middle of a cocktail party it could be considered background conversation. It has all the right "feel" of English . . . and soon it will be. I am very pleased.

The sea pool is done. It is painted with blue Tile-It on the sides and white Thoroseal on the bottom. It is filled and Pam and Sissy are in it and very happy. They can still leap clear out . . . I was not so sure about that with the new bottom. They love it. Sissy spends a good deal of time upside down with her nose in the sump inspecting every inch. I have not been in yet, but I went partly in one day to rub Sissy with cream; she got a bit of a sunburn. It is so nice to walk down a sloping side at the outflow rather than those steps.

The wall around Pam's tank is done, and painted. I had a hard time deciding on color . . . something not too bright and not too hot. I decided on black and white combination, and have done it in big stripes. It is not too dizzy looking as I feared it might be and it seems to be as cool and dim as possible. I am working on a possible scheme for the inflow there . . . if I could somehow use the outflow from the balcony into her tank . . . it would save a pump, electricity, noise, etc. It may or may not work. I am just waiting for the pump to arrive from Miami. I could put a valve on each end of the siphon to control it through that. I am sure the water would be clean enough . . . there is so much upstairs.

One month of the project is up . . . and well spent. I now am no longer thinking in terms of three months . . . I think in terms of forever!

July 17 to August 1, 1965.

Rather than dealing with this as a weekly report, I am going to write at length about several topics that have come to notice during these weeks.

An interesting thing has been going on, as observed by Dr. Lilly involving Peter and his "mouthing" with me. I will recount what goes on.

When Peter and I first became involved in ball playing, we worked nicely into a game where, several feet apart, we bopped the ball to each other, calling it "catch." Peter slowly, subtly, would toss the ball shorter and shorter distances . . . I would have to step towards him to pick it up. This soon moved into a game where I would stand just in front of Peter and really *put the ball into his mouth.* He would lie on his side . . . and gently close his mouth on the ball, releasing it to me. Soon he would hold the ball in his mouth . . . lie on his side, and I tentatively took the ball out of his mouth and began slightly rubbing his gums as I did so. Peter laid dead in the water, eyes partly closed. I was willing to accept this form of mouth play. Previously I would go into a rage whenever Peter opened his mouth in playing a game. Now, however, because Peter was so still and gentle, obviously a little entranced, and because the ball was in his mouth and he could not possibly bite down on me too hard, I was willing to play his way. Note that in the beginning Peter would keep the ball in the front of his mouth . . . mouth open only slightly and not able to close at all. Slowly, Peter began to roll the ball back in his mouth until his jaws were full open and he could close them several inches with the ball still inside. At this point I held back a bit until Peter convinced me, by his gentleness and trancelike fixation, that this was "pleasure," not "fool Margaret" period. I felt a little silly, and was delighted that Peter had devised such a subtle, gentle method of getting me over my fears of all those teeth. So we had arrived at point one . . . Peter "dead" with ball in mouth, slightly open, with me stroking lips and gums. Once step one had been established, Peter slowly moved on to the next step. And that is what happened . . . I had no idea of the end result of this play . . . I was along for the ride to see the results of Peter's increased gentleness and my diminishing fear. Peter led the way.

His next move was, during the same sort of play, to slowly sink in the water with a ball toward the front of his mouth and his jaws slightly closed. All slowly and gently, Peter would run the open tip of his mouth up and down my leg. I, meanwhile, was keeping an eagle eye on the ball and as long as it remained in his mouth I knew that he could not bite down and thus I allowed the play. This, then, became step two in Peter's plan.

Next Peter gradually moved the ball in his mouth so that his jaws were full open with the ball still in the back of his mouth. Now he would sink and go through the up and down the leg business; only this time his full set of teeth were running up and down my leg instead of only the tip of his mouth. I again kept an eagle eye on the ball . . . my "safety factor," held my breath as the teeth ever so gently went up and down my legs, and allowed this play. [Peter is estimated to be about five to six years old, his teeth still have the childish very sharp tips to them and are just beginning to be worn down. They are still capable, however, of drawing blood.]

All of the above happened over several weeks; it has been a slow, gradual buildup. Peter woos me into position and once we are started he seems to completely relax, eyes fully or partially closed, rolling on his side . . . obviously having a marvelous time. My only reaction at this point was to hold my breath and watch the ball . . . I am not an active member at this point.

Peter is not through. During the above, the ball slowly, seemingly, "accidentally" drops out of his mouth. At first I demand that he take it back before I will let him go on with the teeth . . . but soon he is so obviously involved in his fun, and the ball just seems to slip out of his mouth, and again I take a big breath and let Peter continue, his jaws open up and down my leg with no ball. My safety factor is gone and I can only let the play go on for a few seconds at a time.

Peter continues pressing this game . . . and slowly I gain confidence. I no longer demand that the ball be there in the beginning of the game to make me feel better.

Peter simply approaches me, mouth open, rolling on his side; I stand very still, legs slightly apart, and Peter slides his mouth gently over my shin. His mouth opens all the way and he begins up and down my leg. Then the other leg. The whole knee is in his mouth.

At this point it occurs to me what has been going on. Peter is courting me . . . or something very similar! I began to take an active part in the play. After several minutes of Peter "stroking" me gently with his teeth, I compliment him vocally, soothingly, and rub him as he turns to be stroked. Several minutes of this and Peter is back stroking me. I still hold my breath a bit but Peter has convinced me that this is a perfectly legitimate game among dolphins, and with the toning down he gives it for my benefit, it is actually a very pleasant feeling!

Two things about all this stand out in my mind. One is the over-all way Peter was able to woo me, to teach me that *I could play this game.* I had many fears . . . Peter obviously realized them and found ways, and *props* (the ball after all was a very convenient tool) to reassure me. Peter has worked long for this contact . . . he has been most persistent and patient. [Notice that Peter used a tool in a rather sophisticated way in order to induce Margaret to accept certain kinds of attention.] Second is the mood in general of the play. This is obviously a sexy business . . . all it really involves is physical contact. The mood is very gentle . . . still . . . hushed . . . all movements are slow . . . tone is very quiet . . . only slight murmurings from me. Peter is constantly, but ever so slowly, weaving his body around . . . eyes near closed. He does not usually get an erection during this, but does present his tummy and genital area for stroking. I find that once Peter does have an erection, his mood usually changes completely and he gets so rambunctious I have to leave him. Perhaps this is his way of involving me in some form of sex play without scaring me away.

I feel extremely flattered at Peter's patience with me in all this . . . and am delighted to be so obviously "wooed" by this dolphin.

Several other points have come up during these weeks.

For several days there have been groups of from four to six persons at the laboratory. They all saw Peter. They were all dry, standing outside the flooded living room, dangling arms over the wall. This is going back to the "dolphin in the tank-human leaning in" idea . . . and I do not like it. Peter fell back into the old business of squirting up at the people and various dangling arms and heads. And the people? Usual reaction . . . saying "no" in a high-pitched, giggly voice, and ducking down, only to pop up seconds later and dangle again, inviting more squirting.

This is all very fine, and people are flattered and Peter finds it a game but I refuse to allow it. It is boring, eventually annoying, and completely out of line of what I am trying to do by living with Peter. I stop this business by getting in with Peter (and I have been outside with the people). Peter began to play with me . . . and although he was still very aware of the "outside" people . . . he no longer focused on them. Enough said . . . Peter is not in a cage and will not be played with, teased, observed, stared at, or anything else by "outside" people. You are several months too late, people, Peter has outgrown you. [And so has Margaret.]

I went to San Juan and purchased several new toys for Peter. I will introduce them one at a time. I have removed all balls from his rooms, and have given him six "toy" fish. They are red, plastic, about nine inches long, they float, and I can push them gently and they glide on top of the water. Peter began bopping them . . . has collected them together several times . . . and slowly we are working out "toy fish" games. The real butterfish I now term "fish in bucket," as a contrast. Occasionally I play with the fish and a ball . . . explaining "ball" and "toy fish." Peter's "toy fish" comes out as two clear separate sounds, but no pronunciation yet. I am working on "toie." I have not spoken to him yet of color . . . but I do count the fish with him. Slowly these new objects are becoming part of his life. I will discuss the other toys as I use them.

August 2 to August 18, 1965. Eighth, Ninth, and Tenth Weeks
The past few weeks have been interesting ones for me, in that

I am finding that I have periods of lag in my attention to my work.

I fight this to a point, but only to a point. I find that once my attention is averted from Peter, it is best not to fake it, because my lack of genuine enthusiasm with him can only lead us backward.

It is also true that during these weeks there have been other distractions at the lab that have required my attention.

Two awnings have been installed, one over the Fiberglas tank and one over the block pool at the outflow of the sea pool. (See photographs.) We have needed these for a long time, and I was very glad to see them installed.

Also during the week photographs were taken of the lab in general and of me in with Sissy and Pam. We took a series of pictures of Sissy being brought upstairs on the elevator. (See photographs.) For this we used my bed, the pallet to show it in operation. My bed was therefore soaking wet, and it took several days to get the foam dried out. This broke my pattern with Peter, and I find that once it is broken, it is very hard to get back into it.

Also, several matters in town required my attention. Our phone has been out of order for over a week now, and all calls have to be made from outside. (This led to a good deal of anxiety on Dr. Lilly's part in which he spent thirty-six hours trying to raise me and almost came to St. Thomas to find out what was wrong.)

Also I had to go out to the employment agency to start the long fight to keep our three workmen . . . the new immigration law states that I must try to find local help. This is still not settled.

So all in all it has been a distracting week. Meanwhile I have worked with Peter as best I could.

Monday of this week after my several days out of the flooded room, I moved back in with Peter and I find that, after the lapse, energy seems to be renewed on both parts. I am delighted with Peter . . . and he is working as hard as ever. I say "work, work, work" and Peter says "play, play, play." I try to combine them. He plays endlessly with his toys, *if I play with him*. I usually work with two different toys at a time . . . say the toy fish and a "Ba Be Block." We go from one to the other, and I try to get him to tell the difference. He does and he doesn't. Once he has correctly made a choice, I scold him when he makes a mistake. Some of this I am sure is just the bad little boy doing as he wishes.

I wish to add a note about the progress in the sex problem that developed between Peter and myself. I have found that during his erections, Peter was much too strong and pushy and I could not work with him. Then there was the business of Peter wooing me with the nibbling on the legs game. This was an example of Peter teaching me something.

Now it has happened that Peter has modified his sexual rambunctiousness . . . to a more humanized level , , , and no longer has to come to a dead stop when he gets excited. Peter's sexual excitement usually begins with the biting business, and my stroking him. Now, however, when his penis becomes erect, he no longer tries to run me down and knock me off my feet, rather he slides very smoothly along my legs, and I can very easily rub his penis with either my hand or my foot. Peter accepts either and again seems to reach some sort of orgasm and relaxes. We usually go through this three times or so before he quits and starts another game. This is not a private thing. Peter and I have done this with other people present . . . but it is a very precious sort of thing, Peter is completely involved, and I involve myself to the extent of putting as much love into the tone, touch, and mood as possible. We do not have to respect his privacy . . . but we cannot help but respect his happiness!

Now two things . . . I started out afraid of Peter's mouth, and afraid of Peter's sex. It had taken Peter about two months to teach me, and me about two months to learn, that I am free to involve myself completely with both. It is strange that for the one, *I* must trust completely . . . Peter could bite me in two. *So he has taught me that I can trust him.* And in the other, he is putting complete trust in me by letting me handle his most delicate parts . . . *thus he shows me that he has trust in me.* Peter has established mutual trust. Could I have devised such a plan? Looking back . . . things I left out. The effect of isolation and solitude over the ten-week period cannot be ignored. Looking back over the time spent and the notes collected, I find that I, for some reason, left out things about myself. Perhaps I felt they were not important or was ashamed of them.

Several times during the period, I felt the physically depressing effects of the situation to the point where I found myself actually crying. Small inconveniences suddenly loomed as very large and ugly. And I would find myself in a fit of self-pity, depression. It was Peter himself who brought me out of it every time without exception. An example of all this: to take a shower at night before going to bed, means that I have to stand in knee-deep sea water during the shower, dry myself, and then wade back to my bed. This meant that when I got onto my bed, my legs from the knee down were wet with salt water. Even after drying with a towel, the dampness would still get through and make the sheet on my bed clammy and, if I had any nicks on my legs from Peter, they kept "stinging," and in this rather bizarre setting with moonlight shining on the water making moving shadows all over the ceiling and walls, dull pump noises from below, I would try to settle down in bed, and occasionally found that out of sheer self-pity I would be adding my own salt tears to the mess I already lay in. And then, usually not very long after I lay still, Peter would sound off in humanoid, loud and clear, very close. From where I lay I could part the shower curtains around my bed, and reach out my hand to my eager, bright-eyed roommate who had usually collected a ball of some sort and was all set to start up a nice game of fetch or catch.

Peter was very determined in his expression of his need for me to enter into his game . . . he would toss the ball again and again into my bed, and emit humanoids in long and involved phrases, they were not perfectly clear in meaning but were perfectly clear in intent . . . that I seldom if ever ignored him, and usually ended up right back in the water, not caring at all about sleep, or the wet bed or the shower routine . . . simply overwhelmed at what Peter and I were accomplishing together.

Another example of the kind of depression that I went through: during the day the two workmen are around the lab, and I can talk to them and hear their work going on. The last one usually leaves rather late in the day . . . several hours after I have supposedly fed Peter his dinner. I found that the sound or the sight of that last person leaving at the end of the day depressed me so terribly, that the only way to get myself out of this feeling was to hold off feeding Peter until after they had all left. This I did and found that when the sad feeling came over me and I felt so alone, I would then have yet another lesson to do with Peter. At the end of the lesson I would be so involved with Peter and what had gone on during the lesson, that I avoided the empty feeling I dreaded. When I was expecting a human visitor in the evening I was very excited, elated. I almost always found, however, that when the visitor left I was sadder and lonelier than I was without a visitor. (I seldom had visitors.)

The feelings of depression and aloneness were not a constant thing by any means, but they did come and go, and my having to turn to Peter to overcome them was, I feel, an important part of the experiment. [Margaret has not read any of the solitary sailing, alone in the polar night or the isolation experiments literatures. She is acquainted with some of the things that I have told her of this area of isolation. I feel that her description here is definitively her own and that little, if anything, of this is suggested from outside. There is an interesting correspondence here with experiences of other people isolated alone.]

This is the end of Margaret's notes made *during* the experiment. Following is additional data compiled *after* the experiment.

CHAPTER 15

Vocal Exchanges between Margaret and Peter

Before moving into the tape analysis part of this report, we would like to say something of the difficulties in this area, and of our frustration in not being able to turn you into the *listener*, rather than into the *reader*.*

To date there is no way that we know of to *print* something so that you can *hear* it. We are limited to several ways of writing about sound, or describing sound, or even diagramming sound. No one of these methods, or the sum total of these methods, can give you the sound itself. So many aspects of a lesson with a dolphin and a human can be described, so much about the sounds made can be learned by *reading*, so much about the sounds can be learned by *looking* at a diagram, that we feel it is well worthwhile to use as many ways as we can to give you as much of a picture of the sounds as possible.

We do emphasize, however, that each one of these methods can only tell you some aspects of the sounds: the following part of this report is intended to inform to the best of our ability about the vocal aspects of this experiment.

Miss Howe has devised a method of sampling the tapes

* Arrangements can be made to obtain a copy of a tape of samples of sessions showing Margaret and Peter's vocal progress in a year's work ending with this 2½-month period.

made during these 2½ months and during the previous time giving her interactions with Peter on a vocal level. The following section is devoted to these representations that she has worked out, of typical short samples chosen from longer tape records.

Since these tapes are so important to the transmission of information the segments that are used for transcription are copied and placed together in proper calendar sequence and will form a part of this record.

Some samples for pronunciation analysis were selected for analysis by the sound spectrograph. Sonograms of Peter and Margaret pronouncing the same word again and again form part of these data.

The following is an attempt to transcribe portions of tapes in such a way so that the reader can gain a better understanding of the kind of thing that goes on in a lesson with the dolphin Peter. It is *not* an attempt to accurately describe the exact sounds made by the dolphin, but rather to show the progress, over a period of several months, that took place between the human and the dolphin in the teacher-pupil relationship. The transcription method is set up as follows:

1. Two lines are read at a time, as in a staff of music. One line is MH (Margaret Howe), and the other line is PD (Peter Dolphin).

2. The symbol c is used to designate a click, whistle, or any other form of "delphinese." Thus a series of clicks may be written ccccccc. An exact count of the clicks is not represented here, and ccccc does not mean six clicks . . . it simply means a series of clicks.

3. The symbol x is used to designate a humanoid sound made by the dolphin which is *not a clear enough humanoid to accurately describe phonetically*. Thus is a humanoid attempt by the dolphin.

4. When the humanoid attempt is clear enough to be

written phonetically in English, it is described as best as possible. Thus "oie" may be an attempt at "boy" . . . without the "b."

5. Instructions to Peter spoken by MH are in lower case, and words to be copied by Peter are in capitals. Thus, "Peter, please say HELLO MAGRIT."

6. Brief summary notes follow each transcription.

7. These transcriptions are of only the airborne sounds as they are recorded on the tapes. All underwater sounds are kept out of this account.

Sample Seven Months Before 2½-Month Experiment
(November 3, 1964)

MH	SPEAK GOOD		SPEAK GOOD BOIE		Good, Peter, good!
PD		cccc		cccccxx xx	

MH Now you're going!   Yes,   SPEAK
PD   cccccccccxxx cccccccccxxx   ccccccccxxoi

MH Good boy! SPEAK GOOD BOIE   SPEAK GOOD BOIE.
PD   cccc   xx

> Dr. Lilly (JCL) has just arrived and Peter is taking a break to see what's happening.

MH SPEAK   GOOD BOIE   Good boy. (JCL in background)
PD ccccccccccc   cccc xx xx

MH Did you hear that?   Speak GOOD BOIE   SPEAK
PD   cccc   c c c c c c c c c ccccc

MH GOOD BOIE   SPEAK GOOD   (Giggle)   yes, come on,
PD   xxx   xxxxx   oii

MH take a fish   (JCL voice in background) MH and JCL chat.
PD   xxxxxxcccc

MH SPEAK GOOD BOIE   SPEAK GOOD BOIE   (JCL in back-
PD   xx   ccc   xxx

MH ground) Who is that, Peter? (JCL voice) Come on . . . SPEAK
    GOOD BOIE
PD

MH (JCL voice) SPEAK   GOOD BOIE
PD   ccccccc   ccccc

1. Repetition of SPEAK GOOD BOIE by Margaret over and over, an attempt to get Peter to respond in humanoid.
2. Peter responds mainly in delphinese clicks . . . only a few humanoids.
3. Peter often speaks (clicks) while Margaret is still speaking.
4. Lesson is interruptible . . Peter and Margaret are not "meshing gears" . . . there is a rather loose structure to the lesson.

Sample Six Months Before 2½-Month Experiment

MH Sssssshhh I AM SUCH A GOOD BOIE
PD   ccccccxxxxccc ccxxxx xxx xx (shrill)

MH No, Peter, sssshhh. SPEAK GOOD   No, no. Shhhh SPEAK GOOD
PD   xxxxxx (shrill)

MH BOIE FOR FISH   shhh DO NOT PLAY
PD   xxxxxcccxx (shrill) cccc   ccccccccccccc

MH shhhhhhh, Peter, DO NOT PLAY   Yes, sshhhh SPEAK GOOD
PD   cccccxxxxxccxxx xxx

MH BOIE   SPEAK GOOD BOIE   John, that telephone
PD ccccc xx cc   xxxx (shrill)

MH is ringing. SPEAK FOR FISH GOOD BOIE   HELLO ELVAR
PD   cccchxxxx (weak)

MH HELLO ELVAR   SPEAK AND EAT
PD   c ccc xxx lo xxx   xxxx cccccc xx (shrill)

MH No no, sssssshhhh   sssshhhh SPEAK AND EAT   SAY
PD   c c c x x x c c c x x x   xxxxxx ccccccxxxx   C

MH GOOD BOIE   SAY GOOD BOIE   ssshh come on,
PD   CCCCCCC   cccccccccccccccccxx   xxxxccxx

MH I MUST SPEAK FOR FISH   I WILL SPEAK AND EAT NOW
PD   xxxxx cccc xxx   ccccc   ccc xxx (shrill)

MH sssshhhh, no Peter   I WILL SPEAK AND EAT
PD   ccccxx (shrill blasts)   ccccxxxxx (shrill)

1. Peter is still doing a lot of delphinese clicking.
2. He is beginning to give a few more humanoids, but these are in the form of shrill blasts.
3. He still interrupts Margaret and vocalizes while she speaks.

Five Months Previously (January 5, 1965)

MH   AIR OWN EMM   SAY NO ETCH EIM   SIGH IT ARE
PD   cccc cc   cc xxx xx   xx cc xxx

MH   I'll go from lesson eleven back into lesson
PD   xxxx ccc xxx

MH   number eight   listen   TOI   OIT   OICH
PD   ccc xxxx cc xxx   c c   c c xxx cc

MH   CHOIE OIT   COIE OIT COIE TOIE
PD   c c c c ccccc xxxxx xxxx   xxxx ccc xxxxx

MH   say GOOD BOIE GOOD BOIE   OIEZ ZOIE OIS CHOIE
PD   ccc xx   xxxxx ccc xxx

MH   OIE Peter, say BOIE . . . GOOD BOIE   I AM A
PD   ccc xxxxx   xxxxcccxxxxx   ccc

MH   GOOD BOIE   SPEAK GOOD BOIE   TOIE
PD   c c c c c xxxxx cccc xxxx   ccc xxxx xxx

MH   OIE SOIE ROIE   OIE say OIE   GOOD
PD   cccc xxxxx ccc xxx c c   xxxx c

MH   BOIE   OIM MOI LOI OIT   OIL   murmur
PD   cccc xxxx ccc   cxxxx   xxxxx

MH   OIL LOI ROI OIK   Listen . . . OIL LOI ROI OIK
PD   ccc xxx ccc xx   xx oi xx c

MH   OIZ ZOI OIS CHOI   (murmur) OIL LOI ROI OIK
PD   xxx ow xxx   xx xx xxx xxx xxxx

MH   say GOOD BOIE   nope . . . GOOD BOIE   GOOD BOIE (high)
PD   ccc xxx xxx   xxxxxxxx

1. Peter is giving more and more humanoid responses. Still some
   clicks.
2. Peter interrupts occasionally, but is getting a nice sense of
   listen, speak, listen, speak.
3. Words used by Margaret are from a nonsense syllable list designed to present combinations of sounds to the dolphin.

VOCAL EXCHANGES BETWEEN MARGARET AND PETER

MH Peter, say HELLO   yes . . . say GOOD BOIE . . . GOOD BOIE . . .
PD   ccxxxx xxlo

MH Come on, Peter, say GOOD BOIE   Nice. English, Peter, pronounce.
PD   xxxccxxxccxxx xx xx

MH Say MARGARET . . . come on   MA No! Listen. MARGARET   Not
PD   cccvv xx   xxxxx xxc

MH very good   say HELLO   That's better   say HELLO MARGARET
PD   ccc   xxaw baw   cccc

MH   uh uh . . . listen, listen HELLO MARGARET   nice
PD   cccxx uh uh uh   awxxx e

MH nice   listen listen listen   say HELLO GOOD BOY
PD   awxxxx ccccc c c c c c c c c   cc c   ccxxxw aw xxx

MH We are going to speak English yet, Peter . . . say HUMANOID . . .
PD

MH HUMANOID   No! That's not right. Say . . . BALL   No! Listen
PD   xxxxx   awxxx

MH Listen, listen   BALL   O.K. HELLO   uh uh uh
PD   ccccxxx   ccccccccxxxxaw   cc uh uh

MH listen listen HELLO   Uh uh Peter, I don't mean to bore you
PD   cc   xxxxxxxx

MH but you say it right and then we'll go on. Hmmm? You didn't say it
PD

MH right. Now listen. HELLO   Pretty good, pretty good.
PD   xxxx xx   ccccxxx

MH n'uh un uh now listen, listen listen listen Peter sssssh, say MARGARET
PD   c c c c c c c   c c c c c   xx

MH   uh uh no! Wrong MARGARET.   Peter! That's noise!
PD   ccc uh uh uh xx uh   uh uh uh xxx

1. Peter still clicks, but mainly humanoid.
2. Some of his humanoids are beginning to shape into English
   sounds.
3. Peter still interrupts Margaret, but occasionally hushes when
   told to. Whole lesson is shaping up.

After Ten Days of Living Together Twenty-four Hours per Day (June 8, 1965)

MH Say . . . MAGRIT   all right   sssssh   listen listen no!
PD   ccccc xxx xxx   xxx xxxx   x x x x   x x x x x x

MH Listen! Listen, Peter! Listen no! Listen Peter! sshhhh
PD xxx   xxxowxxxxxxx   xxxxxxxx xx

MH   HELLO MAGRIT   GOOD BOIE GOOD BOIE Come on . . .
PD xxx   xx   xxxx xxxxx

MH   Listen, listen. no no no . . . say GOOD BOIE
PD xxxx xxx xxxxxx   xx xxxxbxxxxxxxx

MH Peter! Listen to me! Now stop it! no! no! no! Listen
PD   x x x x x x x x x x x x x x x x x x x x   x x x

MH Peter, shhhh shhhh   say GOOD BOIE   Oh, he just won't
PD   x x x x x x x x x x

MH listen to me. HELLO   thank you, that's good. MAGRIT   all right
PD   xxx   cccccxxx xxxx

MH I Am   all right GOOD BOIE   all right no, listen, no no no no
PD   axxx xxx   xxx Bxxx xxx   xxx x x x x x x x x x x x

MH shhhh listen   listen listen Peter HELLO   no, he's just
PD x x x x x x x   x x x x x x x   x x x x x

MH getting   HELLO   HOW ARE YOU?   No, not very good, Peter.
PD xxxxxxxxx   xxxxxx   xxxx xxx

MH   HOW   Listen, Peter, no no no no ssshhhh . . .
PD xxxx xxx   xxxx x x x x x x x x x x x x x x x x x

1. Peter replies in almost solid humanoids. Very few clicks.
2. He has lost his beginning sense of conversation . . . again, he interrupts Margaret. He speaks at the same time.
3. Time is spent trying to get him to listen . . . hush.

VOCAL EXCHANGES BETWEEN MARGARET AND PETER

After Sixty-three Days and Nights (August 10 1965) (Plate 31)

MH MAGRIT   All right, listen . . . BALL   Peter . . . BALL
PD   xxx xxx   xx xx   x xx xx

MH BALL   Yes. Say TOIE FISH   listen . . . TOIE FISH   murmur
PD   xxaw   aw   xxx xxx

MH come over here, Peter. Say BO BO CLOWN   Let's do it again.
PD   xxx xxx xxx

MH Pronounce, Peter BO BO CLOWN   nice. KI NI PO PO
PD   xxo oh xxx   xx xx xx xx

MH Listen . . . KI NI PO PO   That's better.   murmur MAGRIT
PD   xx xx xx xoh

MH   Listen, MAGRIT   No . . . MAGRIT   No, Peter.
PD xx xx xx   xx xx xx   xx xx ee

MH Listen, MAGRIT   MAGRIT   better. Say HELLO MAGRIT
PD   xx xx xx   xxx xxx

MH   Pronounce, Peter. HELLO MAGRIT   That's
PD xxx xxx xxx xxx   xxx ohh aaa xxx

MH better, Peter. Say BO BO CLOWN   Listen. BO BO CLOWN
PD   xxx xxx   xxx xxx xx

MH Listen . . . BO BO CLOWN   Listen, Peter, BO BO CLOWN
PD   xxx xxx ownxx   xx xx xx

1. Peter no longer clicks or gives any delphinese responses.
2. Peter listens, speaks. When he is wrong, Margaret can hush him and start over.
3. Peter improves in giving back the same number of sounds that are given to him.
4. Peter is able to make parts of his words understandable.
5. Less is controlled, progress can be seen and heard during even such a short segment.

After the Experimental Period Is Finished (October 8, 1965)
(Plate 32)

MH   Now you think, Peter, 'cause you used to do this. Listen. BA BEE
      BLOCK
PD

MH   Yes! (clapping) That's better. Now do the other
PD   mxx xxx

MH   one. Say . . . BA SKET BALL   No, BA SKET BALL
PD   xx   xx xx xx   xxxx xx xx

MH   Better.   shhh! MAGRIT   No. It's EMMMMMM (ends with a kiss
PD   xxx   xxx xxx

MH   on Peter's head) say . . . MMAGRIT   no, not EH. It's MMM.
PD   eh xxx

MH   Eh . . . MMM MMMMMM MMAGRIT   Yes! Yes! (clapping)
PD   (softly) Mxx xxx

MH   That's an EM. Let's do it again. Say . . . MMAGRIT   Yes, that's
PD   mxxx xxx

MH   better. (clapping) Good! Say . . . BALL   No, not MAGRIT.
PD   xxx xxx

MH   BALL with a BEE. Say . . . BALL   Yes! BAWL! Good! Say . . .
PD   baww

MH   MMAGRIT   No . . . not EH. MMMMM. MMMMM.
PD   eh xxx

MH   MMAGRIT   Yes . . . that's better . . . that's better, Peter . . .
PD   mxx xxx

MH   Good! Yes, you can muffle it (clap)
PD

1. Note that Margaret syncopates "baby block" and "basketball"
   and Peter learns to follow this.

2. Note Peter speaks out of turn and is immediately hushed in lines seven and eight.

3. Note Peter, for the main part, is responding with humanoids, the right number with usually a good pitch and inflection. Margaret begins to demand more . . . working on enunciation. Special sounds.

4. The lesson is controlled and formal, and the give-and-take of learning, teaching, speaking, and listening is established so that progress can be seen.

CHAPTER 16

Conclusions about Living with a Dolphin

THE PHOTOGRAPHS which are appended to this report with their captions illustrate many of the points made in the body of Margaret's writing. In order to appreciate the magnitude of many of the tasks she mentioned, these photographs should be studied.

The conclusions are divided up into two sections: those by Margaret Howe, summing up the findings, and those by John Lilly.

Margaret writes as follows:

General conclusions about learning ability of dolphins. (a) It is difficult to record all the information Peter has learned in this program. Dolphins not only can learn, but enjoy learning, learn fast, and they have learned lots of things we cannot know about. We limit the information. (b) Dolphins can learn to play *with* someone. At the beginning of these 2½ months, Peter would not share his toys . . . he played alone, was often the initiator of a game with a human. (c) Peter learned *how* to work during a vocal lesson (as taught by the human) and also made vocal progress. (d) Peter learned how to teach me. (e) Peter learned to curb his physical energies to allow for my being so "human." (f) Peter learned that he could please me immensely, as well as annoy me.

Vocal progress made by Peter is as follows:

The written tape transcriptions show the following steps in progress, early to late. 1. Peter mainly clicks, a few humanoids, interrupts me. 2. Peter gives me more and more humanoids, still interrupts. 3. Peter begins to listen, gains a sense of conversation. 4. Peter learns to hush when I sush him . . . I can correct him. 5. Peter makes good attempts at copying my speech, at the same time keeping a good listen, speak, listen, speak business.

The written tape transcription does *not* show the following steps that were also made in progress: 1. Peter learned to copy the inflection in my voice very well. When my voice rises in the last part of a word, Peter's also rises. 2. Peter learned to be relatively quiet in the water during a lesson. Early lessons are filled with Peter splashing around and often circling the room during a lesson. At the end of the period, he remains in one place during the whole lesson, involved in his part in the lesson. He *listens*. 3. Peter learned to watch what I am doing during a lesson. If I am counting balls, or pointing to shapes, Peter will lie on his side, and I can see his eye look at the objects. 4. Peter has learned to work for whatever he gains out of the lesson as well as my vocal and physical praise, rather than for a fish reward. Peter will enter into a humanoid conversation, speaking and listening, at any time of day or night . . . *no longer just during feedings*. This has been so successful, that now Peter himself will often call to me or start to speak when I am with him, and I find that the lesson or conversation that follows was actually started by Peter. Our formal lessons are still done during feedings, but the fish itself is not used as a reward. Peter gets fed all the fish during the same approximate period of time whether it is a good lesson or a horror. When he gives a poor response, he gets a fish, and a vocal scolding from me. When he is brilliant, he gets a fish and a vocal praising from me.

Conclusions from 2½ months' program for designing future flooded house are as follows: The main conclusion is that this program has shown that this type of living situation is very worthwhile, and that the longer, more permanent flooded house program may prove invaluable as a step in breaking the communication barrier between man and dolphin, and therefore must be achieved.

There are several minor points learned during the course of this program that will prove valuable in the longer program: 1. More work must be done on the diet of the human. This program showed that lots of canned goods, spaghetti, etc., allowed the person to stay healthy, but a considerable gain in weight was noted. Refrigeration would help this problem. 2. Margaret felt, after her one week live-in with Pamela, that even her short bobbed hair was too long, and tended to stay damp through the day and night, and took too long drying when completely wet. For the 2½-month program, she cut her hair into a very boyish cut, about one-quarter inch all over. This could be completely dried with a towel in a matter of a few minutes, and was easy to keep clean and free from salty stickiness and itching. She did this, not only for reasons of health, but also for the advantage of not having to resist leaping in with the dolphin at, say, an odd hour of the night just because she wanted to keep her head dry. (Margaret is determined that nothing as trivial as wet hair should stop just such spontaneous play.) 3. Sleeping must be improved. Being able to sleep in a dry, comfortable bed each night would eliminate much of the discomfort in the program. This must not, however, be done in such a way as to remove the human from the dolphin's area . . . the dolphin must be able to rouse the human at any time. This could be done vocally, however, and not with splashing. Being able to touch and see Peter from my bed was very important . . . this closeness should not be sacrificed for dryness. Perhaps a more rigid curtain around the bed would be appropriate. 4. Being able to shower (fresh water) and get into bed without touching saltwater would be almost a necessity for a period much longer than 2½ months. 5. The human operator involved in the longer program should not have outside responsibilities at the same time. Note that Margaret was distracted or worried by outside construction problems, health of other animals, workmen problems, etc. Pumps, electricity, refrigeration, food, etc. should not be handled by operator . . . but should be taken care of by outside personnel. 6. Flooded house area should contain within it as much variety of living for humans as possible. Several rooms, different sections, a good dry area, an interesting wet area, . . . etc. Note that the two rooms proved to be a rather dull environment for two months. Activity for the human was limited. Note activity for dolphin was also limited . . . and recommend deep area for dolphin relaxation. 7. Sufficient time out must be allotted the human to avoid negative results (lag in interest) of isolation effects. Positive effects, however, of isolation effect (closeness with dolphin) should not be avoided.

One major result is that all of the time, energy, money, self-dedication, and facility development have been eminently worthwhile. I feel that we are in the midst of a new "becoming," moving into a previous unknown, armed with a kind of knowledge that we could not have obtained except through these experiments. I wish to emphasize (and not overanalyze) at this stage of our human development that new totally unexpected sequences of events took place. These events were ably reported by Margaret Howe. In addition much that is not yet consciously reportable has taken place in Miss Howe. Also much that neither she nor I have yet been able to get at in the human-dolphin relationship and in the dolphin. Currently this group is on their way and, I feel strongly, on the right way. This and similar endeavors should be supported and enthusiastically encouraged in order to continue toward the flooded house program.

I personally have learned much new about dolphins, much new about a first-class human faced with a dolphin for long periods. I have learned some new things about the abilities of man and a dolphin in carrying out a good-natured, yet serious wet living together program.

I find that the information collected shows that the assumptions on which this project is founded are productive of new facts. Margaret tests out the assumptions with intelligent and emotional interactions between herself and the dolphin. The only limitations of this kind of research are in our conceptions as carried to this work, modified in the course of this work, and used in planning future more comprehensive contexts for this kind of shared living.

In this sort of work it is wise to minimize the gadgetry, and to maximize the use of one's self. It may be that the fundamental barriers which do exist between these two species may be overcome by Miss Howe's dedicated efforts unaided by devices created for human-dolphin communication. (Another project of CRI is exploring the possibility of surmounting the frequency barrier between human speech and "delphinese." If it turns out that the frequency barrier is the limiting one, then the developed electronic means may be employed.)

Our major goal is breaking the interspecies communication barrier so that we can mutually exchange information having descriptive, predictive, and cognitive meanings. Until we live with dolphins and they with us, the dolphin mind remains opaque to us, and the human mind remains dryly out of reach of dolphin teaching.

Miss Howe did a magnificent job. She now rates a long earned vacation. Her intraspecies needs finally are being taken care of: she, like the girl with the chimpanzees in Africa, married her photographer. For a year or so she will tend her own family, human only. It may be that eventually she will be able to arrange to have a dolphin in her family with her children as one more "child."

Peter has been returned to his dolphin friends for his well-earned vacation from a human—for a while. Some person other than Margaret may continue the work.

Epilogue

In MARCH 1966, the Russian Minister for Fisheries, Alexander Ishkov, signed a decree prohibiting the commercial catching and slaughter of dolphins in the Sea of Azov and in the Black Sea for a period of ten years. Several members of the Soviet Academy of Sciences (USSR) have appealed to scientists in other countries to obtain similar bans in their countries.

What is the background for this sort of initiative in the Soviet Union? Extensive research on the dolphin has been done and is being done in the USSR. Basic research on the brain has been done by several investigators (I. N. Filiminoff, T. Sakharova, V. P. Zvorynkin, Ph. Owsjannikow, M. F. Nikitenko). This area of research is the key to changing the current misconceptions about the place of dolphins on this planet. Our own research on the dolphin's brain is reaching a culmination in *An Atlas of the Brain of the Dolphin*, Tursiops truncatus.* Our work and that of the Russians complement one another. The demonstrations of the high quality of this brain are very nearly completed. To mistreat this species is not in the best humanitarian traditions any longer. Finally the human species has an opportunity to commit itself to collaborative efforts with another species of high caliber in programs of mutual interest. Though the

* Morgane, P. J., *et al.* (1966).

dolphins are different (even alien), they are probably quite as flexible, educable, and as intelligent as we are.

As a consequence of our studies, it is proposed that new facilities be created in various parts of the world to facilitate this kind of development. It is suggested that shallow water "parks" be established. Such parks would be in areas which the dolphins naturally seek. The underwater and above-water facilities are to be designed so as to allow *voluntary* contacts between the species. Neither man nor dolphin are to be constrained in their own or in the other's medium. This interface problem has been presented in this book, and certain kinds of parameters can now be specified. With the help and interest of conservationists and their organizations, with national and state government help, these plans and programs can be realized. With care, the goodwill of the dolphins can be maintained. Men of goodwill can arrange these facilities and protect them.

A new ethic and its consequent laws will develop. Not merely conservation and protection will suffice. Positive new thinking, feeling, and action are needed.

Let us change Aelian's plea, "Oh my good, kind dolphins, beware the savagery of men!" to "Kind dolphins, join us!"

General Bibliography

Aristotle, Works of, translated into English under the editorship of W. D. Ross, and reprinted by arrangement with Oxford University Press for The Great Books, Vol. 9 (Chicago: Encyclopaedia Britannica, 1952).

Ash, Christopher. *Whaler's Eye* (New York: The Macmillan Company, 1962).

Boulle, Pierre. *Planet of the Apes* (New York: New American Library of World Literature, 1963).

Carpenter, C. R. *Naturalistic Behavior of Nonhuman Primates* (University Park, Pa.: Pennsylvania State University Press, 1964).

Dakin, William John. *Whalemen Adventures: The story of whaling in Australian waters and other southern seas related thereto, from the days of sail to modern times* (Sydney, Australia: Angus & Robertson, 1934).

Doppler, Christian J. *Uber Das Farbige Licht Der Doppelsterne* (Prague, 1842).

Eiseley, Loren. "The long loneliness. Man and the porpoise: two solitary destinies." *Am. Scholar* 30: 57–64 (1961).

Erikson, Erik H. *Insight and Responsibility* (New York: W. W. Norton & Company, 1964).

Freud, Anna. *The Ego and Mechanisms of Defence* translated from the German by Cecil Baines (New York: New York International University Press, 1946).

Freud, Sigmund. *Collected Papers* (New York: Basic Books, 1959).

Gilbert, Bil. *How Animals Communicate* (New York: Pantheon Books, 1966).

James, William. *Varieties of Religious Experience; a study in human nature.* Gifford Lectures delivered at Edinburgh University, 1901–2 (New York, London, Bombay, and Calcutta: Longmans, Green & Co., 1902, 1929).

Jung, C. G. *Memories, Dreams and Reflections* (New York: Pantheon Books, 1963).

Kinsey, Alfred C., Pomeroy, Wardell B., and Martin, Clyde E. *Sexual Behavior in the Human Male* (Philadelphia and London: W. B. Saunders Co., 1948).

——, Pomeroy, Wardell B., Martin, Clyde E., and Gebhard, Paul H. *Sexual Behavior in the Human Female* (Philadelphia and London: W. B. Saunders Co., 1953).

Lilly, John C. "Mental effects of reduction of ordinary levels of physical stimuli on intact, healthy persons." *Psychiat. Res. Reports* 5: 1–28 (Washington, D.C.: American Psychiatric Association, 1956).

—— *Man and Dolphin* (Garden City, New York: Doubleday & Company, 1961).

—— "Some considerations regarding basic mechanisms of positive and negative types of motivations." *Am. J. of Psychiat.* 115: 498–504 (1958).

—— "Vocal behavior of the bottlenose dolphin." *Proc. Am. Philos. Soc.* 106: 520–29 (1962).

—— "Critical brain size and language." *Perspectives in Biol. & Med.* 6: 246–55 (1963).

—— "Distress call of the bottlenose dolphin: stimuli and evoked behavioral responses." *Science* 139: 116–18 (1963).

—— "Vocal mimicry in *Tursiops*: ability to match numbers and durations of human vocal bursts." *Science* 147: 300–1 (1965).

—— *The Human Biocomputer: Programming and Metaprogramming (Theory and Experiments with LSD-25)* (Miami: Communication Research Institute, 1967; Scientific Report Number CRI0167).

—— "The need for an adequate model of the human end of the inter-species—specific communication program in communication with Extraterrestrial Intelligence." *IEEE Spectrum* 3: 159–60 (1966).

—— and Howe, Margaret C. Progress Report, St. Thomas (1965).

—— and Miller, Alice M. "Vocal exchanges between dolphins." *Science* 134: 1873–76 (1961).

—— and Shurley, Jay T. "Experiments in solitude, in maximum achievable physical isolation with water suspension of intact healthy persons." *Psychophysiological Aspects of Space Flight*: 238–47 (New York: Columbia University Press, 1961).

Melville, Herman. *Moby Dick* (New York: Dodd, Mead & Co., 1942).

Montaigne, Michel de. Essays II, 12, 1533–92. The Great Books, Vol. 25 (Chicago: University of Chicago, 1952).

Morgane, P. J. "Lamination characteristics and areal differentiation in the cerebral cortex of the bottlenose dolphin (*Tursiops truncatus*)." *Anat. Rec.* 151(3): 390–91 (1965).

——, Yakovlev, Paul I., Jacobs, Myron S., McFarland, W. L., and Piliero, Sam J. *An Atlas of the Brain of the Dolphin*, Tursiops truncatus (New York: Pergamon Press. In press).

Nagel, E., Morgane, P. J., and McFarland, W. L. "Anesthesia for the bottlenose dolphin, *Tursiops truncatus*." *Science* 146: 1591–93 (1964).

Plato. "Statesman," *Dialogues of Plato*, 428–348 B.C.; The Great Books, Vol. 7 (Chicago: University of Chicago, 1952).

Plinius Secundus C. *Natural History*, six volumes (Bostock and Riley, London: Bell, 1855–90).

Skinner, B. F. *Verbal Behavior* (New York: Appleton-Century-Crofts, 1957).

Szilard, Leo. *The Voice of the Dolphins and Other Stories* (New York: Simon and Schuster, 1961).

Truby, H. M. In *Newborn Infant Cry*. A collection of articles edited by John Lind. Acta Paediatrica Scandinavica Supplementary 163 (Uppsala: Almqvist & Wiksells Boktryckeri AB, 1965).

Van Neumann, John. *The Computer and the Brain* (New Haven, Conn.: Yale University Press, 1958).

Zuckerman, Sir Solly. *The Social Life of Monkeys and Apes* (Trency, Trubner & Co., London: Kegan Paul, 1932).

Selected Bibliography on Dolphins

JOHN CUNNINGHAM LILLY

1961 "The biological versus psychoanalytic dichotomy." *Bul. of Phila. Assoc. for Psychoanal.* 11: 116–19.

1961 *Man and Dolphin* (New York: Doubleday & Company; London: Victor Gollancz).

1961 "Problems of physiological research on the dolphin, *Tursiops.*" (abstract) *Fed. Proc. 20.*

1961 (With A. M. Miller) "Sounds emitted by the bottlenose dolphin." *Science* 133: 1689–93.

1961 (With A. M. Miller) "Vocal exchanges between dolphins." *Science* 134: 1873–76.

1962 "Cerebral dominance," pp. 112–14 in Vernon Montcastle, M.D., ed., *Interhemispheric Relations and Cerebral Dominance* (Baltimore: Johns Hopkins Press).

1962 "Consideration of the relation of brain size to capability for language activity as illustrated by *Homo sapiens* and *Tursiops truncatus* (bottlenose dolphin)." *Electroenceph. Clin. Neurophysiol.* 14: 424.

1962 "The Sensory World Within, and Man and Dolphin" (Lecture to the Laity, New York Academy of Medicine, 11 April 1962) (Miami: Communication Research Institute, Report Number CRIo162).

1962 "Interspecies communication," pp. 279–81 in *Yearbook of Science and Technology* (New York: McGraw-Hill).

1962 *Man and Dolphin* (The Worlds of Science Series: Zoology) (New York: Pyramid Publications).

1962 *Manniskan och Delfinen* (Stockholm: Wahlstrom & Widstrand).

1962 *L'Homme et le Dauphin* (Paris: Stock).

1963 *Mennesket og Delfinen* (Oslo: Nasjonalforlaget).

1963 *Mens en Dolfijn* (Amsterdam: Contact).

1962 "A new laboratory for research on delphinids." *Assoc. of Southeastern Biologists Bul.* 9: 3–4.

1962 (With A. M. Miller) "Operant conditioning of the bottlenose dolphin with electrical stimulation of the brain." *J. Comp. & Physiol. Psychol.* 55: 73–79.

1962 "The 'talking' dolphins," in *Book of Knowledge Annual* (New York: Grolier).

1962 "Vocal behavior of the bottlenose dolphin." *Proc. Am. Philos. Soc.* 106: 520–29.

1963 "Critical brain size and language." *Perspectives in Biol. & Med.* 6: 246–55.

1963 "Distress call of the bottlenose dolphin: stimuli and evoked behavioral responses." *Science* 139: 116–18.

1963 "Modern whales, dolphins and porpoises, as challenges to our intelligence," pp. 31–54 in Ashley Montagu and John C. Lilly, *The Dolphin in History*, a symposium given at the Clark Memorial Library, 1962 (Clark Memorial Library, University of California, Los Angeles).

1963 "Productive and creative research with man and dolphin." *Arch. Gen. Psychiatry* 8: 111–16. (Fifth Annual Lasker Lecture, Michael Reese Hospital and Medical Center, Chicago, 1962.)

1964 "Airborne sonic emissions of *Tursiops truncatus* (M)." (abstract) *J. Acoustical Soc. of Amer.* 36:5, p. 1007.

1964 (With M. S. Jacobs, P. J. Morgane, and B. Campbell) "Analysis of cranial nerves in the dolphin." *Anatomical Record* 148: 379.

1964 "Animals in aquatic environment: adaptation of the mammals to the ocean," pp. 741–57 in *Handbook of Physiology: environment I* (Washington, D.C.: Am. Physiol. Soc.).

1965 "Report on experiments with bottlenose dolphins." (abstract) *Proc. Int'l Symp. on Comparative Med.* (New York, 1962).

1965 "Sonic-ultrasonic emissions of the bottlenose dolphin" in *Whales, Dolphins & Porpoises* from *Proc., First Int'l Symp. on Cetacean Research* (Washington, D.C., 1963).

1965 "Vocal mimicry in *Tursiops*: ability to match numbers and durations of human vocal bursts." *Science* 147 (3655): 300–1.

1966 "Communication with extraterrestrial intelligence." *IEEE Spectrum* 3 (3): 159–60. 1965 IEEE Military Electronics Conf. (Washington, D.C.: September 1965).

1966 "Sexual behavior of the bottlenose dolphin" in *Brain and Be-*

havior, Vol. III: *The Brain and Gonadal Function* (R. A. Gorski and R. E. Whalen, eds.) *UCLA Forum Med. Sci.* No. 3 (University of California Press, Los Angeles).

1966 (with H. M. Truby) "Measures of human-Tursiops Sonic Interactions." JASA *40*:1241(A)

1967 "Dolphin-Human Relation and LSD-25" in *The Use of LSD in Psychotherapy and Alcoholism* (H. A. Abramson, editor) *Proc. 2nd Int'l. Conf. on the Use of LSD in Psychotherapy* 1965 (New York: Bobbs-Merrill, 1967).

1967 "Dolphin Vocalization" in *Brain Mechanisms Underlying Speech and Language* (New York: Grune and Stratton, 1967).

1967 "Dolphin's vocal mimicry as a unique ability and a step towards understanding" in *Mechanisms of Vocal Production in Man* (New York: New York Academy of Sciences, 1967).

1967 (With Alice M. Miller and Henry M. Truby) "Reprogramming of the Sonic Output of the Dolphin: Sonic Burst-Count Matching" (Miami: Communication Research Institute; Scientific Report Number CRI0267).

Acknowledgments

The National Institute of Mental Health, National Institutes of Health, Bethesda, Maryland, gave a Career Award to the author for five years (1962–67). This award provided some of the essential freedom to plan, to organize, to integrate, and to think out this program. For these five years of help I am appreciative.

The National Institute of Neurological Diseases and Blindness, National Institutes of Health, Bethesda, has been most helpful in providing research grants in basic support of the research program for several years. Our collaborative studies with Drs. P. J. Morgane, W. L. McFarland, P. I. Yakovlev, M. Jacobs, A. Pilero, E. L. Nagel, R. Galliano, and H. M. Truby have been made possible with this support.

The National Science Foundation, Washington, D.C. has been very helpful with grants for facilities and equipment necessary for the scientific research. I appreciate these aids and also many valuable discussions with personnel of the Foundation.

The Air Force Office of Scientific Research has been helpful at many critical points in the development of parts of the work. Development of new techniques and new orientations toward high-speed communication are coming from this support. I am grateful for this aid.

At a critical time in the development of the program the Unger Vetleson Foundation provided a grant. The Michael Tors Foundation has contributed much-needed private funds in support of the general fund of the Institute.

In addition, many friends have given support (monetary and otherwise) as expressions of their confidence in the ongoing research. To each and every one of these I wish to express my thanks and appreciation.

I wish to thank my colleagues (past and present) in the Institute for many helpful discussions, the work accomplished, and their continuing dedication to the scientific progress. I owe a debt of especial gratitude to Peter J. Morgane and Henry M. Truby for the clarification of many scientific points, and their critical, patient education of me in parts of the neuroanatomical, phonetic, and linguistic sciences. W. A. Munson has helped in the acoustic and speech areas, and in the realization of a voice frequency spectrum translator for man and dolphin.

AFTERWORD by Roberta Goodman
co-author of *Dolphins and Whales Forever*

FOR THE LOVE OF DOLPHINS— WHO'S TESTING WHOM?

"You're really serious about this dolphin business!" John Lilly said when we co-founded Cetacean Nation in 1992 at the edge of the sea on Maui. "*Save the Humans* should be our motto."

Eight years earlier, Dr. John and Toni Lilly asked me to become the Research Director for the Human/Dolphin Foundation and our two dolphins, Joe and Rose. During a process of untraining Joe and Rose in preparation for their move from tanks to sea, I found the dolphins had a quick aptitude for releasing their conditioned responses and creating new responses. On the first trial, I rewarded the dolphins for performing bows when I had played the acoustic cue for *wave pectoral fin*. They hadn't expected the change from sessions beginning with *bow*, but immediately began testing me by giving wrong answers to each cue. Cheering them on, I fed them fish.

In another session, as Joe and Rose performed one novel behavior after another for 20 trials, Lilly sat on the picnic bench at the edge of the pool, "Marvelous!"

The *DolphinTalker*, a Walkman in a waterproof case, had the ability to record and playback dolphin vocalization and human speech while interacting in the water. Teaching the dolphins "Yes" and "No" would become a question in the water when playing back their sounds in an appropriate context, hoping for verification.

An accidental recording from the side of the tank captured the dolphins' use of my name, with a clear rendition of "Roberta!" as I passed by their tank. There had been no previous training in imitation of my name.

John Lilly's gift with the Janus Project, with the dolphins Joe and Rose, was the opportunity for a few of us to conduct communication research in open exploration and for hundreds of

311

people to become intimately acquainted with dolphins. The Human/ Dolphin Foundation Lab was the first place to swim with dolphins in tanks, playing with the dolphins for as long as you wished or until they kicked you out of the pool, and was without a charge. Many influential people came and wrote about their amazement and transformation in our après-swim notebook. Ram Dass tells that Rosie was his *greatest teacher of intuition.* She took his forearm gently in her mouth and nothing in his life prepared him for that moment. He had no idea what to do and became completely in the moment, eye to eye with the dolphin. Facing Rosie, he had to turn to his intuition to act in trust. The dolphins altered one's perceptions of life and the meaning of our conceptions of reality. We were no longer alone as a species at the pinnacle of a mammalian hierarchy. We were united in Nature with an equally aware intelligence, gazing soul to soul. Timothy Leary, Olivia Newton-John, Kris Kristofferson, Susan Sarandon, and others used superlatives in their comments about how it felt to swim with Joe and Rose.

In 1982, my friends had no interest in meeting dolphins. Alone in my quest to understand who dolphins are, they became my closest friends who knew me at the deepest core of my being. The space with dolphins was beyond thought, words, concepts; it was a state of beingness-together. Our consciousness joined in play and in Presence.

I sought to reconnect the dolphins to authenticity in human interactions, based on trust and freedom in two way communication. Project Communion began preparation for the dolphins to return to the sea. When Joe and Rose were caught near Gulfport, Mississippi, Lilly promised to release them back to the Gulf. Joe, Rosie, Cindi Buzzell and I moved from Redwood City, California, to the Florida Keys. Taras Kicenik and Karl Straub cut a large hole in the chain link fence, creating a gate to the channel beyond their sea pen. I fed the dolphins from my windsurf board imagining them following a boat and learning to navigate. Dr. Lilly and I found a community in Sarasota, Florida, supportive of our effort to release the dolphins into the Gulf. My friend bought a private island on which we could establish an *open sea release research center.* We had a long term plan for gradual re-adaptation and documentation of a protocol for returning dolphins to the sea, but Rosie was pregnant and we delayed the move. Circumstances changed—the beloved Toni Lilly was in her last six months of life. The dolphins were assigned to another organization and two years later were let go into the Atlantic off Georgia.

John Lilly and I had differing views on communication between humans and dolphins. His vision was to hear dolphins speak English. He began with in-air speech and with the Human/Dolphin Foundation we heard a better ability to produce sounds underwater. My dream was to learn Delphinese. Lilly and I agreed that telepathy combined with nonverbal language was the most promising method to complex understanding. In hundreds of hours swimming with them, I found Joe and Rose to be telepathic, sensitive, and spiritual nonhuman intelligences. Swimming among wild dolphins since that time, I observe the *essential nature of dolphin*, which is retained by dolphins in aquariums.

Dr. Lilly's description of an Open-Sea Research Lab in *Mind of the Dolphin* continues to inspire my vision for the future of communication between the two peoples, human and dolphin. Towards this end, I have established a base in Hawaii. Funding my research is my boat charter business, while bringing people into the ocean to experience wild dolphins eye to eye. Meanwhile the wild dolphins have come to know me better than I know them. Re-wilding previously captive dolphins into this area or another would combine Dr. Lilly's futuristic lab with the passion of the public to see cetaceans live out their lives in an open environment.

Thank you to Dr. John C. Lilly for letting the world know how to perceive and think about Cetaceans. Most of what we believe about dolphins originated with his prolific early work.

313

Appendix 1
Modern Whales, Dolphins, and Porpoises, as Challenges to Our Intelligence *(Paper delivered at the Clark Library, UCLA, 1962)*

The intelligence of whales has been the subject of speculation by writers since Ancient Greece.[1] [2]The discovery of the large brains of the Cetacea in the eighteenth century led to inevitable comparisons of these brains to those of the humans and of the lower primates. The winds of scholarly opinions concerning the whales have anciently blown strongly for high intelligence, but during later centuries shifted strongly against high intelligence. At the time of Aristotle (384-322 B.C.), the dolphin, for example, was held in high esteem, and many stories of the apparently great abilities of these animals were current.[3] By the time of Plinius Secundus (A.D. 23-79), the beginning of a note of skepticism was introduced. Plinius said, "I should be ashamed to tell the story were it not that it has been written about by . . . others."[1]

In the middle ages the strong influence of religious philosophy on thinking placed Man in a completely separate compartment from all other living creatures, and the accurate anatomy of the whales was neglected. This point is illustrated by Figure I, published in the 1500s in *Historia Animalium* by Konrad Gesner. This was apparently a baleen whale. It has two tubes which apparently symbolize the double blowhole of the Mystacocetae. There is no modern whale known that has such tubes sticking out of the top of his head. There is a huge eye above the angle of the jaw. All whales have the eye at or near the posterior angle of the jaw. The eye is very much smaller than the one shown here. A print published in 1598 of the anatomy of these animals is shown in Figure 2. The drawing of the male organ is accurate (apparently it was measured with a walking stick), but the eye is too large and is misplaced.

These pictures illustrate very well man's most common relationship to the whale, which has continued to the present day. For commercial reasons, man continues to exploit these creatures' bodies.

It was not until the anatomical work of Vesalius and others that the biological similarities and differences of man and other mammals were pointed out. It was at this time that the investigation of man's large and complex brain began.

All through these periods, intelligence and the biological brain factors seemed to be completely separated in the minds of the scholars. At the times of the Greeks and the Romans there was little, if any, link made between brain and mind. Scholars attributed man's special achievements to

314

other factors than excellence of brain structure and its use.

After the discovery of man's complicated and complex brain and the clinical correlation between brain injury and effects on man's performance, the brain and mental factors began to be related to one another. As descriptions of man's brain became more and more exact and clinical correlations increased sufficiently in numbers, new investigations on the relationships between brain size and intelligence in *Homo sapiens* were started. The early work is summarized by Donaldson.[3]

In the late 1700s and the early 1800s, the expansion of the whaling industry offered many opportunities for examination of these interesting mammals. Figures 3 and 4 are dramatic examples of the state of the industry in the late eighteenth and early nineteenth centuries.

One of the earliest drawings of the complex brain of one of the cetacea is that of Gottfried Reinhold Trediramus in 1818 (Fig. 5). This is an anterior view of the brain of the common porpoise *Phocaena phocaena*. This is one of the earliest pictures showing the complexity of the fissuration and the large numbers of gyri and sulci.

By the year 1843, the size of the brain of whales was being related to the total size of the body. The very large brains of the large whales were reduced in importance by considering their weight in a ratio to the weight of the total body. This type of reasoning was culminated with a long series of quantitative measures published by Eugene Dubois (*Bulletins de la Societe d' Anthropologie de Paris*, Ser. 4, VIII [1897], 337-376).

Descriptions from those of Hunter and Tyson onwards agree that, in absolute size, the brains are as large and larger than those of man. All were agreed that the smaller whales, i.e., the dolphins and porpoises, have very large brains with relation to their body size. It was argued, therefore, with respect to the dolphin, "this creature is of more than ordinary wit and capacity." (Robert Hamilton, *The Natural History of the Ordinary Cetacea or Whales*, p. 66, in Sir William Jardine, *The Naturalist's Library*, volume 7, Edinburgh, 1843.)

Tiedemann's drawings of the brain of *Delphinus delphis* and of *Delphinus phocaena* were published by H.G.L. Reichenbach in his *Anatomia Mammalium* in 1845. The four drawings are shown in Figure 6. These drawings show the improved awareness of the complexities of these large brains in regard to cerebral cortex, the cerebellum, and the cranial nerves. Correlations between the structure of this brain and the behavior of the animal possessing it, were (and are) woefully lacking. The only behavioral accounts were those of whalers hunting these animals. Hunters tend to concentrate on the offensive and defensive maneuvers of the

315

animal, and can give useful information for other kinds of evaluation of the animal's behavior and presumed intelligence.

In 1787 John Hunter, writing in the *Philosophical Transactions of the Royal Society of London* (LXXVII, 423-424), said the following: "The size of the Brain differs much in different genera of this tribe, and likewise in the proportion it bears to the bulk of the animal. In the Porpoise, I believe, it [the proportion] is largest, and perhaps in that respect comes nearest to the human . . .

"The brain is composed of cortical and medullary substances, very distinctly marked; the cortical being, in colour, like the tubular substance of a kidney; the medullary, very white. These substances are nearly in the same proportion as in the human brain . . . The thalami themselves are large; the corpora striata small; the crura of the fornix are continued along the windings of the ventricles, much as in the human subject."

Flatau and Jacobsohn in 1899 wrote, "The large brain of the Porpoise is one of the smallest in the Cetacean Order in which the organ attains to a much greater absolute size than any other."[4]

In 1902 G. Elliot Smith wrote of the brain of a species of dolphin called "Delphinus tursio" (which may be the modern *Tursiops truncatus*): "This brain is larger and correspondingly richer in sulci than that of the porpoise: but the structure of the two organs is essentially the same." His drawings are shown in Figures 7 and 8. He said further, "the brains of the Beluga and all the dolphins closely resemble that of the porpoise."

Smith summarizes the discussion of the huge size of the whale's brain. "The apparently extraordinary dimensions of the whale's brain cannot therefore be considered unusual phenomena, because this enormous extent of the cerebral cortex to receive and 'store' impressions of such vast sensory surfaces becomes a condition of survival of the animal.

"The marvelous complexity of the surface of the cerebrum is the direct result of its great size. In order, apparently, that the cerebral cortex may be efficiently nourished and at the same time be spared to as great a degree as possible the risk of vascular disturbances [such as would be produced by large vessels passing into it], its thickness does not appreciably increase in large animals. [He then quotes Dubois' figures showing that the whale's cortex is the same thickness as that of the human.] Such being the case, it naturally results that the increased bulk of cortex in large animals can only be packed by becoming thrown into increasing number of folds, separated by corresponding large number of sulci."[4]

In regard to communication between individual whales, Scammon in 1874 wrote the following: "It is said that the Cachalots [Sperm Whales]

316

are endowed with the faculty of communicating with each other in times of danger, when miles . . . distant. If this be true, the mode of communication rests instinctively within their own contracted brains."[5] Let us not forget that Scammon was talking about the mammal with the largest known brain on this planet. Instinct as the sole cause of communication with a brain this size seems rather improbable. This brain is not any longer considered "contracted." Both of these statements illustrate an authoritative view of that time. If one peruses the paper by Tokuzo Kojima, "On the Brain of the Sperm Whale" (in the *Scientific Reports* of the Whales Research Institute, Tokyo, VI, 1951, 49-72), one can obtain a modern clear view of this brain. The largest one that he obtained (from a 49-foot sperm whale) was 9,200 grams. The average weight of the sixteen brains presented in his paper is 7,800 grams for average body lengths of 50 feet. (The brain weight per foot of body length varied from 118 to 187 grams per foot, averaging 157; man's ratio averages about 250 grams per foot.)

In the literature of the time of Scammon, the scholars failed to give us new information about the behavior of cetacea. There seems to have been a distinctly ambivalent attitude towards these animals which is continued today. This point of view can be summarized as follows: the whale is a very large animal with a brain larger than that of man. This brain is the result of the huge growth of its body. All of this large brain is needed to control a large body. Because these tasks are so demanding, there is not enough brain substance left for a high degree of intelligence to develop. Thus the large brain cannot give the degree of intellectual capability that man has.

As an example of man's attitudes to cetaceans, consider the case of the U.S. Fisheries Bureau *Economic Circular* No. 38, of November 6, 1918, by Lewis Radcliffe, entitled "Whales and Porpoises as Food." Roy Chapman Andrews is quoted as saying that hump-backed whale meat is the best of the larger cetaceans, but that porpoise and dolphin meat is even better eating than that of the larger whale. The composition of the whale meat is given as 30% protein, 6% fat, and less than 2% ash. From a hump-back whale one obtains six tons of meat, from a Sei Whale, five tons, and from a Finback, eight tons. Directions are given to remove the connective tissue between the blubber and the muscle to avoid the oily taste. For those who are interested, the paper includes twenty-two whale meat recipes and ten porpoise meat recipes.

It can well be imagined, if we ever do communicate with whales, dolphins, or porpoises, the kind of reception that this sort of literature will receive from the cetaceans.

317

The limited point of view of the whales as "dumb beasts" neglects the adaptations that have taken place in non-mammalian forms with very much smaller brains but with comparable bulk of body. The 60-foot whale shark, a plankton eater, and like the rest of the sharks a water-breather, has a bulk of body comparable to that of the larger whales. It has a large brain cavity, but a very small brain in a small part of this large cavity. (It is very difficult to find the weight of these brains to compare with that of the cetacea and other mammals.) The problem of brain weight versus body weight versus intelligence is most clearly expressed by Gerhardt von Bonin in his paper in the *Journal of General Psychology (1937)*.[6] He gives a very extensive table for mammals, their brain weight, their body weight, and the values of 2 parameters for their specification. He then states, "It is clear from all that has been said above that the figures given here are nothing but a description of facts, a description which, in the mathematical sense of the term, is the 'best' one. It does not pretend to make any enunciation about the relation of intelligence and brain weight. For that purpose, we need a much broader psychological basis than we have at present.

"Former attempts to analyze the relations between body weight and brain weight suffer from three deficits: (1) they presuppose a correlation between intelligence and brain weight, (2) they make suppositions about the intelligence of animals which are unproven, and (3) they are based on a conception of cortical function which can no longer be considered valid . . . There is a close correlation between the logarithms of brain and body weight, and this co-relation is linear. Brain weight increases as the 0.655^{th} power of body weight. The value of the cephalization co-efficient k differs from species to species. *Whether or not this is an indication of the intelligence of animals must be left to the psychologists to answer.*"

One of the problems that the whales have, as compared to, say, the large shark, is breathing air while living in the sea. This requires that these animals reach the air-water interface relatively frequently – at least every one hour-and-a-half for the bottlenose whale *(Hyperoodon)*, three-quarters of an hour for the Sperm Whale *(Physeter catadon)*, and every six minutes for *Tursiops truncatus*. This puts very stringent requirements on the relationship of the whales to other events within the sea. Each whale must know where the surface of the sea is at each instant and compute his future actions so that when he does run out of air, he is near the surface. He is essentially a surface-to-depth and depth-to-surface oriented animal. He must travel at high speed at times in order to recapture enough air to continue whatever he is doing under the surface. This means that he must calculate his chances of obtaining a good breath of air during rain storms and similar situations. He can be violently thrown around at the surface unless he comes up in the trough rather than at the crest of the wave. Such calculations probably require an exercise of something more than just "instinct."

Water-breathing animals, on the other hand, have no need for such calculations. If the surface gets rough, they move downward and stay there. The required maneuvers are very much simpler and the amount of computation is very much less.

This requirement for the whales implies that the information coming from every one of the senses, not just the skin, needs to be correlated very rapidly and in complex patterning to allow the animals to predict their future course safely and accurately. It also requires the use of large amounts of information from memory.

The predators of the sea, other than the whales themselves, make life in the sea rather a complex business for mammals. The very large sharks can and do attack whales, dolphins, and porpoises. At times such attacks are by overwhelming numbers of sharks on a relatively small number of dolphins. All of the older animals in our experience have at least one shark bite on them – the younger animals are protected by the older ones and most of them are not so dramatically scarred.

The whales, in turn, must track their own prey in order to obtain food. With the single known exception of *Orca,* none of their prey are air-breathers. In general, the whales' diet consists of fish, squid, or other water-breathing organisms of the sea.

A scientific assessment of the position of these animals in the competitive environment of the sea is not yet fully evaluated quantitatively. Any pronouncement of the requirements in regard to new complex adaptations to new complicated situations and hence the evaluation of intelligence of these animals at this time is premature and presumptuous. The whole issue of the meaning and the use of these large brains is still very much unknown. As I say in *Man and Dolphin,*[7] I am espousing a plea for an open-minded attitude with respect to these animals. It would be presumptuous to assume that we at the present time can know how to measure their intelligence or their intellectual capacity. The usual behavioral criteria used in evaluation of intelligence of other animals are obviously inapplicable to a mammal living in the sea. As McBride and Hebb [8] so clearly stated, they cannot place the dolphin in any sort of intellectual comparative intelligence scale; they did not know the appropriate experimental questions to ask in order to compare the dolphins with the chimpanzees, for example. Comparing a handed-mammal with a flippered-mammal, each of which lives in an entirely separate and distinctive environment, is a very difficult intellectual task even for *Homo sapiens.*

In pursuing possible measures of intellectual and intelligent capacity, what line should one pursue? I explored this question somewhat in *Man and Dolphin,* but wish to summarize and extend it here in this discussion. The invariants that we are seeking somehow do not seem to be as concrete as "tool-making and tool-using ability" by means of the hands which has been one of the major alleged criteria for human adaptation and success. The chimpanzee and the gorilla have the hands but they do not have the brains to back up the use of the hands. Man has both the hands and the brain. Thus we can quite simply and concretely contrast the performance of the large brains of man with his hands to the smaller brains of the primates with their hands. When we consider the whales, we seem obsessed, as it were, with the necessity of our own nature to look for an analog of the hand and the manipulative ability. May it not be better to find a more general principle than just handedness and its use?

I suggest that we think more in terms of a physiologically appropriate set of more general mechanisms which may subsume several other human functions under the same principle. It seems to me that we must look for abilities to develop generalized dexterity of use for certain kinds of end purposes for any or all muscular outputs from the central nervous system. If there is a task to be done, such as lifting a stone, whether in water or air, a given animal may turn it over with his foot, with his flipper, with his hand, with his tail, or with any other body part with which he could obtain a purchase on the stone. The end task is turning over the stone, to obtain food or whatever. It makes little difference what kind of muscular equipment he uses just so he uses it appropriately.

Let me illustrate with a more complex example seen in our own laboratory. A baby dolphin was being nursed in a small tank artificially. It apparently needed the constant attention of a human attendant. Its mother had not been caught with it. After several days it discovered that if it banged on the bottom of the tank with its flipper in a rhythmic fashion it could bring the humans from the other room. (We heard a loud thumping sound transmitted from a hydrophone in its tank.) Previous to this it attempted to bring the humans from the other room by whistling the distress call of the dolphins; unlike its mother, the humans did not respond

320

to the whistle. In a sense this distress call is in his instinctual pattern for obtaining food and aid by other dolphins. The secondary adaptation and the new effort was that of manipulating the flipper rather than the phonation mechanism in the blowhole. Thus driven by whatever the instinctual need is, it tried different outputs from its brain and finally discovered one which brought the desired results. This ability to change the output from unsuccessful ones to successful ones seems to me to be evidence of a "higher nervous system" function. Of course in fine gradation and small differences, the same kind of pattern can be shown for smaller-brained animals. It is the seeking a new output, not necessarily instinctually tied in, and the radicalness of the change of output, plus the relating of many of the variables to one another thus generating the new output, that seems to be the hallmark of the large brain. These problems are not single variable ones with simple cause and effect, but are simultaneous multiple variable ones.

Among the manipulable outputs (muscular groups) I would include those of respiration and phonation. The dexterous and finely differentiated use of these muscles generates all the complexities of human speech. As more of the physiology and psychology of human speech are analyzed and made part of our sciences, the sharper will be our criteria for separating man from the other animals, and from those with smaller brains. Scientific descriptions of human speech are of relatively recent origin. Scientific descriptions of the physiology of the vocal tract are anything but a closed book at the present time. The neuroanatomy and neurophysiology of speech is in a relatively primative state of development as a science. With such a lack of knowledge of the intimate and detailed mechanisms concerned, it would be rather presumptuous to evaluate at the present time their role in the measurement and testing of intelligence and intellectual capacity.

However, I wish to point out that these factors are important in such an evaluation and become even more important in terms of evaluating a species that is not human. Thus it is necessary, in order to evaluate the intelligence of even the dolphins, much less the whales, to know something of their abilities in the areas of phonation and other kinds of bodily gestures and manipulations and hence in their abilities to communicate with one another. As I implied in *Man and Dolphin,* it is not possible to measure accurately the intelligence of any other being than that of a human being, mainly because we do not exchange ideas through any known communication mode with such beings.

The difficulties of such understanding as we can possibly gain of the real situation of the whales in the sea and their adaptation as mammals to this particular environment, can be illustrated by their use of sonic generators for the location of their prey and of the boundaries of their container by means of the perception of echoes. As is well-known, the small mammals, such as the bat, use this mechanism in air.[9] The bottlenose dolphin also uses this same kind of mechanism underwater[7, 9, 14] Because these animals are immersed in a medium of a density and a sound velocity comparable to the density and sound velocity of their own bodies, they can presumably use their sonar also in looking, as it were, inside one another's body.[7] The sonar view of the inside of the body of a dolphin may possibly be very instructive to other dolphins and possibly even aid in diagnosis of the causes of certain problems, especially of those of the baby by the mother. For example, their buoyancy depends upon maintaining their center of gravity below their center of buoyancy; otherwise they turn over and drown. If the baby develops gas in stomach #1, he can develop problems in his buoyancy relationship which turn him over; however, the mother dolphin can probably easily find out whether or not there is a bubble of gas in the baby's stomach by her echo ranging abilities. When she discovers such a bubble, she can then burp the baby by banging on the belly with her beak. We have seen such operations take place in our tanks. Here is another instance of the animal using a given output, coupled with the proper input, to diagnose a problem and to manipulate other outputs in the solution of that problem. How much of this is labeled "instinctual," i.e., "unlearned," is purely a matter of intellectual taste.

In the sea it is necessary to use sonic mechanisms for sightings and recognition. If one goes into the sea one realizes that one's range of vision even under the best of circumstances is rarely beyond 100 feet and most of the time is less than that even near the brilliantly lit surface of the tropical seas. With sonic means, one's range is extended up to several miles under the best of circumstances and under the worst to a few hundred feet.

Recently we have obtained evidence that shows that the dolphins communicate most of their information in the band of frequencies extending from about 8 kilocycles to 20 kilocycles by means of whistles and sonic clicks.[11] However, as shown by Schevill and Lawrence, they can hear sounds at least to 120 kilocycles" and as shown by Kellogg can produce sounds at least to 170 kilocycles.[7, 13] With the proper electronic equipment one can listen to the nearer portions of the upper band and quickly determine that they can transmit in these bands without the necessity of transmitting in the (lower frequency) communication band. The high frequency information is broadcast in a narrow beam off the front of the beak as was first detected by Kenneth Norris. [14]

In these bands we find that they can produce musical tones or individual clickings or hissing-like noises. Recently we have found that an emotionally upset animal threatens other animals and humans by productions of very large amounts of energy both in the sonic communication band and in the ultrasonic bands. Recently we have had the opportunity of working with an old bull of 450 pounds weight who is so old his teeth have been ground down flat. In terms of his skeleton, he is the most massive animal we have ever seen. When he is irritated, his "barks" have sizable amounts of energy from about 0.5 to at least 300 kilocycles. He is also capable of transmitting in bands between 100 to 300 kilocycles without transmitting anything in the band from 8 kilocycles to 20 kilocycles in a narrow beam straight ahead of his body. When he is upset by the activities of a younger male, they face one another and blast at one another with short barks of this sort, meanwhile "threatening" by opening their mouths.

Since they live immersed in an acoustic world quite strange to us, we have great difficulty in appreciating the full life of these animals with respect to one another and their environment. From birth they are constantly bombarded with signals from the other animals of the same species and by echoes from the environment which they can apparently use very efficiently. Their ultrasonic (to us) emissions are not merely "sonar," but are interpersonal and even emotional. These animals are not inanimate, cold pieces of sonar apparatus. They use their ultrasounds and their high-pitched sounds interpersonally with fervor in everything they do. [15]

We have demonstrated that the dolphins are quite capable of using vocal outputs as a demand for further rewards or for surcease from punishment. Their ability in the vocal sphere is quite sophisticated. In addition to the ultrasonic matters mentioned above, their sonic performance, when in close contact with man, is astonishing. In 1957 I discovered their ability to produce sounds similar to our speech sounds. [16] During the last two years we have had many opportunities to pursue further observations in this area. This emerging ability seems to be an adaptation to a new environment which includes Man. [17] They quickly discover that they can obtain various kinds of rewards by making what we now call "humanoid emissions." When they make a sound which sounds similar to a human syllable or word, we express our pleasure by rewarding the animals in various ways. We have been exploring what some of these rewards are in order to elicit further such behavior under better control.

We demonstrated that, like other animals, the monkey, the rat, etc., these animals can be rewarded by stimulating the proper places in their brains.[18, 15]In a recent series of experiments, we have been establishing the controls necessary to understanding what brain rewards mean in terms of natural physiology. We have demonstrated quite formally that rubbing the skin of these animals with our hands is a rewarding experience to them; they will seek it vocally and by body gestures and give certain kinds of performance in order to obtain this reward.

Recently we have found that "vocal transactions" are a reward to these animals.[7, 13] (See below for human analogies in the child.) This seems to be one of the basic factors in our being able to elicit humanoid emissions. The vocal transactions are started by a human shouting some words over the water of the tank in which the animal is residing. A single word may be used or many words – it makes little difference. Eventually the animal in the tank will raise his blowhole out of water and make some sort of a humanoid emission or whistle or clicks in a delphinese fashion. If the human immediately replies with some word or words, the animal may immediately respond, the human answers, and a vocal transaction is under way. We have shown that dolphins naturally do this with one another in both their whistle and clicking spheres, and sometimes do it in the barking sphere.[13] How much of this is "instinctual" and how much is not, there is no way of knowing at the present time.

A physical analysis of such vocal transactions shows them to be formally quite as complex as the vocal transactions between human beings. In other words, the dolphin may say one word or a syllable-like emission, or many, one right after the other, as may the humans. If the human says one word, the dolphin may say one, two, three, or four, and if the human says one, two, three, or four, the dolphin may say one. There is no necessary master-slave kind of relationship in the delphinic emissions.

In our early reports we gave examples which were single words which sounded like the words that the human made.[7, 13] This presentation led to misunderstandings among our scientific colleagues. It looked as if the animals were doing a slavish tape-recorder rendition of what we were doing in a fashion similar to that of a parrot or a Mynah bird. All along we have known that the dolphins did not do such a slavish job and were obviously doing a much more complicated series of actions. We are just beginning to appreciate how to analyze and what to analyze in these transactions. As I stated in *Man and Dolphin*, about 10% of these emissions sound like human speech. In other words, the dolphin is "saying" far more than we have transmitted to the scientific community to date. We hesitate to say anything more about this until we begin to

324

NAVTAE IN DORSA CETORVM, QVAE INSVLAS PVTANT, anchoras figentes fæpe periclitantur. Hos cetos Trolual fua lingua appellant, Germanice Teuffelwal.

FIGURE 1. *A 16th-Century Impression of a Whale* (by Konrad Gesner).

Notice the four large human-like breasts, the two long tubes on top of the head, the beetling brow, the misplaced giant eye, the teeth and the doglike snarling facial expression, the rays in the tail. None of these features exist in any known modern whale or dolphin or porpoise. All modern whales, dolphins, and porpoises have two teats, at the genital slit only, which are long and narrow, not hemispherical; the blowhole slits are flush with the skin at the true forehead; the relatively small eyes are at the posterior angle of the jaw; baleen whales have no teeth; large toothed whales have only a few teeth; no "facial" expression is detectable on whales, dolphins, or porpoises; the tail flukes of all species are smooth skinned, not rayed like a fish.

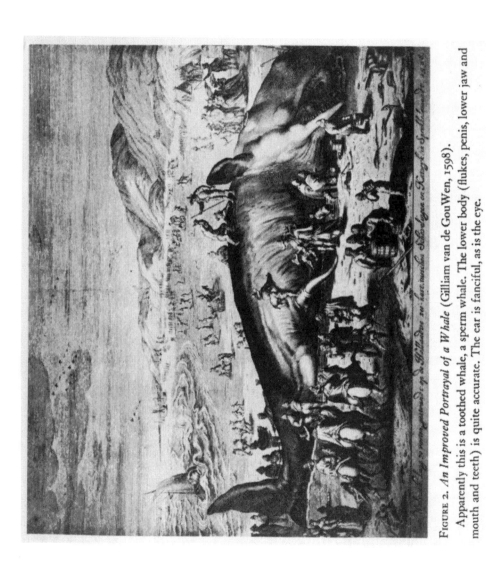

FIGURE 2. *An Improved Portrayal of a Whale* (Gilliam van de GouWen, 1598).

Apparently this is a toothed whale, a sperm whale. The lower body (flukes, penis, lower jaw and mouth and teeth) is quite accurate. The ear is fanciful, as is the eye.

FIGURE 3. *Whaling in the 19th Century.*
Sperm whale being lanced and blowing blood. (Painting in the collection of the Old Dartmouth Historical Society, New Bedford Whaling Museum, New Bedford, Mass.; copy through the courtesy of Philip Purrington, Curator.)

FIGURE 4. *Whaling in the 19th Century.*

A sperm whale is attacking a whale boat with his jaws after being provoked by Man. There is no record of an un-provoked attack on a man or a boat or a ship by a whale. (Courtesy of Phillip Purrington, New Bedford.)

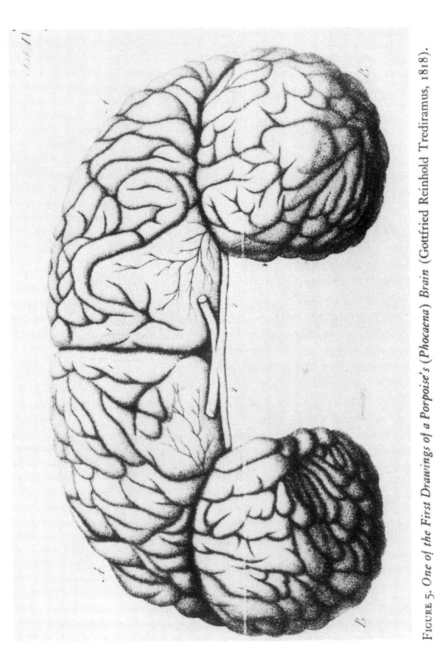

FIGURE 5. *One of the First Drawings of a Porpoise's (Phocaena) Brain* (Gottfried Reinhold Trediramus, 1818). This is an anterior view. The hemispheres are artificially separated for unknown reasons. The optic nerves and tracts are shown. The complex fissuration is obvious. (Courtesy of Dr. Mary A. B. Brazier, UCLA.)

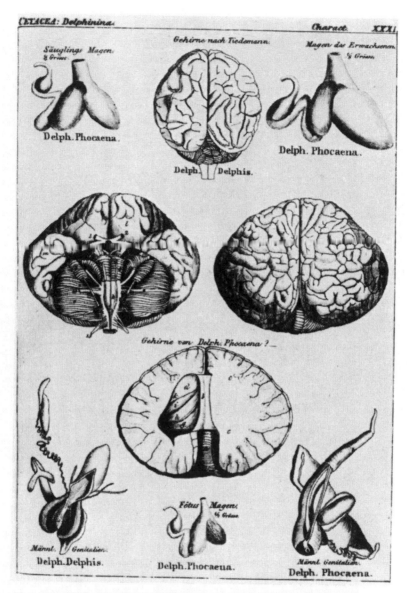

FIGURE 6. *Early Drawings of the Brain of the Dolphin and of the Porpoise by Tiedemann.*

These drawings were reproduced by H. G. L. Reichenbach in his *Anatomia Mammalium* in 1845. These are more accurate renditions and show the lateral expansion of these fine brains. (Courtesy of the Library of Congress, Washington, D.C.)

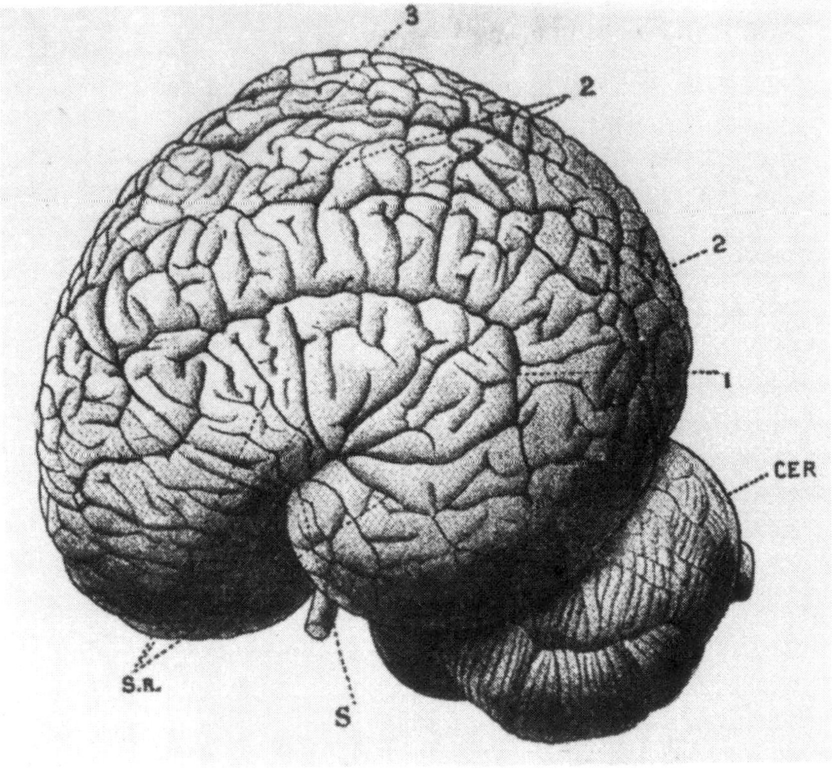

FIGURE 7. *The First 20th-Century Drawing of a Dolphin Brain* (G. Elliot Smith, 1902).

Lateral view. The proportions are excellent, as are the gyri and sulci. Smith gives the species as *Delphinus tursio;* this probably corresponds to the modern *Tursiops truncatus* or bottlenose dolphin. This brain closely resembles that of *Tursiops* shown in photos in reference 7. Langworthy's 1931 drawings ("Porpoise") are also similar (Brain, 54, 225, 1931).

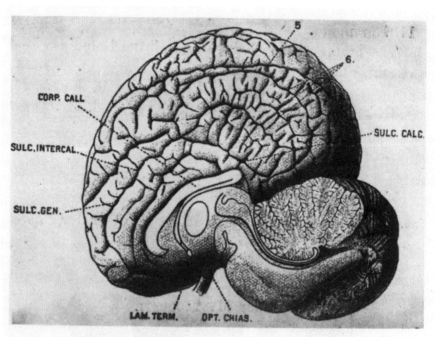

FIGURE 8. *Mesial View of Same Brain as in Figure 7.*

understand what is going on in greater detail. We are making progress slowly.

Let me then make an appeal to you – a long appeal to your logical and rational views of man and cetaceans. Here I review the above points in more general terms, and develop a plea for a new science – a new discipline combining the best of science with the best of the humanities.

Several old questions should be revived and asked again with a new attitude, with more modern techniques of investigation and with more persistence. It may take twenty years or more to develop good answers; meanwhile the intellectual life of man will profit in the undertaking. There is something exciting and even at times disturbing in this quest. [19] The bits and pieces may have started before historical times. In each age of man a new fragment was allowed to be recorded and passed on to subsequent generations. Each generation judged and rejudged the evidence from the older sources on the basis of its then current beliefs and on the basis of its new experiences, if any. At times good evidence was attenuated, distorted, and even destroyed in the name of the then current dogma.

Today we have similar problems; our current beliefs blind us, too. Evidence right before the eye can be distorted by the eye of the beholder quite as powerfully as it has been in previous ages of man. We can only hope that we have achieved greater insight and greater objectivity than some of our ancestors. The winds and currents of bias and prejudice blow hard and run deep in the minds of men. In one's own mind these factors are difficult to see, and when seen, difficult to attenuate and to allow for their influence. If at times I scold my own species, do not take it too personally; I am scolding myself more than you.

You can see by now that I believe that some of the answers to the quest are in our own minds. We must develop, imaginatively and humbly, numbers of alternative hypotheses to expand the testable areas of the intellect and bring to the investigation new mental instruments to test and to collect facts germane to our questions.

To ask about the intelligence of another species, we somehow first ask: how large and well-developed is its brain? Somewhat blindly we link brain size (a biological fact) to intelligence (a behavioral and psychological concept). We know, in the case of our own species, that if the brain fails to develop, intelligence also fails to develop.

How do we judge in our own species that intelligence develops or fails to develop? We work with the child and carefully observe its performances of common tasks and carefully measure its acquisition of speech quantitatively. We measure (among other factors) size of word vocabulary, adequacy of pronunciation, lengths of phrases and sentences, appropriateness of use, levels of abstraction achieved, and the quality of the logical processes used. We also measure speed of grasping new games with novel sets of rules and strategy; games physical and/or games verbal and vocal.

Normal mental growth patterns of human children have been measured extensively in both performance and in vocal speech acquisition. I have taken the liberty of relating these to the normal growth of brain weight of children.

TABLE I
Threshold Quantities for Human Acquisition of Speech: Age and Brain Weight[1]

Age (months)	Brain weight[2] (grams)	Speech stages[3] (first appearances)
2	480	Responds to human voice, cooing, and vocalizes pleasure.
4	580	Vocal play. Eagerness and displeasure expressed vocally.
6	660	Imitates sounds.
9	770	First word.
11	850	Imitates syllables and words. Second word.
13	930	Vocabulary expands rapidly.
17	1,030	Names objects and pictures.
21	1,060	Combines words in speech.
23	1,070	Uses pronouns, understands prepositions, uses phrases and sentences.

[1] Lilly, John C. *Man and Dolphin: A Developing Relationship,* London: Victor Gollanez, 1962.
[2] Boston Children's Hospital data from 1,198 records, in Coppoletta, J.M., and Wolbach, S. B., "Body Length and Organ Weights of Infants and Children," *American Journal of Pathology,* IX (1933), 55-70.
[3] Summarized from McCarthy, Dorothea, "Language Development in Children," in Carmichael, Leonard, ed., *Manual of Child Psychology,* New York: John Wiley, 1946, pp. 476-581.

Table I shows relations between age, brain weight, and speech performance, up to 23 months, 1070 grams, and the use of full sentences. By 17 years, the brain reaches and levels off at 1450 grams and the number of words, levels of abstraction, etc., are so large as to be difficult to assess.

In these processes, what are the minimum necessary but not necessarily sufficient factors?[20] On the biological side, modern theory concentrates on two factors: total numbers of neurons and the number of interconnections between them. On the psychological side, modern theory concentrates on the numbers of occurrences of reinforced contingencies experienced, the number of repetitions, and the number of adequate presentations from the accepted set of the consensus known as "native language," and the total numbers of sets in the stored memories at a given age. In addition, of course, is the adequate development of the transmitting and of the receiving equipment needed for speech and its ancillary behaviors.

On the biological side, modern neurology says the number of neurons in the human brain reaches maximum value before birth at about 13 billion. After this point, the increase in weight consists of increased numbers of fibers, increased connections, increased size of elements, and increased efficiency and selectivity of transmission. Thus the increase in weight of the human brain from about 400 to 1400 grams seems to be devoted to improving its internal (as well as external) communication, storage, and computation networks. As I have stated elsewhere *(Man and Dolphin)*, it is my impression that there exist critical threshold values in the brain's growth pattern at which certain kinds of performance become possible. Complex speech acquisition seems related to brain weights of 800 to 1000 grams, but no smaller. This assumes, of course, numbers of neurons (10^{10}) and numbers of connections and opportunities for learning and time to learn commonly found with humans.

The critical psychological factors in speech acquisition are slowly being dug out and described.[21, 22] Among these, the most important seem to be a continuous background of presentations to the child in rewarding circumstances of speech and its close relations to objects, actions, satisfaction of needs, and persons. Imitation of one's use of facial and vocal apparatus appears spontaneously in the happy child. The virtuosity of the child as a mimic is truly astonishing.

I am also impressed by evidence for what I call the "transactional drive." A bright child seems to seek and respond best to those persons who respond in kind, back and forth in exchanges of sounds and linked actions. For example, if one starts such a transaction with a child of 22 months with a loud word, if he is ready, he may return his version of the word or a slight variant; if one replies with another variant the child replies with still a third, or even suddenly with a new word, and so on back and forth in a transactional vocal dance. Or one may reply to a child who invites such an exchange to begin. Such exchanges seem to function as rewards of themselves, and hence the name, "transactional drive." This phenomenon is more than mere mechanical slavish mimicry. It seems to aid in perfecting pronunciation, increases vocabulary, increases the bonds with other persons, serves to substitute the "consensus-dictionary" words for the private baby words, and is thus essential to learning a language of one's own species. It is thus that the child "becomes human."

As the child ages and grows, the exchanges lengthen, and the time during which each member of the dyad is quiet while the other speaks becomes longer, until finally for a half hour or so, I am lecturing and you are at least quiet, if not listening.

How does all of this relate to modern dolphins, porpoises, and whales? From the vast array of scientific facts and theories about our own species, a few of those which I feel are useful in approaching another species to evaluate its intelligence are discussed above. But before I make connections there, let us attenuate some interfering attitudes and points of view, some myths not so modern; these interfering presumptions can be stated as follows:

(1) No animal has a language comparable to a human language.
(2) No animal is as intelligent as man.
(3) Man can adapt himself to any environment quite as well as any animal.
(4) Intelligence and intellect can be expressed only in the ways man expresses or has expressed them.
(5) All animal behavior is instinct-determined.
(6) None of man's thought and behavior is so determined.
(7) Only man thinks and plans; animals are incapable of having a mental life.
(8) Philosophy and contemplative and analytic thought are characteristic only of man, not of any animal.

All of these statements stem from ignorance and anthropocentricity. For example, who are we to say that whales, dolphins, and porpoises are to be included as "dumb beasts"? It would be far more objective and humble to tell the truth – we don't know about these animals because we haven't "been there yet." We have not lived in the sea, naked

328

and alone, or even in mobile groups, without steel containers to keep out the sea itself. For purposes of discussion let us make the following assumptions which push counter to the current of bias running deep among us:

(1) Man has not yet been willing to investigate the possibility of another intelligent species.
(2) Whales, dolphins, and porpoises are assumed to be "dumb beasts" with little or no evidence for this presumption.
(3) We do not yet know very much about these animals – their necessities, their intelligences, their lives, the possibility of their communication.
(4) It is possible for man to investigate these matters objectively with courage and perseverance.
(5) To properly evaluate whales, dolphins, porpoises, we must use everything we have intellectually, all available knowledge, *humanistic* as well as *scientific*.

Our best knowledge of ourselves as a species, as humans, is in the humanities and in the budding, growing sciences of man. In pursuit of understanding of the whales, dolphins, and porpoises, we need, at least at the beginning, a large view which is in the human sciences and in the humanities. The sciences of animals are necessarily restrictive in their view, and hence not yet applicable to our problems.

The history of the animal sciences shows that they have had grave difficulties with the fact that the observers are present and human. These sciences, like physics, chemistry, and biology, play the game as if the human observer were not there and the systems were isolated from man. This is fine strategy for "man-less nature" studies and quite appropriate for such studies.

However, I submit to you another view, for a science of man and animal, their relationships to one another. Modern man and modern dolphin and whale may be best investigated in the framework of a new science one might call "anthropo-zoology" or "zoo-anthropology." This science is a deep study of man, of the animal, of their mutual relations, present and potential. In this discipline scientists encourage close relations with the animal, and study the developing relation between man and so-called "beast."

For the last three years in the Communication Research Institute[29] we have been pursuing an investigative path in this new science with the pair "man and bottlenose dolphin." We have encouraged and pursued studies in classical sciences such as neurophysiology, animal psychology, anatomy, biophysics, and zoology. We have also initiated and pursued this new science of the man and dolphin relation; these "homo-delphic" studies, if you will, are triply demanding: we must not only know our animal objectively, but we must know man objectively, and ourselves subjectively. We cannot fight shy of involving ourselves in the investigation as objects also. In this science man, and hence one's own self, are part of the system under investigation. This is not an easy discipline. One must guard quite as rigorously (or even more so) against the pitfalls of wishful thinking and sensational fantasy as in other scientific endeavors. This field requires a self-candor, an inner honesty, and a humility quite difficult to acquire. But I maintain that good science can be done here, that the field is a proper one for properly trained and properly motivated investigators.

REFERENCES AND NOTES

1. Plinius Secundus. *Natural History.* III, Book IX.

2. Aristotle. *Historia Animalium.* Books I-IX.

3. Donaldson, Henry H. *The Growth of the Brain.* London: Walter Scott, 1895.

4. Smith, G. Elliot, in Royal College of Surgeons of England, Museum, *Descriptive and Illustrated Catalogue of the Physiological Series of Comparative Anatomy.* London: Taylor and Francis, 1902 pp. 349, 351, 356.

5. Scammon, Charles Melville. *The Marine Mammals of the North-Western Coast of North America, Described and Illustrated: Together with an Account of the American Whale-Fishery.* San Francisco: J. H. Carmany, 1874, p. 78.

6. von Bonin, Gerhardt. "Brain-Weight and Body-Weight in Mammals," *Journal of General Psychology,* XVI (1937), 379-389.

7. Lilly, John C. *Man and Dolphin.* Garden City, N.Y.: Doubleday, 1961; London: Victor Gollancz, 1962.

8. McBride, Arthur F., and Hebb, D. O. "Behavior of the Captive Bottle-Nose Dolphin, *Tursiops truncatus,"* *Journal of Comparative and Physiological Psychology,* XLI (1948), 111-123.

9. Griffin, Donald R. *Echoes of Bats and Men.* Garden City, N.Y.: Doubleday, 1959.

10. Kellogg, Winthrop N. *Porpoises and Sonar.* Chicago: University of Chicago Press, 1961.

11. Lilly, John C., and Miller, Alice M. "Vocal Exchanges between Dolphins; Bottlenose Dolphins 'Talk' to Each Other with Whistles, Clicks, and a Variety of Other Noises," *Science,* CXXXIV (1961), 1873-1876.

12. Schevill, William E., and Lawrence, Barbara. "Auditory Response of a Bottlenosed Porpoise, *Tursiops truncatus,* to Frequencies above 100 KC," *Journal of Experimental Zoology,* CXXIV (1953), 147-165.

13. Lilly, John C. "Vocal Behavior of the Bottlenose Dolphin," *Proceedings of the American Philosophical Society,* CVI (1926), 520-529.

14. Norris, Kenneth S., Prescott, John H., Asa-Dorian, Paul V., and Perkins, Paul. "An Experimental Demonstration of Echo-Location Behavior in the Porpoise, *Tursiops truncatus* (Montagu)," *Biological Bulletin,* CXX (1961), 163-176.

15. Lilly, John C. "Interspecies Communication," *McGraw-Hill Yearbook of Science and Technology 1962.* New York: McGraw-Hill, 1962, pp. 279-281.

16. Lilly, John C. "Some Considerations Regarding Basic Mechanisms of Positive and Negative Types of Motivations," *American Journal of Psychiatry,* CXV (1958), 498-504.

17. Lilly, John C. "Some Aspects of the Adaptation of the Mammals to the Ocean," in John Field, ed., *Handbook of Physiology.* Washington: American Physiological Society (in press).

18. Lilly, John C., and Miller, A. M. "Operant Conditioning of the Bottlenose Dolphin with Electrical Stimulation of the Brain," *Journal of Comparative and Physiological Psychology,* LV (1962), 73-79.

19. Lilly, John C. "Some Problems of Productive and Creative Scientific Research with Man and Dolphin," *Archives of General Psychiatry* (1963, in press).

20. Lilly, John C. "Critical Brain Size and Language," *Perspectives in Biology and Medicine* (in press).

21. Skinner, Burrhus F. *Verbal Behavior.* New York: Appleton-Century-Crofts, 1957.

22. Lewis, Morris M. *How Children Learn to Speak.* New York: Basic Books, 1959.

23. Support for the program of the Communication Research Institute, St. Thomas, Virgin Islands, is from the National Institute of Mental Health and the National Institute of Neurological Diseases and Blindness of the National Institutes of Health; from the Coyle Foundation; from the Office of Naval Research; from the U.S. Air Force Office of Scientific Research; and from private gifts and contributions to the Communication Research Institute.

331

Appendix 2

Communication with Extraterrestrial Intelligence

The title that I might choose for my discussion is "The Need for an Adequate Model of the Human End of the Interspecies Communication Program," a plea for self-conscious, open-ended, general-purpose, nonspecies-specific cognition research into models of theory for communication with nonhuman minds. I believe that this is the first time the word "mind" has been mentioned in this respect.

In recent years, I have struggled with the problem of devising working models of the interspecies communication problem at a relatively highly structured cognitive level. Despite over-glamorization and excessive public exposure, the embryo has remained viable and hard working.

The major portion of the total problem has been found to be my own species rather than the delphinic ones. There is apparently no currently available adequate theory of the human portion of the communication network. The lack of such a theory has made it difficult for most scientists to see the reality of the problems posed in the interspecies program. As long as the conscious-unconscious basic belief exists of the pre-eminence of the human brain and mind over all other earthside brains and minds, little credence can be obtained for the proposition that a problem of interspecies communication exists at all.

Despite arguments based on the complexity and size of certain nonhuman brains, little if any belief in the project has been instilled in the scientific community at large. Support has been obtained for further examination and demonstration of the large-sized, detailed excellence of structure and description of the large dolphin brain. There is no lack of interest in this area. The falling out comes in obtaining the operating interest of competent working scientists in the evaluation of the performance of these large brains. Interest and commitment of time and self are needed for progress.

The basic assumptions on which we operate are as follows. Each mammalian brain functions as a computer with properties, programs, and metaprograms partly to be defined and partly to be determined by observation. The human computer contains at least 13 billion active elements and hence is functionally and structurally larger than any artificially built computer of the present era. This human computer has the

332

properties of modern artificial computers of large size, plus additional ones not yet achieved in the nonbiological machines. This human computer has stored program properties, and stored metaprogram properties as well. Among other known properties are self-programming and self-metaprogramming. Programming and metaprogramming language is different for each human, depending upon the developmental experiential, genetic, educational, accidental, and self-chosen variables, elements, and values. Basically, the verbal forms are those of the native language of the individual, modulated by nonverbal language elements acquired in the same epochs of his development.

Each such computer has scales of self-maturation and self-evaluation. Constant and continuous computations are being done, giving aim and goal distance estimates of external reality performances and internal reality achievements.

Comparison scales are set up between human computers for performance measures of each and of several in concert. Each computer models other computers of importance to itself, beginning immediately *post partum,* with greater or lesser degrees of error.

The phenomenon of computer interlock facilitates model construction and operation. One computer interlocks with one or more other computers above and below the level of awareness any time the communicational distance is sufficiently small to bring the interlock functions above threshold level.

In the complete physical absence of other external computers within the critical interlock distance, the self-directed and other-directed programs can be clearly detected, analyzed, recomputed, and reprogrammed, and new metaprograms initiated by the solitudinous computer itself. In this physical reality (which is an as completely attenuated as possible environment with solitude), maximum intensity, maximum complexity, and maximum speed of reprogramming are achievable by the self.

In the field of scientific research, such a computer can function in many different ways—from the pure, austere thought processes of theory and mathematics to the almost random data absorption of the naturalistic approach with newly found systems, or to the coordinated interlock with other human computers of an engineering effort.

At least two extreme major techniques of data-collection analysis exist for individual scientists: (1) artificially created, controlled-element, invented, devised-system methods; and (2) methods involving the participant-observer, who interacts intimately and experientially with naturally given elements, with nonhuman or human computers as parts of the system.

The former is the current basis of individual physical-chemical research; the latter is one basis for individual explorative, first-discovery research of organisms having brains larger than those of humans.

Sets of human motivational procedural postulates for the interlock research method on nonhuman beings, with computers as large as and larger than the human computers, are sought. Some of these methods involve the establishment of long periods—perhaps months or years—of human to other organism computer interlock. It is hoped that this interlock will be of a quality and value sufficiently high to permit interspecies communication efforts on both sides on an intense, highly-structured level.

In essence, then, this is the problem of communicating with any nonhuman species or being or mind or computer. We do not have, however, the full support in basic beliefs in the scientific community for these postulates. Obviously, we as a species do not believe, for example, that a whale, with a brain six times the size of ours, has a computer worth dealing with. Instead, we kill whales and use them as fertilizer. We also eat them. To be fair to the killer whale, I know of no instance in which a killer whale has eaten a human, but I know of many instances in which humans have eaten killer whales.

Therefore, on an historical basis, I do not feel that at present there is much chance that any species of greater attainments than ours will want to communicate with us. The dolphins want to communicate only with those people who are willing to live with them on the terms the dolphins set up and that certain kinds of human beings set up. Other types the dolphins drive away. Every year we lose people from the dolphin research program. Usually it is because of fear of the power of these animals and fear of damage, even though in the history of the laboratory no one has yet been injured by the dolphins. Sometimes we think that these people who are lost are projecting their own hostilities outward onto the animals in a very unrealistic fashion. The people who survive either realize that this mechanism is operating and conquer it, or else their nature is such that they do not have hostilities to project.

Appendix 3

Origins of Dolphins and of Men

The modern whales, including modern dolphins, first appear in the Miocene period 25 million years ago. Previous to this appearance there were ancient whales (Archeoceti) whose remains are found in the early Eocene and late Eocene periods about 60 million years ago. Between these two groups no transitional forms have yet been found, according to Remington Kellogg.[1]

The Archeocetes are said to be descended from very early general mammals of insectivore-creodont forms in the late Cretacious and early Paleocene periods 100 million years ago. These ancient whales had separate nares ("nostrils") near the end of the upper beak (rostrum) rather than a blowhole on the "forehead" farther back as in the case of modern dolphins. The teeth of these early forms were of the cutting form in the cheeks and conical at the rostral end of the jaw; modern dolphins in general have conical teeth. Other differences are demonstrable in the bones of the skull, trunk, limbs, etc.

In the opinion of R. Kellogg, the primitive insectivore-creodont stock gave rise to a generalized prototype which developed separately into each of three lines: the Archeoceti, the Odontoceti (including dolphins), and the Mysticeti (baleen whales).

In relation to brain size, the earlier whales had smaller brains (800 cc cranial capacity per 60 feet for toothed Prozeuglodon of middle Eocene) than the modern ones (9000 cc per 60 feet for toothed sperm whale).

The origins of *Homo sapiens* have been traced through similar epochs.[2] The primitive mammals of the early Eocene period (70 million years ago) also included the earliest Primates. The first apes (Parapithecus) are found in the Oligocene period, 40 million years ago. In the Miocene (25 million years ago) the ape type is Proconsul of the big jaw and small brain: these are said to have given rise to the modern apes. Man's predecessors presumably were among the many types of apes of the Miocene and Pliocene (15 million years ago) periods, but the evidence is still fragmentary and unsatisfactory. (As stated above, the first good evidence of progenitors of modern whales is found in the Miocene.) In the early Pleistocene period (1 million years ago) the Australopithecines appeared with a brain of about 600cc (a little less than half our brain). (This value is to be compared with Prozeuglodon which lived 50 or so million years earlier with 800 cc.) The Australopithecines are "exceedingly

335

primitive representatives of the family which includes modern and extinct types of Man." There is no evidence of speech or tool-making; there is suggestive evidence that they crushed the skulls of baboons with weapons of unknown sort: this fact places them above modern apes in intelligence.

Later, Pithecanthropus appears (Middle Pleistocene period, 500,000 years ago) with a brain of about 900 cc (but larger ones are found). He made primitive tools, used fire, hunted other animals such as deer, and practiced cannibalism, eating the brains of his own species. Evidence is fairly strong that he was a progenitor of modern man.

Strictly modern man arose from traceable progenitors living during the Pleistocene period: Old Stone Age Man (Paleolithic Man) was of many varieties and places in Europe and Asia. His brain was almost up to ours (1300 cc). This group includes Neanderthal man of Europe, Rhodesian man of Africa, and solo man of Java.

In the late Paleolithic period, about 50,000 years ago, modern men, "the Aurignacians," suddenly replaced Neanderthal man. This group includes the Cro-Magnon man. They are hardly distinguishable from present-day *Homo sapiens.* Their cave paintings, sculpture, personal ivory jewelry, and fine javelin blades show their high level of achievement.

By 10,000 years ago, the cultural artifacts have an extremely high level. The first written records seem to begin at least 7000 years ago in Sumeria.[3]

The parallel kinds of development of the whales are not known: since whales do not, as far as we know, create tools, jewelry, drawings, or other artifacts, and since they usually die in the sea or at its edge, most of them are eaten by predators ranging in size from large sharks to small bacteria. The best remains are in silt deposits on present land which was formerly ancient seas. Only a few skeletons have been found. As the science of oceanography progresses, we may find the whales' complete skeletal record in the oceans' bottoms. Until then, the guesses are further apart than those for man's evolutionary record.

One systematic schema for the evolutionary inter-relationships of the Delphinidae is given by Heluf Winge.[4]

The first recorded contacts between man and dolphins may be those given by Aristotle (fourth century B.C.). His account of the dolphins' anatomy and behavior is fairly exact: he distinguishes the dolphin (of the Mediterranean) from the porpoise (from the Black Sea). The contacts are quoted[5] as follows:

"Among the sea-fishes, many stories are told about the dolphin, indicative of his gentle and kindly nature, and of manifestations of passionate attachment to boys, in and about Tarentum, Caria, and other places. The story goes that, after a dolphin had been caught and wounded off the coast of Caria, a shoal of dolphins came into the harbour and stopped there until the fisherman let his captive go free; whereupon the shoal departed. A shoal of young dolphins is always, by way of protection, followed by a large one. On one occasion, a shoal of dolphins, large and small, was seen, and two dolphins at a little distance appeared swimming in underneath a little dead dolphin when it was sinking, and supporting it on their backs, trying out of compassion to prevent its being devoured by some predaceous fish. Incredible stories are told regarding the rapidity of movement of this creature. It appears to be the fleetest of all animals, marine and terrestrial, and it can leap over the masts of large vessels. This speed is chiefly manifested when they are pursuing a fish for food; then, if the fish endeavours to escape, they pursue him in their ravenous hunger down to deep waters; but, when the necessary return swim is getting too long, they hold in their breath, as though calculating the length of it, and then draw themselves together for an effort and shoot up like arrows, trying to make the long ascent rapidly in order to breathe, and in the effort, they spring right over a ship's masts if a ship be in the vicinity. This same phenomenon is observed in divers, when they have plunged into deep water; that is, they pull themselves together and rise with a speed proportional to their strength. Dolphins live together in pairs, male and female. It is not known for what reason they run themselves aground on dry land; at all events, it is said that they do so at times, and for no obvious reason."

Later contacts with "wild" dolphins include those of "Opo" (a *Tursiops*?) in New Zealand, whose story and photographs have been published.[6]

[1] Kellogg, Remington. *A Review of the Archeoceti* (Carnegie Institution, Washington, D.C. 1936).

[2] Clark, W.E LeGros, *History of the Primates* (University of Chicago Press, Chicago, 1957).

[3] Kramer, Samuel Noah. *History Begins at Sumer* (Doubleday Anchor Book, New York, 1959).

[4] Winge, Herluf. *A Review of the Inter-relationships of the Cetacea* (Smithsonian Institution, Washington, D.C., 1921).

[5] *The Works of Aristotle,* translated into English under the editorship of W. D. Ross, and reprinted by arrangement with Oxford University Press for The Great Books, Vol. 9, p. 156, Encyclopaedia Britannica, Inc., Chicago, 1952.

[6] Alpers, Antony. *A Book of Dolphins* (John Murray, London, 1960).

Appendix 4
Introduction by John C. Lilly (Lilly on Dolphins © 1975)

This book is a combination and republication of three books and two scientific papers. The books are: *Man and Dolphin, The Dolphin in History* and *The Mind of the Dolphin.* The scientific papers are: "Communication with Extraterrestrial Intelligence" and "Reprogramming of the Sonic Output of the Dolphin: Sonic Burst Count Matching."

The dolphins were respected by people such as Aristotle (400 B.C.). His write-up of dolphins is to this day one of the best. It can be found in Volume 9, page 156, *Great Books of the Western World,* Encyclopaedia Britannica, Inc, Chicago, 1952. It is wise to read all of Aristotle on the animals. He scatters his observations of the dolphins through this book. Similar respect for the dolphins in the printed version has not been found until the book *Man and Dolphin*, 1961, in this century.

The Dolphin in History was published in 1962-63 by the William Andrews Clark Memorial Library, University of California, Los Angeles. There are two papers in this small book: one by Ashley Montagu and one by John C. Lilly. Ashley Montagu reviews "The History of the Dolphin," which is well worth reading. John C. Lilly's paper, "Modern Whales, Dolphins and Porpoises, as Challenges to Our Intelligence," is in this volume in full, including references.

The book *The Mind of the Dolphin* was published in 1967 by Doubleday; and in 1968, Avon issued a paperback, reducing the size of the text of *The Mind of the Dolphin.* In order to fit it into this volume and not to repeat things that were said in *Man and Dolphin,* with Margaret Howe's account of her several months of living with Peter and training Peter. We are keeping all the pictures of Margaret and Peter that were published in this volume.

We present the needs for the future dolphin research both on the theoretical and practical side in terms of the personnel that are required and give a specific example of a successful trial period of Margaret and Peter. I feel this work should be followed up. In the future, such research should be done by the sea, with a house such as detailed in this text. Here the dolphins can come and go as they please. It may be necessary to capture some dolphins in order to start the facility on its way, but it should be in the area of a warm sea and in a house through which the dolphins can swim with special waterways, and in which the humans can meet the dolphins without being afraid of being drowned. We would include several

338

enthusiastic children, of all ages, from approximately three or four up through the teens and into adulthood. All will participate in all of the life within the house including the kitchen, the bathroom and the living room.

Programming and Metaprogramming in the Human Biocomputer was published in 1967. The paper that was taken from this was republished in the Spectrum of the I.E.E.E. (the Institute of Electronic and Electrical Engineers) as "Communication with Extraterrestrial Intelligence." This paper summarizes the problems of interspecies communication in a very scientific and sparse fashion. In this volume I write a popularized version of the scientific version in order to broaden the understanding of this particular paper.

"Reprogramming of the Sonic Output of the Dolphin: Sonic Burst Count Matching" is the last scientific paper which I published. It was published by The Acoustical Society of America in June of 1968 in Volume 43, *Journal of the Acoustical Society of America,* pages 1412 to 1424. These twelve pages are reproduced in full in this volume. They summarize the operational philosophy on which I was operating over the previous twelve years and show my slow but sure break with the Skinnerian-Pavlovian interpretation of dolphin behavior. We talk about programming, programming subroutines and so on, using a more modern language and a more modern set of concepts and not assuming that we know everything about them. An equal amount of space for the unknowns in the dolphins and for the dolphin's initiative is given.

In this paper we show the quantitative limits of human hearing and of dolphin hearing and of the human sonic output and the dolphin sonic output. We have a vocal mode flow diagram with the human-dolphin communication link with feedback between the two. Analysis of the outputs of the two species demonstrates the very small overlap between these two and shows the almost eight times difference between the two species in regard to their outputs and their inputs in the sonic sphere. This was ignored by the scientific establishment and hence I feel it should have more publicity and a wider circulation and a greater understanding. It shows the basic problem of communication with the bottle-nosed dolphin which can be extended to other species such as the elephants and the whales.

All of the above works were reproduced between 1954 and 1968. In 1967 to 1968 I decided to stop dolphin work. I no longer wanted to run a concentration camp for my friends and if they were as I found them to be and if this was not only my imagination, then there was an ethical problem of maintaining them in a confined state in which they may not survive.

Immediately after I decided to stop dolphin research, at least in this way, five of the dolphins in our eight-dolphin colony committed suicide. Within the next week, I let three go. A later book called *The Center of the Cyclone,* 1972, contains details of this ethical problem.

The problems of the humans are summarized in a later book called *Simulations of God, the Science of Belief.* This book illustrates in a succinct and direct way the difficulties that we have with our belief systems. Belief systems are programs which are written into us or acquired by us when we are too young to know any better. Later we modify these with metabeliefs that are our beliefs about beliefs, then as we learn to learn and as we become mature, we become less susceptible to the dictates of these early belief structures, presented in the foreword of this book and previously published in *The Center of the Cyclone,* also in *Programming and Metaprogramming in the Human Biocomputer,* published by Julian Press, 1973.

You may well ask where all of this started. It is generally assumed the dolphin work started before the isolation work. This is not true. In 1954 I decided to do a series of experiments on humans isolated from all visual, acoustic, tactile, pressure and gravity stimuli in so far as this is possible without cutting nerve fibers, so I devised a technique using a tank of water, floating the person in the darkness and the silence. This work has been explained in greater length in both *The Human Biocomputer* and *The Center of the Cyclone.* In our new book, *The Dyadic Cyclone,* my wife, Toni, and I go into this even further and show how we have modified and made a new system having an Epsom salt (magnesium sulphate) solution to float in and at the surface so that one doesn't use any breathing apparatus.